A Centennial Celebration of *The Brownies' Book*

Children's
Literature
Association

Children's Literature Association Series

A CENTENNIAL CELEBRATION OF

The Brownies' Book

Edited by
DIANNE JOHNSON-FEELINGS
and JONDA C. MCNAIR

Foreword by RUDINE SIMS BISHOP

UNIVERSITY PRESS OF MISSISSIPPI / JACKSON

The University Press of Mississippi is the scholarly publishing agency of
the Mississippi Institutions of Higher Learning: Alcorn State University,
Delta State University, Jackson State University, Mississippi State University,
Mississippi University for Women, Mississippi Valley State University,
University of Mississippi, and University of Southern Mississippi.

www.upress.state.ms.us

The University Press of Mississippi is a member
of the Association of University Presses.

First printing 2022

∞

Library of Congress Cataloging-in-Publication Data

Names: Johnson-Feelings, Dianne, editor. | McNair, Jonda C., 1970– editor.
| Bishop, Rudine Sims, writer of foreword.
Title: A centennial celebration of the Brownies' book / Dianne
Johnson-Feelings, Jonda C. McNair, Rudine Sims Bishop.
Other titles: Children's Literature Association series.
Description: Jackson : University Press of Mississippi, 2022. | Series:
Children's literature association series | Includes bibliographical
references and index.
Identifiers: LCCN 2022031558 (print) | LCCN 2022031559 (ebook) | ISBN
9781496841230 (hardback) | ISBN 9781496841247 (trade paperback) | ISBN
9781496841254 (epub) | ISBN 9781496841261 (epub) | ISBN 9781496841278
(pdf) | ISBN 9781496841285 (pdf)
Subjects: LCSH: African American children—Periodicals—History and
criticism. | African American children—Race identity. | African
American children in literature. | African Americans—Juvenile literature.
Classification: LCC PN4835 .C46 2022 (print) | LCC PN4835 (ebook) | DDC
051.089/96073—dc23/eng/20220810
LC record available at https://lccn.loc.gov/2022031558
LC ebook record available at https://lccn.loc.gov/2022031559

British Library Cataloging-in-Publication Data available

We dedicate this volume to all the scholars whose work illuminates the history of African American children's literature.

CONTENTS

FOREWORD

RUDINE SIMS BISHOP

I was introduced to *The Brownies' Book* through Dianne Johnson-Feelings's 1996 anthology, *The Best of "The Brownies' Book."* It is possible that I, in turn, introduced it to Jonda C. McNair during her studies with me at The Ohio State University. Johnson-Feelings and McNair are currently both highly respected scholars in the field of children's literature and, given their focus on African American children's literature, particularly suited to produce this volume. No one is better qualified, and I am delighted to contribute to this effort.

In the United States in 1920, African American children's literature was virtually nonexistent. When Black characters appeared in the children's literature of the day, they were what Langston Hughes called clowns and caricatures. So, in part, *The Brownies' Book* was intended to counter those images, seeking to supplant them with realistic representations of Black people and Black lives. As we celebrate the one-hundredth anniversary of *The Brownies' Book*, it is appropriate to take a scholarly look back at its significance and its influence.

Jessie Redmon Fauset was the literary editor of both *The Brownies' Book* and *The Crisis*, the official organ of the National Association for the Advancement of Colored People (NAACP). Langston Hughes called her a midwife of the Harlem Renaissance because, by publishing some of its authors' early work, she helped to launch the careers of a number of the writers who gained prominence in that era, including Hughes himself. It is not surprising, then, that contemporary critics are interested in Fauset, her work, and her influence.

This volume also recognizes the significance of biographies for Black youth and the importance of reader response, in the form of letters to the editor published in the column called "The Jury." In addition, it highlights the role that *The Brownies' Book* may have played in the creation of children's sections featured during the 1920s in prominent African American newspapers such as the *Chicago Defender*.

It would be more than another four decades after *The Brownies' Book* before a substantial body of work that can legitimately be called African American children's literature began to develop. In the essay focused on Mildred Taylor's Newbery Award–winning novel *Roll of Thunder, Hear My Cry*, this volume recognizes the continuity between *The Brownies' Book* and contemporary African American children's literature in relation to their themes and the values they espouse.

Taken together, the essays in this volume confirm the significance of *The Brownies' Book* as foundational to contemporary African American children's literature. Although it sought to engage and entertain readers, it was also purposeful, even didactic to some extent. Its stated objectives are echoed by later twentieth-century Black writers and artists in their statements about their work. It published a variety of genres: fiction, folklore, nonfiction, biography, history, and poetry, all of which are echoed in the contemporary body of work produced by a talented group of writers and artists.

Let us celebrate *The Brownies' Book*!

INTRODUCTION

DIANNE JOHNSON-FEELINGS AND JONDA C. MCNAIR

This volume, celebrating the centennial of the publication of *The Brownies' Book*, appears at a pivotal time in American history. The cry of the Black Lives Matter movement reverberates nationwide and worldwide. And like other movements throughout history, in the United States and around the globe, young people are at the forefront. A century ago, the National Association for the Advancement of Colored People (NAACP) recognized the importance of the youth constituency—largely, but not limited to, the children of its membership. To speak directly to this audience, each year the NAACP published a "Youth Number" of its official publication, *The Crisis*.

Editors Jessie Redmon Fauset and W. E. B. Du Bois, along with business manager Augustus Granville Dill, created *The Brownies' Book*, a monthly magazine designed especially for their youngest readers, as a response to the popularity of that annual issue. The magazine was foundational and forward-looking. It included fiction, current events, games, songs, biographies, letters to the editor, a section titled "Little People of the Month" that highlighted young people's accomplishments, and more. Produced from January 1920 through December 1921, *The Brownies' Book* stands as a testament to the early commitment of Black communities, intellectuals, writers, artists, and families to the unwavering belief that Black Lives Matter, and that the youngest members of the community matter.

When announcing the upcoming publication of *The Brownies' Book* in the October 1919 issue of *The Crisis*, Du Bois wrote that one of the objectives of this magazine was "to make colored children realize that being colored is a normal, beautiful thing" (286). How astounding and sobering it is that Black people a century later still have to think about the normalcy of being comfortable in the skins in which we were born. This concern has been a preoccupation of African American children's literature creators throughout this past century. Fortunately, countless writers, illustrators, publishers, editors, educators, parents, and others have been working steadily to build upon the foundation fostered by Fauset and Du Bois. There are countless books now designed to normalize and celebrate the Black body—the myriad and beautiful hair textures, skin colors, and facial features.

These twenty-first-century books would have been appreciated by many readers of *The Brownies' Book*, including young Alice Martin, of Philadelphia, Pennsylvania. In the June 1920 issue, she wrote:

> Sometimes in school I feel so badly. In the geography lesson, when we read about the different people who live in the world, all the pictures are pretty, nice-looking men and women, except the Africans. They always look so ugly. I don't mean to make fun of them, for I am not pretty myself; but I know not all colored people look like me. I see lots of ugly white people, too; but not all white people look like them, and they are not the ones they put in the geography. Last week the girl across the aisle from me in school looked at the picture and laughed and whispered something about it to her friend. And they both looked at me. It made me so angry. Mother said for me to write you about it. (178)

This letter is remarkable in several ways. First, it reminds adults not to underestimate the insight and intelligence of young people. Martin is a sophisticated cultural critic who understands the complicated nature of a cultural concept such as beauty. Almost intuitively, she understands that the cultural, the social, the political, and the educational are all connected. More specifically, she understands the power of visual images and how those images can be used and manipulated. Her posing of questions to the editor of *The Brownies' Book* shows that she values her elders' experience and insight and, simultaneously, that she appreciates the value of sharing ideas across generations. Her own intelligence shines in the letter.

Not only was *The Brownies' Book* shared across generations, but it bridged countries, cultures, and civilizations. Yes, readers of *The Brownies' Book* learned about peoples of Africa. But they also learned about an entire international community, largely through the "Where the Crow Flies" section, which focused on current events worldwide. In addition, young readers from many countries sent in letters, songs, games, and stories from their own societies. Similarly, in this present geopolitical moment, young people in the United States and worldwide have added passionately to the chorus of voices crying out that Black Lives Matter.

Black children's literature matters. Though the absolute numbers of children's books created by African Americans and other creators of color have increased over time, these books still account for an extremely small percentage of the total number published each year in this country. A long-standing and reliable source for statistics is the University of Wisconsin's Cooperative Center for Children's Books' *Annual Statistics on Multicultural Literature in Publishing* (which shares "publishing statistics on Children's/YA Books about People of Color and First/Native Nations and by People of Color and First/Native Nations Authors and Illustrators"). Black children's literature mattered for Black children in the 1920s. Its existence is critical for Black children, and for all children, in 2021 and beyond. How appropriate it is that this project is part of a Centennial Series. There could be no anniversary more timely.

The contributors to this volume have written essays that both stand alone and speak to each other in numerous ways, offering original and important insights into the enduring significance of the magazine and placing it within a larger cultural history.

It is fitting that the first essay is "The Blind Maze of Thought: Jessie Redmon Fauset, *The Brownies' Book*, and the Measure of a Movement." Julia S. Charles-Linen highlights Fauset's brilliance and her contributions to African American cultural history, something not yet fully explored by scholars. She elucidates Fauset's editorial vision, designed to offer Black children tools "to navigate a nation in racial turmoil."

In "Black Heroes and 'The Jury': *The Brownies' Book* Biographies as Counter-Memories for Black Children," Sara C. VanderHaagen explores how others have, indeed, navigated this landscape successfully. She argues for the importance of "biography as a tool for recovering Black voices from the past and thereby empowering the Black children of her present." These biographies are no less important for young people of the twenty-first century.

It is not only the present moment that concerns Michelle Taylor Watts in "'My Soul Calls for Larger Things': Voice, Vision, and Justice in Children's Letters to the Editor." Complementing Julia S. Charles-Linen's work on Fauset, Watts explores what can be gained by reading Fauset's work "through the lens of Black futurity."

Paige Gray's "'Let Us Make the World Know That We Are Living': *The Brownies' Book*, African American Newspapers, and Black Childhood Identity" explores some of the powerful and forward-thinking ways in which popular periodicals of the day—"prototype[s] for social media"—contributed to the shaping of identity and community for Black children.

The final essay, by Jani L. Barker, is titled "Mildred D. Taylor's *Roll of Thunder, Hear My Cry*: A Worthy Successor to *The Brownies' Book*." It is an important contribution to the work of continually creating a literary history of African American writing for youth. How exciting that it is being published just a few years after publication of the final book in Taylor's multivolume saga—both the saga and this essay tying together the past, the present, and even the future.

The Brownies' Book will always matter and always be integral to any scholarship on American children's literature. Everyone who has contributed to this volume furthers our appreciation of just how time-specific, yet timeless, this groundbreaking publication was. The full run of *The Brownies' Book*, so stunning in both its written and visual content, is available through the Schomburg Center for Research in Black Culture and through the Library of Congress. Our hope is that this collection of essays offers information, context, and insight that moves scholars across disciplines to continue to look closely at the original publication and to spread word about it far and wide. How wonderful it would be for teachers, parents, and other adults to share these volumes with children today. We are pleased to include here facsimiles of the first and final issues of the publication.

In the spirit of those Fauset and Du Bois referred to as "the true Brownies," we hope that you delight in and are edified by this volume which, in the end, can merely hint at the richness of this literary and historical treasure.

Works Cited

Du Bois, W. E. B. "The True Brownies." *The Crisis*, vol. 18, Oct. 1919, pp. 285–86.
Martin, Alice. "The Jury." *The Brownies' Book*, vol. 1, no. 6, June 1920, p. 178.

A Centennial Celebration of *The Brownies' Book*

The Brownies' Book

JANUARY, 1920

One Dollar and a Half a Year   Fifteen Cents a Copy

THIS IS

The Brownies' Book

A Monthly Magazine
For the Children of the Sun

DESIGNED FOR ALL CHILDREN,
BUT ESPECIALLY FOR *OURS*.

It aims to be a thing of Joy and Beauty, dealing in Happiness, Laughter and Emulation, and designed especially for Kiddies from Six to Sixteen.

It will seek to teach Universal Love and Brotherhood for all little folk--black and brown and yellow and white.

Of course, pictures, stories, letters from little ones, games and oh--everything!

One Dollar and a Half a Year
Fifteen Cents a Copy

W. E. B. DU BOIS, ... Editor
A. G. DILL. . . . . . Business Manager

Address: THE BROWNIES' BOOK
2 West 13th Street   New York, N. Y.

THE BROWNIES' BOOK

Published Monthly and Copyrighted by DuBois and Dill, Publishers, at 2 West 13th Street, New York, N. Y. Conducted by W. E. Burghardt DuBois; Jessie Redmon Fauset, Literary Editor; Augustus Granville Dill, Business Manager

VOL. 1.   JANUARY, 1920   No. 1

CONTENTS

FIFTEEN CENTS A COPY; ONE DOLLAR AND A HALF A YEAR
FOREIGN SUBSCRIPTIONS TWENTY-FIVE CENTS EXTRA

RENEWALS: The date of expiration of each subscription is printed on the wrapper. When the subscription is due a yellow renewal blank is enclosed.

CHANGE OF ADDRESS: The address of a subscriber can be changed as often as desired. In ordering a change of address, both the old and the new address must be given. Two weeks' notice is required.

MANUSCRIPTS and drawings relating to colored children are desired. They must be accompanied by return postage. If found unavailable they will be returned.

Application pending for entry as second class matter at the Post Office at New York, N. Y., under the Act of March 3, 1879.

Underwood & Underwood.

Her Royal Highness, Zaouditou, Queen of the Kings of Abyssinia, Empress of Ethiopia

The Brownies' Book

Vol. 1   JANUARY, 1920   No. 1

Cumpkin Land.

A STORY

PEGGY POE

IN the Land of Sure Enough, away down South, in a most wonderful land named Georgia, lives a little colored boy called Happy. He is fat and round as a brown cookie, with eyes like two round moons, and these eyes just sparkle. Now this little boy's really name isn't Happy—he has a long, solemn name written in his Mammy's Bible, but somehow that long name didn't just fit the boy. It seemed as if that name was too long, just like it was when he tried on his daddy's pants; besides when you looked at him, you felt jolly all inside and outside and just up and said that that boy's name must be Happy; so everyone called him Happy.

He wasn't very big, because he liked candy; and he wasn't very little, because he had a real knife in his pocket. He was just as high as this, but not quite as low as that; he could whistle "Bob White!" Sometimes he got a spanking; sometimes he got pennies.

He lived in a funny little house made of logs, all nice and white; there was the biggest yard, and in it was a great big China-berry tree; under the tree was a bench so big and so untippy that Happy often played that it was a boat. He had a little dog, with a very long tail; a big black rooster and a little red hen,—all his own.

Now this very day Happy was sitting on the bench under the China-berry tree, waiting for his Mammy to come home with the syrup from the cane mill,—real, ribbon cane syrup that only southern girls and boys know about, and which is far nicer than any candy. Happy saw his Mammy coming away down the white road. His mouth began to water, his round little stom-ick away down inside of him begged for that syrup; so Happy's little fat legs said to his little fat feet, "Get up, Feet," and Happy almost knocked Mammy Tibblets over, begging for a bit; but she walked right straight into the kitchen, put the bucket on the table, and said to Happy—

"Now, Happy, you go on and play. Don't you bother that syrup, and for supper I'll bake you a pile of waffles most as high as yourself and you can swim them in that syrup. I am going over to Captain Jones' and get their clothes to wash. Now don't you bother that syrup."

Happy turned cart-wheels out the door and landed on the bench under the China-berry tree. He tried very hard not to think about that syrup. He made a whistle with his "Sure Enough Knife;" he fed the old black rooster and the little red hen, although it wasn't near time; and all the while a small voice kept saying, "My, but ribbon cane syrup is sure good."

After a while, although Happy did not tell them to, his right little leg started to the house and, of course, the fat little left leg followed, back to the kitchen door, right up to the kitchen table. There sat the bucket of syrup, and that little voice said again, "Oh, Happy, don't you want a little bit?" And, really, a big drop rolled over the bucket's side, right down on to Happy's fat finger. Pop! right into Happy's mouth went that little finger, and Happy's little stom-ick said, "My, that's good."

So Happy went over to the cupboard and got a spoon,—he was sure it was Mammy's littlest spoon,—right up on the table he climbed and sat down beside the bucket of syrup. He took just a tiny bit; then his eyes got rounder, and old Mister Temp-ta-tion came out of the shadowy place and helped Happy hold the spoon, and said, "Help yourself, Happy. It's so good it won't hurt you."

My, what big spoonfuls old Mister Temp-ta-tion helped Happy dip from that bucket, until— Oh,—what a hurting came into Happy's stom-ick, just like a whole paper of pins hopping about in it. Right then old Mister Temp-ta-tion gave an awful mean laugh and ran away, never saying he was sorry one bit, while poor Happy, kicking about to get that pain away, kicked the bucket of syrup on to Mammy Tibblets' clean floor. In half a minute Happy grabbed the bucket up, before all the syrup could get out; but there on the floor was a lake of syrup, big enough to sail a toy boat on; beside it lay the spoon, not Mammy's little spoon, but oh, dear, it was her big corn-bread spoon.

Happy looked up and saw Daddy Henry's razor strop dancing on the wall, just like it was trying to jump off the nail. Now the little boys away down south in Georgia wear very thin pants and Happy was afraid that Mammy Tibblets would come home and help that razor strop off its nail, so Happy ran away,—out the back-gate, past the garden-patch, where old Mister Rabbit was stealing a mess of greens, went Happy, right out through the cotton-patch, where the long white fingers tried to pull out his hair. The fat little right leg and the chubby little left leg, both, tried to be first all the time, until at last they tumbled Happy to the cornfield, where the corn was so tall that no one, that is, really every-day people, could see him. There he found a big pumpkin and sat down.

All the running had scared the pain out of his stom-ick, but it didn't scare the 'fraid away from Happy. The more he thought about what old Mister Temp-ta-tion had made him do, and Mammy's sticky floor, the more he thought about the razor strop.

"Oh, I cannot go back to my old home, and I haven't a new one. What will I do?" Just then old Mister Sun began to shake up his pil-

lows for a night's nap, the corn stalks made the longest, blackest shadows, right in the tree above the fence, and Mister Crow began to laugh at Happy—"Haw, Haw, Haw." Then Happy felt like a balloon that had to burst, enough, anyway, so that a few tears could squeeze out. One little tear dropped on his big toe and made a mud cake. Then came more tears, until Mrs. Ladybug hurried all her children under a pumpkin leaf, thinking it was raining.

Just then someone said as clear and friendly, "Well, Happy, you can come and live with me." Happy looked around and there stood a tiny man, a kind of nice little Elf, with the nicest green clothes, a yellow hat, and a yellow face. Happy thought at once how much like Mammy's pumpkin pie, with cinnamon sprinkled on it, this little man's face looked; but, of course, the cinnamon-like spots were freckles. "I am the Pumpkin-Man, if you please," and the Elf bowed mighty polite and nice.

Happy felt better, and it is nice to be bowed to when one is very little. At first Happy had been afraid it was old Mister Temp-ta-tion calling him.

"Where is your house, Mister Pumpkin-Man?" asked Happy.

"You are sitting on it, Sir," said the Man.

Happy jumped up in a hurry; although he had picked out the biggest pumpkin, he never dreamed it was a house.

"Oh, excuse me, Mister Pumpkin-Man, I didn't mean to sit on anybody's house."

"Oh, that's all right, Happy; come right in and I'll give you a bite to eat; come right in and make yourself at home."

The Elf was so polite it made Happy feel good, but he did wonder how the Elf knew his name—really, the Elf had just looked at him and guessed his name.

"Where's your door?" Happy asked.

"Right here," and the Pumpkin-Man pulled aside a big leaf, showing a nice little open door in the pumpkin. "Walk right in, Sir."

Happy looked at the small door and his fat, round self.

"I'd like to, but I never could get in that door," Happy said.

"Did you ever T-R-Y?" the Pumpkin-Man asked.

"No, and it wouldn't do any good; see how big I am." Happy puffed out kind of proud.

"T-R-Y; why try has made all the wonderful

things in the world,—ships, trains, wagons, ice cream, and candy—they were all made by try."

Happy thought if try could do all, that he had better try to get into that pumpkin-house, as the shadows in the corn-rows were getting very black. So he poked his fat hand into the pumpkin-house door, and it slipped right in; so he tried the other hand, then his curly head bobbed right in, too, and quick as a wink in walked all of Happy.

How nice it was in that pumpkin-house,— little chairs, a table, a bed, a dandy fire-place to bake sweet potatoes in. While Happy's eyes grew big looking at things, the Pumpkin-Man came in and pulled out a company chair.

"Now you just make yourself at home, while I get you a bite to eat. It sure seems good to have a little boy about."

While the Pumpkin-Man cooked the nicest smelling things, Happy tried to figure out how small he really was. Just then the Pumpkin-Man invited Happy to supper, and it was a nice supper,— pumpkin pie, pumpkin butter—so many good things, and not one drop of syrup on them. Somehow Happy didn't like syrup any more and was glad the Pumpkin-Man didn't have any.

After a while the Pumpkin-Man helped Happy into a soft bed, and Happy sailed away into sleepy-land.

The next morning when Happy awoke, the Pumpkin-Man had breakfast ready. He seemed in a terrible hurry about something. Scarcely had Happy swallowed his breakfast when the Pumpkin-Man handed him a shovel and a sack.

"Hurry, Happy, we must get to work." He jumped out of the door with Happy following.

" HAPPY "

"Say, Mister Pumpkin-Man, I don't want to work."

"Oh, that don't make any difference; everyone works here," and the Pumpkin-Man looked so in earnest that Happy thought he had better see how hard the work was; so he watched the Pumpkin-Man go among the big, yellow pumpkin flowers.

"Now, Happy," said the Man, "You look into these pumpkin flowers and you will see that some of them are just loaded with gold powder; but they are too stingy to give part of it to their poor neighbors who haven't any, so you and I must shovel that gold powder into our sacks. When you get your sack full, you call me."

Then the Pumpkin-Man went to work filling his sack; so did Happy, and at first it seemed lots of fun climbing in and out the big yellow flowers; but at last when the sack was so full he could scarcely wiggle it, he was mighty glad to call the Pumpkin-Man, who came on a run.

"Now I can play," said Happy, skipping about so crazy-like that he kicked Mister Grasshopper on the knee.

"Not yet, Happy, we don't play in Pumpkin Land until all our work is done."

"But I did fill the sack," Happy panted.

"You are only half-done; now take your sack of gold powder, go among the flowers and when you find a pumpkin flower without any gold, you put in a shovelful and very soon that lazy flower will turn into a big, yellow pumpkin,— just like magic. Only in the Land of Sure Enough things do that way without magic."

The Pumpkin-Man hurried away and Happy sat down, exclaiming, "I'm not going to work."

Just then Old Mister Bumble-Bee came along with his fiery stick, singing a war song.

Happy had met Mister Bumble-Bee before and he didn't like him; but anyway he said, "Howdy," mighty friendly.

"Why, hello, Happy. Are you working?"

"Yes," said Happy. "What are you doing, Mister Bumble-Bee?"

"Me? Oh, I am the corn-field policeman. I see that everyone keeps at their work; goodness, I do get tired; but you bet I don't stop until play-time."

Mister Bumble-Bee gave such a mad hum that Happy almost upset himself putting gold powder into the flowers. Before he knew it, there wasn't a grain left in his sack and when he got to the Pumpkin-Man's house, the Pumpkin-Man was already there, with the table just loaded with good things. Why he seemed to just fairly rake the roundest, brownest goodies right out of the fire-place; and all the time the Pumpkin-Man was smiling so that it seemed as if Mister Sun was in the house.

When they had eaten all the good supper, the Pumpkin-Man grabbed Happy's fat little hand, and sang:

"Come play, Come play,
No more work for us this day."

Dancing and singing out among the tall corn, they went for the best really good time Happy ever had,—he never dreamed one could have just such a good time in a corn-field.

All the Grasshopper family came and brought their fiddles; the Cricket family brought their mandolins; Miss Katy-did and the three Frogs sang songs; even old Mr. Bumble-Bee hung his fiery stick on a corn leaf and sang a funny song.

Everybody danced until their legs got tired, then they played games, until at last Happy just couldn't even prop his eyes open, and he tumbled into bed.

For a long time Happy lived with the Pumpkin-Man, working and playing. He liked the great yellow flowers, and they would tremble with delight and nod so gayly when he passed among them. At last, one day, the Pumpkin-Man looked so sad he wouldn't even eat any of the good things he had fixed for Happy.

"Guess we won't need our shovels today, Happy."

"Why?" asked Happy. "What's the matter?"

"Old Mister Wolf-Wind is going to pay us a visit tonight," said the Pumpkin-Man. "That old, cold, long tongue of his will lick up all the green things."

All that day Happy played as he had never played before, telling each yellow pumpkin flower good-bye; and the flowers drooped their heads when he didn't give them any gold powder, and wondered why he passed them so.

Very late Happy went into the pumpkin-house. How he did wish he could take all the pumpkin flowers in with him and cuddle them warm and safe from the long, white, sharp teeth of Mr. Wolf-Wind, who comes sometimes away down South, in Georgia, for a nice juicy bite of greens.

Somehow, the Pumpkin-Man would not talk that night, so that Happy went to bed; and strange, he thought about going home for the first time since he ran away.

Why, really, he wanted to go back so bad that a tear crept out of his eye, to see how sad he looked; he felt like getting up right then and going home, only he was so small that he was afraid Mammy Tibblets wouldn't know him; so he went to sleep.

It was very late the next morning when Happy woke up, and no wonder—the Pumpkin-Man wasn't there to call him. Happy ran here and there calling him.

Outside everything looked so different,—Old Mister Wolf-Wind had been there, all right, and my! What a mess of greens he had snapped up! Why, he didn't leave a green thing in the corn-field; wherever he had blown his breath, he had left all the pumpkin vines black. Happy called and called the Pumpkin-Man, but he couldn't find any sign of him. He asked Mister Grasshopper if he had seen the Pumpkin-Man, but old Mister Wolf-Wind had bit Mister Grasshopper so that he just couldn't say a word,—he was so cold. To be sure, when Mister Sun woke up and saw Mister Wolf-Wind lapping up all the green things, he was sure mad, and tumbled out of his bed right on to old Wolf-Wind's back and sent him back North again, a-howling and a-hurrying.

Then Happy heard a terrible noise down in the corn-field. He saw coming two big mules, pulling a big wagon, and Captain Jones' colored boy pulling the pumpkins and putting them into the wagon.

Happy hopped into the pumpkin-house and slammed the door tight. Then Happy felt his pumpkin-house lifted up—up, and plunked right down on a pile of pumpkins in the wagon.

"Get up, mules," shouted the colored boy, and the wagon rattled and bumped down the big road, past Happy's own house.

"Whoa," called the colored boy, and the mules stopped.

Happy wondered where he was going, then the colored boy called to someone.

"Say, Aunt Tibblets, do you want to buy a mighty fine pie pumpkin for a dime? It's the biggest pumpkin that I ever saw in a corn-field."

Mammy Tibblets went into the house, got a dime out of the cracked cup in the cupboard, and gave it to the boy for the pumpkin.

"My, it's just as heavy as my boy, Happy," said she, dropping the pumpkin on the table.

While she went for a knife to cut open the pumpkin for pies, Happy tried to get out; but the pumpkin-door had stuck fast. Just then Mammy Tibblets started to cut the pumpkin, but somehow that pumpkin was so hard and she sawed and grunted so hard that the pumpkin

slipped and fell right off the table and rolled under it. There it broke into halves, leaving Happy kicking about, as big as he ever was. Mammy reached under the table and pulled. She thought she had the pumpkin, but she had Happy's fat left leg.

"For land's sakes, Happy, what are you doing under there? That's no place to sleep, besides that syrup isn't anything to hide for." Mammy Tibblets looked so pleased that Happy smiled all over his nice brown face.

"Why, Mammy, have I been asleep? Seems to me as if I have been away in Pumpkin Land for a long time.

"Pshaw, what a funny boy you are," said Mammy.

You see, magic things do happen in the Land of Sure Enough, only they are not magic, and you don't know them, because you never wash your toes in the dew drops.

Then Happy picked up the pumpkin-house and helped Mammy make it into pies.

The Wishing Game
ANNETTE BROWNE

WE gathered 'round the fire last night,
    Jim an' Bess an' me,
And said, "Now let us each in turn
Tell who we'd rather be,
Of all the folks that's in our books."
(Of course, we wouldn't want their looks.)

Bess wished that she'd been Betsy Ross,
The first to make the flag.
one said, "I'd like to do some deed
To make the people brag,
And have the papers print my name,—
If colored girls could rise to fame."

An' I stood out for Roosevelt;
I wished to be like him.
Then Bess said, "We've both had our say,
Now tell who you'd be, Jim."
Jim never thinks like me or Bess,
He knows more than us both, I guess.

He said, "I'd be a Paul Dunbar
Or Booker Washington.
The folks you named were good, I know,
But you see, Tom, each one
Of these two men I'd wish to be
Were colored boys, like you and me.

"Sojourner Truth was colored, Bess,
And Phyllis Wheatley, too;
Their names will live like Betsy Ross,
Though they were dark like you."
Jim's read of 'em somewhere, I guess,
He knows heaps more than me or Bess.

The Origin of White Folks
ANNIE VIRGINIA CULBERTSON

DE white folks nee-nter putt on airs
    About dem wash'out faces,
De culled folks wuz made de fust,
    De oldes' uv de races.
Dey'z kneaded outer mud an' truck,
    An' den stood up in places
Along de fence to bake 'em dry,
    An' dat's de on'liest reason why
Dey's got dem sunburnt faces.

Dey had a scrumpshous time ontwel
    Ole Nick got on deir traces,
An' den dey et dat apple up,
    An' fell in deep disgraces;
An' when dey hearn deir names called out,
    Dey run fer hidin' places,
An' turnt so pale dey stayed dat way,
    An' dat's de reason why, folks say,
Dey's got dem wash'out faces.

A Boy Scout Troop of Philadelphia

"OVER THE OCEAN WAVE"

BETTY and Philip went with Uncle Jim to the "movies" that rainy afternoon, and there they saw a picture of two young colored girls.

"Look, Phil," whispered Betty, "there are some colored folks just like us. Who are they?"

"It tells underneath the picture," said Philip, "but the words are so hard and long. Quick, tell us what it's all about, Uncle Jim."

So Uncle Jim read obediently, "Left and right: Beautiful Princess Parhata Miran, eighteen year old daughter of the Sultan of the Island of Jolo, and Carmen R. Aguinaldo, daughter of the former Filipino bandit, who are now enrolled as students in the University of Chicago, Illinois."

By the time Uncle Jim had finished, the picture had passed on, and the feature picture began. The children were very much interested in this, for it was a Wild West Show, and Uncle Jim thought they had forgotten all about the two Filipinos. He was rather glad of this, for the children could ask a great many difficult questions. Of course, Uncle Jim knew lots of answers, but it is not easy to know something about everything, and if it were not for Children's Magazines, Uncle Jim at times would hardly know what to do.

As it was, Betty and Philip had hardly stepped out into the pleasant, silver rain, before they began.

"Where did you say those girls came from?" asked Betty. "Were they really colored? They looked a little odd, though the fat girl looks like Mabel Ross who sits next to me in school."

"They're from the Philippines," said Uncle Jim with a slight groan, for he knew he was in for it now. "And they are colored,—that is their skin is not white; but they belong to a different division of people from what we do. You see, we colored Americans are mostly of the black, or Negro race; whereas these girls belong to the brown, or Malay race. Do you know anything of the different races in the world, Betty?"

"Yes," said Betty promptly, and standing still in the pattering rain, right in the middle of the street, she began. "There are five races:

the red, or Indian; the yellow, or Mongolian; the white, or——"

"Oh, make her stop that, Uncle Jim!" interrupted Philip. "She got a hundred in an examination on the different races once, and she's been talking about them ever since. Tell us where the Philippines are."

"Well," said Uncle Jim, "let me see if I can make you see them plainly without the map. Do you know where China is?"

"Yes," said Philip, "it's in Asia, right on the Pacific Ocean."

"Good," said his uncle; "now the Philippine Islands are a large group of islands lying in the Pacific Ocean, south and east of China, directly east of French Indo-China, and north and west of Borneo. The China Sea is on the west of these islands, between China and the Philippines, and to the north and south and east lies the wonderful Pacific Ocean. Do you get the picture, Betty?"

"Yes," said Betty, "I do. Aren't the names pretty,—Borneo and the China Sea. It seems to me I smell all sorts of good things. Tell us about some more places with the queer, pretty names."

"I'm not so sure I can remember," said Uncle Jim. "Let's see now, the Philippines form a sort of a capital S, with very shallow upper and lower curves. At the top of the letter is Luzon, and at the bottom Mindanao, and right through the center is a group called the Bisayas. I've forgotten the names of the islands that form the group, but I'll tell you some day."

"Well, here we are right at home, so look it up now," said the children. So they went into the little sitting-room and got out the atlas, and there were the Bisayas, with names that delighted Betty more than ever: Panay, Negros, Leite, Cebu, Samar, and Bohol. Off to the west, and not belonging to the Bisayan group, but still one of the Philippines, lies long, slim Palawan.

"And down here in the corner is Jolo," cried Philip, who had been looking industriously through the pages of his little geography.

"Show it to me," said Uncle Jim, much relieved to find out where it was before the children had forced him to admit his lack of knowledge. So Philip showed him with a pudgy, brown finger, which nearly blotted out the island, for Jolo was so tiny. Sure enough, there it lay, a little speck of an island quite to the south-west of the extreme south-western point of Mindanao. It seemed to be a very important island, however, for to the north and west of it lay the Jolo Sea, and to the south and east of it lay a group of tiny islands called the Jolo Archipelago.

"Archipelago is the name for a lot of islands all jammed up close together," Betty told her uncle.

"Now," said Uncle Jim, "you kiddies have had a fine time of it. Get out and give me a chance to read the paper."

"Just one t h i n g more," begged Philip. "Do tell me what the picture meant when it spoke of the bandit, Aggy-Aggy — w h a t was his name, Uncle Jim?"

"Aguinaldo, y o u mean. Oh, that was the name of a great Filipino leader," said his uncle. "You see, the Philippines used to belong to Spain, but in 1898, as the result of a war between Spain and the United States, the islands were given to us. Aguinaldo, a brave and spirited Filipino, resented American rule and

Princess Parhata Miran   *International.*   Carmen R. Aguinaldo

waged warfare for a long time against the Americans. He was finally captured and banished by the new-comers in authority.

"Of course, according to them he was a bandit, or outlaw,—a person who breaks the laws. But in the eyes of his own countrymen he was probably regarded as a patriot. It all depends," said Uncle Jim, "on how you look at it. As it is, the United States has finally promised the Filipinos their independence, and there is a delegation of Filipinos in Washington this minute to remind us of that promise. I shouldn't be surprised if the influence of Aguinaldo were back of it all. Now I shall not answer another question. Get out."

"It's too bad you're a boy," said Betty, turning to Philip, "because both the people in that picture were girls. I shall play first at being t h e "Beautiful Princess," whose father is Sultan of the funny little island, and then afterwards I shall be the daughter of the bandit."

"Oh," said Philip, "you don't suppose I care. I am going to be the bandit!"

卐 卐 卐 卐

Whole Duty of Children

FROM ROBERT LOUIS STEVENSON

A CHILD should always say what's true,
   And speak when he is spoken to,
And behave mannerly at table,
   At least, as far as he is able.

Some Little Friends of Ours

THE JUDGE

AM the Judge. I am very, very old. I know all things, except a few, and I have been appointed by the King to sit in the Court of Children and tell them the Law and listen to what they have to say. The Law is old and musty and needs sadly to be changed. In time the Children will change it; but now it is the Law.

Before me sit the Children. There are three of them. It may be three hundred, or three million, or—— but at any rate, THREE: first, there is Billikins, who is six; then, there is Billie, who is ten; and finally, there is William, who is astonishingly grown-up, being all of fifteen on his last birthday.

It is my business,—I, the Judge—to say each month a little lecture to Billikins, Billie and William, *and* their sisters who have much prettier names and faces; and also to listen very patiently while the *children* speak to me and to the world.

SAYS BILLIKINS

THIS is winter. There is the shadow of snow in the air: Thanksgiving and Christmas and the New Year are here to make us glad. School work is getting interesting. Flowers are gone. But the sun shines, and it is cold and sweet out-doors even when the bright rain falls. This is the time to play and think and work for Springtime. It is splendid to live in these fine days and study and learn lots and grow big and do things.

I would like to know so much: Why the sun rises, and what the moon is, and who lives in the stars, and why candy is so good. If I listen and try, I shall know most of these things and many others in time. All the time, I must be true. I try to be good. But you cannot always be good. You CAN always be true, and that is better.

Of course, SOMETIMES, almost all times, you can be Good, too. But if you're not good, just say so and try, try again. That's what the world does, and Life is Trying.

ABOUT BILLIE

THERE is no doubt about it, we Children have just got to take hold of this world. The Grown-ups have made an awful mess of it. First and worst, they have forgotten how to Laugh. Now let me say right here: The nicest thing in the world is Laughter—good, big, loud laughs. And next is Smiles, the sort that come before and after. Laughter clears away rubbish and gets things started. Fancy forgetting how to laugh! How *could* they? But they did and then, naturally, they fought. Fighting is mostly wrong and silly. Of *course*, if you're just set upon by a bully and you *can't* laugh it off, why just punch him hard, and then make up. See? *Make up!* Don't try and be mad forever, or for a day. Make up, and try a game of ball. Let him bat if he wants to. He'll probably strike out, and then you'll have your innings.

Of course, we Children know this is easy; but Grown-ups don't. They're awfully dull at times, and if we don't take hold of things and help, I don't know where this old world is going to land. It's a mighty nice world, too. The best ever if you just treat it square. But if you mess it up with blood and hate and meanness, why it's awful. If the Grown-ups keep on, we Children will just have to crowd them right off the edge and take charge of things. Gee! But what a jolly place: marbles, and tag, and funny stories, and pennies, and dolls, and tops, and—oh! everything that really counts.

So look out, Grown-ups, we've got our eye on you, and "Don't let us have to speak to you again,"—as Father says.

THE PROBLEMS OF WILLIAM'S SISTER

I AM what mother is fond of calling "Half-grown"—which is not altogether a nice description. I am very nearly as big as I ever expect to be, and while I shall doubtless learn a great deal more than I now know, yet even now I am by no means an idiot, and I have gotten considerable valuable information—particularly in the last Fifteen years.

I know, naturally, that one cannot have everything one wants in this world—worse luck! I, for instance, would like silk stockings, a hobble skirt, and one of those dreams of hats that look like little beds of nicely tended violets. Mother says we can't afford it, and I presume we can't. Only I want to put the thing this way: Sometimes we can afford some things that I particularly want and when we *can*, why not let me have what I want, instead of always handing me what somebody else wants me to want? Of course, I know I must be a good sport and take my share of hard work and not want everything always; but I insist, let my very own wants count sometimes. Don't always try to do my wishing and thinking for me. It may be that this particular hat is worth a week's work to me and that some people don't fancy it, but why not let me have it if I want it and we can afford it? You see, it's this way: In three or four little years I shall be my own mistress; why not train me for that part, instead of continually mistaking me for Billikins?

WHERETO THE JUDGE REPLIES

BILLIKINS, you're the wisest of the bunch. Be happy and learn. Notice the Weather and the Flowers and have faith in Time. Try hard to be true. I suspect that you are not really, truly, saying all these things yourself, for you are a very little man. But Mother, or God, is interpreting your thoughts for you liberally and nicely.

I ADMIT, Billie, that we Grown-ups ought to be ashamed of ourselves, for we have sinned, and we keep it up. Only, Billie, remember that this world is not simple and easy to understand and guide. There are whole lots of difficulties that you have neither seen nor dreamed of, and which are very hard to explain. Before, then, you lose faith in us entirely, wait—wait a while. Meantime, it is too true that we should dwell close to your simplicity; that we should amid noise and wrong and multiplicity, keep your clear, straightforward view of the bigger world. We must rise to our Children's Laughter—but, ah! Billie-boy, it's a hard thing for *us* to laugh at times; wherefore, perhaps, *you* should laugh all the more.

And do *please*, for our sakes, have just as much fun as you possibly can, so as to set the world a-laughing.

IT is a difficult and ever-recurring question that Wilhelmina brings: a question of Money, Taste, and Guidance for young folk—not "Half-growns," but simply Folk who still have the shining mark of Youth written on their dear foreheads.

If you had all the Money in the World and were—as God send you may be—Mother of a Little Man, would you give him everything he wanted, even though he were Fifteen? Oh, no, —not even though he were Fifty! So here is the first Law:

Not everything we want.

But, surely, some things we want, else what's the use of living? Too true. Moreover, the

"World is so full of a number of things"

that we must choose. Choosing is hard, for it involves Money and Taste. Taste is a sort of rule of Choice. It is the Judgment, not of you or of me alone, but of numbers of thoughtful people, living at all times.

How do you *know* you like that hat? Is it suited to you? Does it really set off your figure and your gown and your smooth, brown skin? Or—and here I have a deep suspicion—do you choose it because Katie Brown has one like it and the Ladies of Avenue K, and—but hold! Who are K. B. and the L. of A. K? Are they persons of taste, or simply of power? Do you imitate them for love, or fear? Does the choice of this hat represent your freedom of thoughtful taste, or your slavery to what the flamboyant Kitty does or to what rich white folk wear?

Mind you, I'm not answering these questions —I'm just asking. We will assume that the hat is becoming and suits you and you want it. Now comes that awkward question of Money. What is the question of Money? Simply this: Of the 1,000 ways of spending this dollar, which is best for me, for mother, for the family, for my people, for the world? If the "best" way of spending it for you makes mother starve, or the family lose the home, or colored folk be ridiculed, or the world look silly—why, the such hat for *you*, and that, too, by is very dull. dear Judgment.   town, but you

On the contrary, if nobody is h d, anyhow, it is want the hat and have the do And there are not get more pleasure in any othe s by sewing rags to- and be happy. You see, de ts and I am going to that is asked of Fiftee OOK, which I am very when hats call. And c best chum's advic   MARY PERKINS.

Waiting for a Howard-Fisk Football Game

rises, ...
the stars, a...
and try, I sha...
many others in
true. I try to be ...
be good. You CAN
better.
    Of course, SOME...
,ou can be Good, too. Bu...
just say so and try, try, again...
....r'd loes, and Life is Trying.

THE JURY

DEAR MR. EDITOR:

Y mother says you are going to have a magazine about colored boys and girls, and I am very glad. So I am writing to ask you if you will please put in your paper some of the things which colored boys can work at when they grow up. I don't want to be a doctor, or anything like that. I think I'd like to plan houses for men to build. But one day, down on Broad Street, I was watching some men building houses, and I said to a boy there, "When I grow up, I am going to draw a lot of houses like that and have men build them." The boy was a white boy, and he looked at me and laughed and said, "Colored boys don't draw houses."

Why don't they, Mr. Editor?

My mother says you will explain all this to me in your magazine and will tell me where to learn how to draw a house, for that is what I certainly mean to do. I hope I haven't made you tired, so no more from your friend,

FRANKLIN LEWIS, Philadelphia, Pa.

DEAR SIR:

I AM a girl fifteen years old and am still in the graded school. I am not so very poor, and would like to take up any course in a boarding school. Do you know of any school that a girl not yet out of graded school could enter? Also, do you know of anyone who would back me in going to the school? I am willing to work my way through school, if I could only get someone to help me get in a school like that.

I am a girl who has never known of a father's love, as my father died when I was very young. I will tell you in the beginning,—I am not a very pretty girl, and for that reason I have not been able to get anyone to help me in my little plan.

I have tried and tried to do something in Seattle, but the people are very down on the Negro race. In some schools they do not want colored children.

I close, hoping you will try and do something for me, leaving with you my address.

—————— ——, Seattle, Washington.

P. S. Won't you answer me just as soon as you can? Please help me, and maybe some day I can help you.

DEAR DR. DU BOIS:

OUR *Crisis* came a few days ago, and I was very glad to see the advertisement of THE BROWNIES' BOOK. I had just been talking to mother about giving me a subscription to some children's magazine and was delighted to know that we shall soon have one of our very own.

I see that you want letters from the children. I shall be glad if you will tell me what kind of a letter you want.

I want to be one of the first subscribers to THE BROWNIES' BOOK.

WENONAH BOND, Washington, D. C.

DEAR SIR:

I AM writing to ask you to refer me to some books on the Negro. I want to learn more about my race, so I want to begin early. I am twelve years old and hope to, when I am old enough, bend all of my efforts for the advancement of colored people.

I want to subscribe for *The Crisis*, but I don't want to subscribe until I go to Covington, Ky., where I go to school. . . .

I hope some day that all detestable "Jim-Crow" cars will be wiped out of existence, along with all prejudice, segregation, etc.

ELEANOR HOLLAND, Wilberforce, Ohio.

DEAR CRISIS:

IN the country where I live, it is very dull. There is a movie in the next town, but you have to sit in one corner. And, anyhow, it is too far away for little girls. And there are not many books. I make pennies by sewing rags together to make rag carpets and I am going to buy THE BROWNIES' BOOK, which I am very glad to hear of.

MARY PERKINS.

Celebratin

Tuskegee

THE OUIJA BOARD

A STORY

EDNA MAY HARROLD

LORIA LORIMER and Betty Fielding came slowly down the steps of the public library, their arms burdened with books piled high.

"It's going to be a great contest, Betty," said Gloria, a round, short maiden of fifteen. "I think it's so nice of Mr. Sellers to offer such a prize, don't you?"

"Yes, it's nice," replied Betty, stifling a sigh, "but it won't do me any good. I just know you'll get the prize. No one has any chance against you."

Gloria, exulting inwardly, cast her eyes modestly toward the ground.

"Of course, I'm not going to win the prize," she protested. "I mean to try for it, but that's no sign I'll get it. There are plenty of girls, and boys, too, in our class who are just as smart as I am."

"But you've led the class all this term," said Betty dolefully. "Oh, dear, I wish I were so smart."

"Why, Betty, you have as much chance to win the prize as I have. And I'll help you. Don't I always help you whenever you ask me? I'm glad we came to the library early and got the best books. It's lucky Maude wasn't at school today. If she had heard about the contest, she would have been at the library picking over books before anyone else had time to turn. I'll call her up, though, and tell her about it."

When Gloria reached home, she hurried to the telephone to tell her friend the news. Barely taking time to inquire about the aching tooth which had kept Maude from school that day, she began:

"Maude, you'd never guess! Miss Dyson told us today in English literature that the president of the school board has offered a prize of five dollars in gold to the pupil who brings in the most comprehensive review of 'Macbeth.' . . . Why, Maude Barstow, what nonsense you talk! Of course, I'm going to try for the prize, but I don't know that I'll get it. . . . What? . . . Oh, that's what Betty said, but I don't know. Try and come to school tomorrow. I'm

going to help you and Betty both with your reviews. We've got two weeks. . . . Good-by."

Gloria turned from the telephone with a pleased expression. For a while she gave herself over to visions of winning the prize, and spending it. In spite of her modest protests to her friends, Gloria was confident that she would win. Hadn't she led her English literature class all the term? Wasn't she the most brilliant scholar in her Latin class? With a satisfied, confident smile, she began to sharpen her pencil.

The time went by, until there remained only four days in which to prepare for the contest. Betty and Maude had valiantly, though reluctantly, declined Gloria's generous offers of help and had decided to do the best they could alone; not that either of them had the faintest hope of winning the prize; they were confident that the gold would go to Gloria.

The contest was to close on Thursday and the prize was to be awarded the following Monday. Friday afternoon when school was dismissed, Gloria approached her chums with an air of mystery.

"I'm going to have my fortune told and I want you to go with me," she whispered, enjoying the shocked surprise of the other girls.

"Gloria, you wouldn't dare!" exclaimed Maude. "Why, that's a sin."

Betty was speechless.

"It is not a sin!" denied Gloria indignantly. "It's just in fun, anyway. Why, I know lots of people who go to Mrs. Gray and have their fortunes told. People who belong to the church, too. It only costs thirty cents. And I guess I've got a right to know what my future holds."

Maude shifted uneasily. "It doesn't seem right," she protested feebly.

"Well, it is right. I'm not asking you or Betty to have yours told. I'm just asking you to go with me. I've always treated you both right and done whatever you wanted me to; and if you're not friends enough to me to do a little thing like that, well—all right."

This argument, although not strictly true, was felt to be unanswerable; so the three started out for Mrs. Gray's.

In spite of her brave exterior, Gloria felt

considerable trepidation when Mrs. Gray responded to her timid knock.

"Come in, girls, come in," invited the seer cordially. "Which one wants to see me?"

Betty and Maude huddled fearfully together, while Gloria moistened dry lips and stammered a husky, "I do."

"Well, now, don't be afraid. Just set right down. I'll give you a twenty minute palm reading for a dollar, or a ten minute card reading for fifty cents. Them's my terms."

Gloria's face fell.

"Why—I—I—someone told me it was thirty cents," she ventured timidly.

"Thirty cents! You see it's hard on me—this medium business is. Sometimes when I give five or six readings a day, I get so wore out that when night comes, I feel just like I'm shrivelling up. So, you see, I have to make it worth my while, Dearie."

"Yes'm." Gloria forced a feeble smile and arose. "I guess maybe I'll have to come back some other day. Thirty cents is all I have, and——"

"Well now, Pet, set right down. You didn't let me finish telling you my terms. I'll give you a five minute reading on the Ouija Board for thirty cents. Here's my Board right here. Now just set quiet, all of you."

The three girls waited with baited breath, while Mrs. Gray, eyes closed and hands moving rapidly over the Board, began in a low tone:

"You are going to be a great woman some day, Derie; the Board tells me so. An' you're going to win great fame and honors, and it won't be so very long till you win them, either. You're coming into money, Dearie,—gold; the Ouija Board tells me it is. You've got some friends and some enemies. Look out for a slim, brown-skin woman. An'—an'—that's all."

Gloria left the fortune teller's with a swelling heart. The girls were half-way up the block before anyone spoke, and then Betty said solemnly, "Isn't she wonderful? The great honors and the gold! Oh, Gloria, now I know you're going to win the prize."

Maude, who had been walking along rapt in thought, stopped suddenly and said, "Look here, girls, I believe that woman's a fake."

Gloria turned angrily upon her and answered hotly, "She isn't a fake, either. I can't help it if you're mad about what she said about my——"

"Humph! I'm not mad," interrupted Maude.

"Didn't I say all along that you'd get the prize? But here's why I say that woman's a fake: it seems to me that I've heard people say that when you work a Ouija Board, you ask it questions and it spells out the answers. Well, if it spells things out, wouldn't you have to look at the letters on it to see what it's spelling; and didn't Mrs. Gray have her eyes shut the whole time? And did she ask it a single, solitary question? Yes, she's a fake and a big one, too."

For a moment even Gloria was stunned by this, but after a bit she retorted, "Sometimes you have to look at a Ouija Board, and sometimes you don't. Real good mediums, like Mrs. Gray, don't need to look because they—they—well, they get the messages through their finger tips."

Even Betty looked skeptical at this, but Gloria continued stoutly, "I guess I ought to know, seeing how much I've read about it. I've read dozens of books just on that one subject, and I can show you the very page in one of the books where it says that first-class mediums get messages through their finger tips. Can either of you show me any book where it says they don't?"

This silenced the others, whether it convinced them or not. Gloria cared not at all that what she had just uttered contained even less than a grain of truth. She had been convinced from the first that she was going to win the prize and Mrs. Gray's statements had only served to strengthen that conviction. Gloria didn't care a jot how Mrs. Gray received her messages; she didn't care a fig for Maude's croakings. Besides, hadn't Mrs. Gray warned her to look out for a "slim, brown-skin woman"? And wasn't Maude "slim and brown-skin"? Most assuredly she was to pay no attention to Maude.

When the news of Mrs. Gray's revelation spread at school Monday morning, Gloria was regarded with a feeling closely akin to awe. Nearly everyone had been certain that Gloria would win the prize and now that certainty was confirmed by supernatural powers. Happy Gloria! How she basked in the light of her school-mates' adulation!

Monday afternoon the class was in a fever of expectation, and Gloria was easily the most popular girl at school. Girls who had not spoken to her for weeks vied with each other for a word, or a smile from the chosen one.

When the time came for awarding the prize,

it was with great difficulty that Miss Dyson obtained order. Mr. Sellers, President of the School Board, sat by Miss Dyson's desk, looking very large and important, while the other judges sat hard by. After a few whispered words with Miss Dyson, Mr. Sellers arose and stepped ponderously forward.

He wasn't much of a speechmaker, he said,—in fact he couldn't make a speech at all. But the other judges had insisted that he present the prize. As every scholar knew, this prize was a five dollar gold-piece, to be given to the pupil who wrote the most comprehensive review of "Macbeth." After a very careful consideration of all the manuscripts handed in, the judges had come to this conclusion: Most of the reviews were good; two or three were excellent; but the one the judges considered the most deserving of the prize was written by Miss Maude Barstow. Therefore, it was with unqualified pleasure that he presented Miss Barstow the gold.

 PLAYTIME

"HARK, HARK, THE DOGS DO BARK"
A Nursery Rhyme Dance
CARRIEBEL B. COLE

FORMATION—Single circle, facing for walking.

"HARK, hark"

> Right hand at ear (listening), walking forward, right and left.

"The dogs do bark"

> Hands at sides, four little scuffling steps forward: left, right, left, right.

"The beggars are coming to town"

> Left hand over eyes (looking), three steps forward, trunk bending, and looking from side to side.

"Some in rags, and some in tags"

> Arms hanging relaxed at sides, four steps forward: right, left, right, left, with high knee bending.

"And some in velvet gowns"

> Right arm extended forward, left backward, three stately walking steps forward: right, left, right, left.

"And some in velvet gowns"

> Repeat, but much slower, and more stately.

DANCE

1. Touch right toe in front.
2. Touch right toe in front.
1. Change weight to left foot, and point right in front.
2. Change weight to right foot, and point left in front.
3. Change weight to left foot, and point right in front.

Repeat all, but start with touching left foot.

1, 2, 3, Change step forward, starting with left foot.
1, 2, 3, Change step forward, starting with right foot.
1, 2, 3, Change step forward, starting with left foot.
1, 2, 3, Change step forward, starting with right foot.

Repeat the whole dance.

———————

NOTE—Change step: step forward right, bring left to it, and
step again right. This resembles the two-step, or is a
catch-step.

Girls School Directed by Nuns, Addis-Ababa, Abyssinia

Y. W. C. A. Girls in New York City

AS THE CROW FLIES

HE Crow is black and O so beautiful, shining with dark blues and purples, with little hints of gold in his mighty wings. He flies far above the Earth, looking downward with his sharp eyes.

What a lot of things he must see and hear and if he could only talk—and lo! THE BROWNIES' BOOK has made him talk for you.

卐 卐

"Ah!" says the Crow, as he sharpens his long, thin beak on his slender leg—"What a year—what a year that 1918 was—all blood and hurt and cries—I thought the world people were mad and would die away and leave the earth to us peaceful crows."

"That was the World War, and it cost 200 thousand million dollars and 8 million lives and 20 million wounded men," piped the Little Boy with the Big Voice.

"Yes," answered the Crow, "and then came THE YEAR OF THE GREAT PEACE, 1919.

"O me, O my," said the Little Voice with the Big Boy, "I hadn't heard of 1919."

"That's because it's so near."

"Well, tell me quick before they stick it into my history and make me study it three times a week at 2:45 p.m. and examination Thursdays, with dates."

"I don't remember dates," said the Crow, "but here are the facts."

⁋ This year was two things: it was the year of the Great Peace and the 300th year since our black fathers settled in America. Perhaps the good God remembered both these things when he made this year.

⁋ The Armistice came November, a year ago, with the black troops nearing Metz, and the 367th colored regiment nearest the Rhine.

⁋ Then the Peace Conference met at Paris, in January, with white men and black men and yellow. There were the President-elect of Liberia, and the Minister from Haiti, and dark Arabs; there were Japanese and Chinese, and they remade the map of Europe.

⁋ Take your atlas: There is no German Empire—it is the Imperial German Republic; there is only a piece of Austria; there is a new Poland, Czecho-Slovakia, Hungary, and a new kingdom of Serbs and Jugo-slavs; a new Jewish state is planned in the ancient Holy Land, 'round about Jerusalem; and Italy and France are much larger.

⁋ Then, too, the Peace Conference formed a new League of Nations—a sort of union government of all the world; and having made the Treaty and made Germany sign it, the Treaty was sent out to the nations of the world for their assent. England, Italy, Belgium, and Japan have signed it.

⁋ China refused to sign the Peace Treaty because the Treaty gives to Japan certain rights to that part of China,—Shantung,—which Germany formerly held.

⁋ The United States has refused to sign the Treaty as yet because a majority of the Senate wish to change some parts of it, so as to limit the power of the League of Nations. It will probably be signed, with some changes, next year.

⁋ Always after a great war there is much unrest, suffering, and poverty. This is because war kills human beings, leaves widows and orphans, destroys vast amounts of wealth, and disorganizes industry. The war of 1914-1918 was the greatest of human wars, and we hope the last. It destroyed untold wealth and turned men from their usual work. The result is great unrest and dissatisfaction throughout the world. People are thinking, they are hungry, and everything costs more.

⁋ The "High Cost of Living" means that today most things cost twice as much as they did five years ago. This is because materials are scarcer, fewer goods have been made, other goods have been destroyed, and more people want what's left. In addition to this, the cost of war was met by promises to pay in the future, (Liberty Bonds, for instance, are promises to pay) and this has increased the amount of things that circulate as money, as compared with the goods which money buys. For all these reasons prices have risen, and the man who could live on $750 a year in 1914 can scarcely get along with $1,500 today.

¶ There is unrest in Ireland because the Sinn Fein, (pronounced "Shin Fayn") representing most of the Irish, want Ireland to be an independent Republic, while others want it to be a part of England, with partial self-government, i.e., Home Rule.

¶ India, with 315,000,000 brown people, is very poor and illiterate. The average earnings of an Indian is only $9.50 a *year*, and 93% of them cannot read and write. Large numbers of Indians want to be an independent country and not a part of the British Empire. The English are seeking to suppress this desire by harsh laws and some concessions.

¶ Egypt, the oldest civilized country in the world, inhabited by mulattoes, has been declared a Protectorate of England since the war. Egypt does not like this, and many riots have taken place.

¶ Russia, during the war, had a revolution by which she overthrew the Empire of the Czar and tried to establish a Republic; but the common people feared the leadership of the rich and powerful even in a Republic, and under Lenine and Trotsky they established a communism of the "Bolsheviki." This movement is an attempt to place all power, both in politics and industry, in the hands of the working class, and the experiment is being watched with fear and excitement by the whole world.

¶ Parts of Russia and all of eastern Europe south of Poland, and on into the Balkans, are still in the midst of revolution. Thousands of Jews have been killed there.

¶ Celebrations to welcome returning soldiers took place all over the United States. Among the first and most notable were the receptions tendered to two colored regiments, the 369th in New York City and the 370th in Chicago. One thousand colored officers took part in the war.

¶ Many hundred strikes took place during the year; the most important were the harbor strike, which stopped all ships from leaving New York; the printers' strike, which kept hundreds of magazines from appearing; the coal strike, which halted the industry of the nation; and the steel strike against the great steel corporation. All these strikes are efforts of workingmen united in unions to increase wages by refusing to work. They claim that in no other way can they make known their wants and sufferings.

¶ Cotton, which in normal times sells at ten cents a pound or even less, has, on account of the war, gone up as high as forty cents a pound. This has brought much prosperity to the South.

¶ Reconstruction is the effort to re-establish normal conditions in the world after the war. It has resulted in many efforts to better the conditions of people and to find out causes of complaint. An Anti-lynching conference has been held in New York City; a new Labor Party has been founded in Chicago; and in South Dakota effort has been made to run certain kinds of public business by the State, so as to avoid giving profits to private merchants.

¶ For the first time an aeroplane crossed the Atlantic Ocean.

¶ At the great commencement season last June, five colored students received the degree of Master of Arts; 379, of whom 60 came from the great northern colleges, received the degree of Bachelor of Arts; and 129 received professional degrees.

¶ Many distinguished visitors have come to the United States since the war. Prominent among these was a delegation from the Empress of Abyssinia who claims descent from the Queen of Sheba; Liberia sent her President-elect, the Honorable C. D. B. King, and his wife; the King of Belgium visited us with his Queen; also the young Prince of Wales, who will sometime be King of England. Cardinal Mercier, of Belgium, and the Spanish writer Ibañez have spent some time in America.

¶ The President of the United States has been made seriously ill by his work at the Peace Conference and his effort since.

¶ There have been many race riots and lynchings during the year. The chief riots were in Washington, Chicago, Omaha; Longview, Texas, and Phillips County, Arkansas.

¶ Mexico is still striving against great odds to make herself a modern country, conducted for the benefit of her citizens instead of for the enriching of great corporations. Some people in the United States would like to have us intervene and help her, but we can scarcely help ourselves, and we ought to let Mexico alone.

❑ Many persons of wide renown died during the year. Chief among them were Theodore Roosevelt and Andrew Carnegie, friends of the

Negro race; George R. White, who was once a colored member of Congress; Madam C. J. Walker, a colored woman who amassed a large fortune by her preparations for the hair; and James Reese Europe, the colored musician.

❑ Nor may we forget the thousand black boys dead for France.

THE GROWN-UPS' CORNER

E are going to reserve a very small bit of this magazine for Grown-ups. It must not, under any circumstances, encroach on the Children's property, but we want to be generous.

This magazine is published for Children, but no one understands the needs of children, or the problems that arise in their training, particularly in colored families, so well as their Parents.

We want, therefore, the constant co-operation of parents, telling us what we ought to do, and what we ought to publish, and what we ought not to publish, and just what their problems are, what they need for themselves and for their children.

We trust that parents will write us freely and continually and let us have the benefit of their wisdom.

GENTLEMEN:

I HAVE just read your article in the October *Crisis*, "True Brownies," and I wish to say that of all the great things which you have undertaken during the publication of *The Crisis*, I think this the greatest. The idea is wonderful, and it expresses a thought which I have long wanted some information on.

We have one darling little boy, who is nine years of age today. We spend our summers here, as my husband's work is here during the summer months. My boy was born here, and I am sorry to say that he simply hates the place. The entire population is white,—colored people come only in the capacity of servants.

The natives are mostly Irish, and the children call my boy "nigger" and other names which make life for him very unpleasant. He comes

to us crying about it, and oh, the resentment I feel is terrible! He will fight the smaller boys, but, of course, the large boys he cannot fight. When we speak to their parents about it, they say that they are very sorry, and promise to stop their children from calling him names.

Now, the difficult problem for us is: What shall we tell him to do, and how best for him to answer them, and instill into him race love and race pride?

He is the first and only colored child in Nahant, and since the Great War and the recent race riots, his color seems to be noticed more and spoken of more by the white children.

One day he said to me: "Mother, the only way to fight these white people is to get an education and fight them with knowledge."

I shall await the TRUE BROWNIES number with great joy, as I believe it will be a great help to all of us. I pass *The Crisis* around among my white neighbors here. I want them to read it.

Enclosed please find $1.00 for one year's subscription to TRUE BROWNIES.

MRS. C. M. JOHNSON, Nahant, Mass.

HON. FRIEND:

FOR two years I have been a subscriber and a delighted reader of that very excellent journal *The Crisis*. I would not be without it.

My children look forward to its arrival with almost as much eagerness as myself. My boy of nine years on seeing and reading the account of that great "Silent Parade" wished he had been in it.

I know the great efforts and sacrifices we make here and there will surely bring better days for our boys and girls.

MRS. HATTIE E. WORNBLE, Rockingham, N. C.

Children in the "Silent Protest" Parade, New York City

KATY FERGUSON

A TRUE STORY

ID you ever hear of Katy Ferguson? I confess I did not until a very short while ago, and yet without my knowing it, Katy Ferguson must have been exerting a great influence over me for at least sixteen years. And unless I am very much mistaken, she has been influencing you, too.

If you are being brought up as I hope you are, you go to school every week-day, except Saturday, and on Sundays you go to Sunday School. There you sit and listen to the really wonderful church music and learn a great many beautiful texts and chat with the other boys and girls and enjoy yourself famously. Then you go home feeling very good and somewhat solemn, not very sorry that Sunday School is over, but on the whole perfectly willing to go back next Sunday.

"But what has Katy Ferguson to do with all this?" I hear you wondering.

Wait a moment.

Long, long ago, in 1774, Katy Ferguson was born to the cruellest fate that ever awaited a child. She was a slave. Stop and think about that a little while, try to picture the horrors of such a condition, and resolve that in no sense of the word will you allow such a fate to overtake you and yours. Evidently Katy thought something like this, for when she was eighteen, due to her own efforts and the fortunate impression she had made on some friends, she became free.

Not long afterwards she married, but neither her husband nor the children who came to her lived very long, and presently she was by herself again, living her life alone in the city of New York.

Now Katy was a very good woman,—tender, kind-hearted, and sensible. She did not let her sorrows crush and enfeeble her. On the contrary, she looked about her to see what her hands could find to do, and having found it, she did it. In her neighborhood in New York there were very many neglected children, both white and colored, and to them she gave her attention. Some she sheltered in her own house, and for others she found positions. During her life-time she helped in this way forty-eight needy children—a tremendous job for a poor woman.

But what interested Katy even more than caring for little children's bodies, was caring for little children's souls. So every Sunday Katy had children to come to her house so she could tell them about "God and the world to come." When her class grew too large and its instruction too much for her limited knowledge, she called in other good Christian folk to help; but of these none, I am sure, worked more willingly or more successfully than Katy.

One wonderful Sunday, Dr. Mason, the kind minister of a church on Murray Street, who had helped Katy in many ways when as a little girl she was beginning to seek "the way, the truth and the light," walked into Katy's house and found her surrounded by a group of interested and happy children.

"What are you about here?" he said. "Keeping school on the Sabbath? We must not leave you to do all this." And off he went and told the officers of his church and some other good people about it, and in a short while the lecture-room was opened to receive Katy's little friends. So the church in Murray Street opened a Sunday School, and it is generally conceded that Katy Ferguson, colored, and once a slave, was the founder of the first Sunday School in New York City.

Of course, Katy did many other things—she toiled hard for her daily bread and she received many opportunities to work, for she was a wonderful laundress and a ravishing cook. She was interested in the cause of missions, too, and let no chance of aiding them pass by. But don't you like best the notion of her getting the little children together and telling them that "of such is the kingdom of heaven?" I do.

And I think that those of you who read this little history will go to Sunday School some Sunday and instead of whispering to the pupil next you, you will look right into the wonderful glory that comes pouring through the stained-glass windows on Sunday afternoons, and in your heart you will say, "Dear God, I am thankful for Katy Ferguson."

So now you know the story of a noble colored woman. But she is not the only colored woman to do great deeds for her race. There are many splendid colored men, too. Think of all the wonderful folks you have still to hear about!

Little People of the Month

A MUSICIAN

OST boys and girls are frightened when they get up to "speak a piece" at the Sunday School concert. But Eugene Mars Martin would not be, because he has been used to facing audiences ever since he was very tiny. When he was not quite four years old, he played on his little violin in the auditorium of the Grand Central Palace, in New York. Since then he has studied at the Institute of Musical Art, in New York, and also under Edwin Coates for piano and Conrad C. Held for the violin. Last year he appeared in Aeolian Hall, one of the finest musical auditoriums in the country. That was his coming-out concert.

Hasn't he had an interesting life in his fifteen years? And best of all, he is the champion pitcher on the Neighborhood Baseball Team!

A SHINING EXAMPLE

WOULDN'T it be wonderful if every child who reads the BROWNIES' BOOK should have a record like that of Lucile Spence? She came from South Carolina to New York City, and has lived there eight years. When she graduated from the grammar school, out of a class of 150, she received the gold medal for the highest average in general excellence. But this was only the beginning of Lucile's career. She went to the Wadleigh High School and there in her second year, as a result of a fine composition, she became a member of the "Scribes," a literary club which usually receives only third and fourth year pupils. Later she became a member of the Arista, a club whose members excel in scholarship and character, and also of a classical club, the Hellenes. Lucile wrote a number of short stories which were published in the *Owl*, the school magazine; then she wrote and helped produce the first play ever given in Wadleigh, which had a colored theme and was produced by colored students.

Throughout her whole high school life she held some class office and in her senior year was an officer of the General Organization, which governs Wadleigh. It is no wonder, then, that this girl on graduating last year received not only the John G. Wight Scholarship, for excellence in scholarship, character, and service to the school, but also the State Scholarship, which is awarded for highest standing in the Regent's examination.

Lucile is now in Hunter College, getting

Eugene Mars Martin   Lucile Spence   Roderic Smith

Lucy Beatrice Miller

ready to teach little readers of THE BROWNIES' BOOK.

A MEDALIST

IMAGINE going to school for thirteen years and never missing a single day! That is the record of Lucy Beatrice Miller when she graduated in 1918 from the Daytona, Fla., Normal and Industrial Institute for Negro Youth. Besides, she has been such a good girl that she helped keep the other pupils good and for this she received the O'Neil Medal in 1916. Then, because she has always stood so well in her studies and has behaved herself so nicely, she received the Bethune Medal in 1918.

How many of you will have a similar record when you graduate?

A LITTLE BUSINESS MAN

OF course, Roderic is proud of his pony. But if the pony only knew, he would be proud of Roderic. For Roderic, think of it—is only eleven years old; yet he has been selling newspapers for four years! Every week he sells fifty copies of the *New York News*, fifty of the *Amsterdam News* and twenty-five or thirty copies of the *Chicago Defender*. Sometimes he sells monthly magazines and in the summer he peddles refreshments.

He lived with his grandmother for a while and then he helped her with his earnings. Now he lives with his mother again, and this year he has bought his shoes and suit for school,—for of course he goes to school,—he is in Grade 6 B-1. During the month of September, this past year, he was one of nine boys whose names appeared on the Honor Roll. Every Thursday morning he is an early bird, reporting to the office of the *New York News* at *five o'clock*, where he puts inserts in the papers until eight. Then he goes home, gets his breakfast, cleans up, and gets to school on time.

Don't you think that the pony and New York City, where Roderic lives, and all of us ought to be proud of him?

VIVIAN JUANITA LONG

THIS little girl, the only child of Abe M. and Amelia Long, left her parents forever August 15, 1919. She is not really dead, though, —she is still living

"In that great cloister's quiet and seclusion,
By guardian angels led."

The Late Vivian Juanita Long

After School

JESSIE FAUSET

AT nine o'clock I always say,
   "I wish there'd be no school today."
And while the rest are at their books,
I give the teacher horrid looks,—
And think, "The minute school is over,
I'll race and romp with Ted Moore's Rover."
No matter what the teacher's saying,
My mind is off somewhere else playing.
But don't you know when Home-time comes,
I think, "I'll stay and work my sums.
I'll do 'four times four' on the board,
Or write how much wood makes a cord."

And Billy Hughes is just like me,
He stays back just as regularly!
He's always hunting out strange places
Upon the globe, and then he traces
A map with towns and states and mountains,
And public parks with trees and fountains!
And this is what's so queer to me—
Bill just *can't get* geography
In school-time, and I'm awful dumb,
I cannot do one single sum.
But just let that old teacher go—
There's nothing Bill and me don't know!

"Ted Moore's Rover"

GYP

A Fairy Story

A. T. KILPATRICK

NCE there was a little fairy named Gyp. The king of fairies gave all of the little fairies work to do. And Gyp's work for that day was to paint apples.

Early that morning Gyp went to the forest to work. He carried all his paints, but more of red and brown because he had a lot of apples to paint red and also the leaves to tint brown.

He soon came to the trees, and leaving the other paints on the ground, he carried the red up to paint apples.

The little children who lived in the forest thought it about time to find ripe apples, and some of them went out that same morning to get some.

After roaming a bit they came to the tree where Gyp was painting and found all his paints on the ground.

They began to amuse themselves by playing with the paints, until the wind blew some apples down.

But they soon tired and fell asleep. Gyp had noticed them meddling with his paints and saw that they liked red and brown best.

When he came down and found all asleep, he wondered what joke to play on them that would be pleasing. So after deciding on many things and changing, he determined to paint their faces, knowing they would be delighted.

So he painted their faces,—some red like the apples, and the others brown like the leaves. When they woke and looked at each other, they were startled and amazed. They went home never knowing why their faces changed colors.

Now their descendants still live. Those children who were at home remained white, but the little red children still love to roam about in the forest and on the plains.

The little brown children can be found most everywhere, carrying happiness and sunshine to all they see.

So when you read of the work of the little brownies, don't forget the good fairy Gyp.

THE BOY'S ANSWER

A. U. CRAIG

NE day, while in a park, I saw a little ten or twelve year old boy sitting on a bench and, on taking a seat by him, he looked at me and and I looked at him; he smiled and I smiled.

"Little man, what are you going to do when you get to be a man?"

"Well," said the little boy, "I am going to be a Civil Engineer, like my father."

The little man's answer was a surprise to me, because most little brown boys of whom I ask the question, "What are you going to do when you get to be a man," usually say, "I don't know." This little fellow gave me his answer at once and said he was going to be a Civil Engineer! (All boys who know what a Civil Engineer is and some of the things he does, hold up your hands).

His next answer to my question surprised me even more, when I put this one to him, "What do you know about Civil Engineering?" Without hesitating, he said: "I can draw a railroad bridge, and its joints; I can draw the sections of the different kinds of sewers; and I can draw a map with the contour lines."

I heard a whistle in the distance and my little friend said, "Mother is calling me." And away he ran, leaving me to think that I had met a little brown boy who would some day become a great Civil Engineer. At the age of ten or twelve this little boy knows more about Civil Engineering than most men do when they enter college to learn Civil Engineering, and so he is sure to be far ahead of his class as he goes through college.

How many boys, who expect to be physicians, can, at the age of—say 15, name one-half of the bones in their bodies, or locate their stomach or liver?

Nearly all great men have shown remarkable interest in their chosen calling when they were still very small boys. Coleridge-Taylor was playing on his violin when he was only five!

POLITENESS is to do and say
The kindest thing in the kindest way.
—*Old Saying.*

The Tale of a Kitten

JAMES WELDON JOHNSON

LOUIE! Louie! little dear!
    Louie! Louie! Don't you hear?
Don't hold the cat up by her tail;
Its strength might of a sudden fail.
Then, oh, what a pity!
You would have a little kitty,
Wandering all around forlorn,
Of her pride and beauty shorn,
And not knowing what to do,
But to sit alone and mew;
For like a ship without a sail,
Would be a cat without a tail.

The Happy Quail

WILLIAM I. WALLACE

(Aged Twelve)

BOB WHITE! Bob White! sings the quail,
    Happily as she sits upon a rail;
In the summer evening air,
    She is thinking of her young ones fair.

She is thinking of the days of spring,
    And slowly and merrily doth she sing;
Sings of the bright May days,
    While Father Quail works and Baby Quail
    plays.

She flies from rail to rail all day,
    Thinking of the bright days of May;
She teaches her children not to fight,
    But teaches them to call, Bob White! Bob
    White!

Singing

FROM ROBERT LOUIS STEVENSON

OF speckled eggs the birdie sings,
    And rests among the trees;
The sailor sings of ropes and things,
    In ships upon the seas.

The children sing in far Japan,
    The children sing in Spain;
The organ with the organ man,
    Is singing in the rain.

Recruit

GEORGIA DOUGLAS JOHNSON

RIGHT shoulder arms, my laddie,
    Step like your soldier-daddy,
The world is yours for taking,
Life, what you will, for making;
Dare boldly, be no slacker,
Black heroes are your backer,
And all your mother's dreaming
Awaits your full redeeming!
Right shoulder arms, my laddie,
Step like your soldier-daddy.

Dedication

JESSIE FAUSET

To Children, who with eager look
Scanned vainly library shelf and nook,
For History or Song or Story
That told of Colored Peoples' glory,—
We dedicate THE BROWNIES' BOOK.

Chapter 1

THE BLIND MAZE OF THOUGHT

Jessie Redmon Fauset, *The Brownies' Book*, and the Measure of a Movement

JULIA S. CHARLES-LINEN

> All of us are passionately interested in the education of our children, our younger brothers and sisters. And just as deliberately, as earnestly as white people discuss tuition, relative ability of professors, expenses, etc., so we in addition discuss the question of prejudice.
>
> —JESSIE REDMON FAUSET, "SOME NOTES ON COLOR"

When W. E. B. Du Bois's *The Souls of Black Folk* was first published in 1903, it was met with collective gratitude from its Black readership. Among the impressive chorus of praise was an English major from Cornell University who, according to Du Bois biographer David Levering Lewis, was "enraptured" by it (292). On the recommendation of Dean Walter F. Wilcox at Cornell, Jessie Redmon Fauset wrote to Du Bois regarding summer teaching opportunities and her appraisal of *Souls*, saying, "Professor Du Bois I am going to thank you, as though it had been a personal favor, for your book *The Souls of Black Folk*. I am glad, glad you wrote it—we have needed someone to voice the intricacies of the blind maze of thought and action along which the modern, educated colored man or woman struggles" (Letter to W. E. B. Du Bois).

Thus begins the storied relationship, both personal and professional, between Du Bois and the woman whom Langston Hughes would later remember as one of the three people who midwifed the New Negro Renaissance (also known as the Harlem Renaissance),[1] having helped give birth to the cultural and artistic explosion centered—at least in part—in Harlem.[2] Their reciprocal relationship resulted in *The Crisis* becoming one of the major publications for Black America. While *The Crisis*—the official magazine of the National Association for the Advancement of Colored People (NAACP)—already had a devoted audience before Fauset joined its staff in 1919, her influence on the magazine during the New Negro Renaissance resulted in *The Crisis* being viewed as a vehicle for young Black writers of the literary movement. In August 1919, an announcement appeared in *The Crisis* about the coming of *The Brownies' Book*—"a monthly magazine for children of the sun" (Du Bois, *The Brownies' Book* inside cover). As the literary editor of both publications (*The Crisis* from 1919 to 1926, and *The Brownies' Book* in 1920 and its managing editor in 1921), Fauset followed in Du Bois's footsteps, but she did not fall in his shadow. Yet she remains among the most prominent yet understudied women of the New Negro Renaissance.

This chapter explores the cultural influence of *The Brownies' Book* and how Fauset used her educational background and her considerable social and political influence to navigate that "blind maze of thought" to which she gestures in her appraisal of Du Bois's work. First, I discuss Fauset's educational trajectory, her philosophies about Black art, and her adult fiction. In the section "The Measure of a Movement," I focus on a select few columns that demonstrate the aim of *The Brownies' Book* and consider how those columns contribute to the lives of Black children and the aim of the New Negro Renaissance more broadly. Then, in the section "The Blind Maze of Thought," I discuss *The Brownies' Book* as an educational tool for Black children. I argue that Fauset's management of *The Brownies' Book* is evidence of her devotion to and cultivation of a specifically Black child readership of the magazine and how the publication itself develops into a yardstick by which we should measure the New Negro Renaissance as a literary and cultural movement that views Black youth as tomorrow's promise.

The following sections demonstrate, similar to the way Nazera Sadiq Wright does of the *Colored American*, that "cultivating black children as sophisticated readers was crucial to the newspaper's promotion of a middle-class identity" (148). While Wright argues this about the antebellum periodical and is specifically dealing with the North, *The Brownies' Book* was not restricted to a geographical region in the United States during the early twentieth century. Rather, the magazine encouraged literacy and political engagement for its Black child readers across the United States. Fauset's investment in the education of Black youth is evident in the more didactic sections of the magazine, as well as in the sections that included games and short stories. "The Blind Maze of Thought" then—as both an ideological perspective and a finite book chapter—examines and underscores the political and educational utility of identity-forging cultural productions for Black children. *The Brownies' Book*, though short-lived, engendered social, political, educational, and cultural dialogues for and about Black children during the New Negro Renaissance. "What Du Bois proposed," according to Violet Harris, "was a model of social action or behavior that would attempt to counter negative images of blacks and black culture then pervasive in children's literature" (36).

FAUSET'S EDUCATION, HER PHILOSOPHIES ABOUT BLACK ART, AND HER ADULT FICTION

Fauset was only twenty-one years old when she first corresponded with Du Bois, who was a man of thirty-five at the time. Yet, despite their nearly fifteen-year age difference, she felt a kinship with him concerning "the blind maze of thought and action." Perhaps Du Bois felt a sameness with her, too, based on her evident association with the class of Black people he had, in his 1903 essay, identified as the Talented Tenth. In her letter to him, she empathizes, "it hurt you to write that book [*Souls*], didn't it? The man of fine sensibilities has to suffer exquisitely, just simply because his feeling is so fine." Fauset's implied difference between Du Bois (and herself by virtue of the tone in her letter) and some of the rest of Black America was almost certainly based on (the pursuit of) education and, by extension, class status. She had experienced her share of clashes between her desire for education and the mitigating factor that jeopardized it: her race.

As valedictorian of her class at the prestigious Philadelphia High School for Girls, Fauset had hoped to attend another esteemed girls' school upon graduation, Bryn Mawr College. She observed the true expense of education when she was ultimately refused the opportunity to attend Bryn Mawr because of her race, and instead, Bryn Mawr's president, M. Carey Thomas, facilitated Fauset's acceptance and paid for her tuition to Cornell. According to Bryn Mawr's 2015 Black Alumni Bulletin:

> In 1901, Jessie Redmon Fauset had just graduated from Philadelphia High School for Girls, then a feeder school for Bryn Mawr with an agreement that the top four graduating seniors would receive a full four-year scholarship to the College. Fauset was one of those young women, and she accepted that scholarship. But when she presented herself, on the first day of classes, it was discovered that she was a young woman of color.
>
> Thomas leapt into action. For about 30 days, Fauset was allowed to attend classes but was quickly shipped off to Cornell. To cover Fauset's tuition, Thomas pledged 10 percent of her personal funds and solicited money from friends, relatives, and other college presidents. (Goff)

The challenges Fauset faced in pursuit of formal academic training left her conflicted and determined to navigate the combined factors of race—or, more aptly, Blackness—with education and class status. Consequently, her letter to Du Bois is simultaneously reflective of her own trajectory and an awareness of his charge to Black America not to "sit silently by while the inevitable seeds are sown for the harvest of disaster to our children, black and white" (Du Bois, *Souls* 55–56). He had already made that position clear in several publications: in *The Souls of Black Folk* and "The Talented Tenth," and through his editorship of *The Crisis*. While Fauset "could be called a member of the Negro cultured class or intelligentsia in her early life" (Sylvander 26), acclimating to life as (typically) the only Black student in her class was not at all an innocuous effort. According to her biographer, Carolyn W. Sylvander, Fauset lamented,

> To this day, it hurts me to think about my childhood. My father was a Methodist minister, and his passion was education, so I was raised to be a teacher. I happened to be the only colored girl in my classes at high school, and I'll never forget the agony I endured on entrance day when the white girls, with whom I had played and studied through the graded schools, refused to acknowledge my greeting. (27)

The pain that accompanied Fauset's many educational efforts stayed with her through her studies at Cornell and the Sorbonne and are doubtlessly the impulse for the way she shaped *The Brownies' Book* to center on education, politics, and culture for Black children in the United States. Thus, this question of how it feels to be a problem permeated her work and her life, real and imagined. Fauset details this feeling in her 1922 essay "Some Notes on Color," when she recalls, "A distinguished novelist said to me not long ago: 'I think you colored people make a great mistake in dragging the race problem into your books and novels. It isn't art.' 'But good heavens,' I told him, 'it's life, it's colored life. Being colored is being a problem'" (76). The recollection and retelling of this anecdote suggest it was a crucial moment in Fauset's public philosophies of Black art; or, perhaps better still, it signifies the confrontation between her race and artistic expression, mirroring Du Bois's approaches to both art and literature, especially that which intends to reflect Black life. Du Bois had already noticed, "Between me and the other world there is ever an unasked question: . . . how does it feel to be a problem?" (*Souls* 1). He later declared in his 1926 essay "Criteria for Negro Art," "Thus all Art is propaganda and ever must be" (Jarrett and Gates 259). Indeed, he unflinchingly asserted, "I do not care a damn for any art that is not used for propaganda" (Jarrett and Gates 259). Jointly, they stitched together adjacent theories of racial identity and artistic expression, finding that what lives at the intersection of those concepts is not too dissimilar from the New Negro ideology that had already materialized at the time.

As Du Bois unapologetically tethered art to propaganda, so too had Fauset espoused that view, recognizing that it had the ability to disrupt the harmful view of Black folks across the nation. He saw Fauset's work—with *The Brownies' Book* as well as her novels—to erode the perceived authority that the white public and political sphere had over the image of Black folks in the United States. By the time Fauset published her third novel, *The Chinaberry Tree: A Novel of American Life*, the Depression was already altering the landscape of Black life in Harlem and elsewhere. In the novel, which is preoccupied with the issue of "bad blood," she deals head-on with the condition of being mixed race and impoverished. Still, at its core, the novel is about a desire to "marry up" and escape the pitfalls that darker-skinned Black folks face—a subject on which she expands in her final novel, *Comedy: American Style*.

Inasmuch as her fiction often featured mixed-race characters who were ever on the cusp between the Black and white worlds, her work and that of many in her cohort became the catalog of fiction *about* the nation during post-Reconstruction (Charles 133). Fauset's essay on color tells us something that her fiction may not: that she was a champion for the Black race. She and her cohort of Black writers[3]—many of whom she featured in *The Brownies' Book*—knew how the mixed-race figure could help expand representations of Black people in the mass market. They depicted "That Middle World"[4] through sustainable mixed-race communities that confronted and usurped—rather than acquiesced to—the color line. Indeed, their very existence in literature warrants reflection on the enduring effect of color biases on US racial politics, even into contemporary American culture. The mixed-race figure in Fauset's fiction became a useful tool through which to probe the arbitrariness of the color line. It was but another of her strategies for representing Black life in realistic, if uncommon, ways.

Because of all her representations of mixed-race, middle-class characters, some critics felt that Fauset's characters were not "Black" enough. To her credit, her hope was to expand the public's otherwise static perceptions and expectations of Black folks in America:

> That attitude and the sort of attitude instanced by a journalist the other day who thought colored people ought to be willing to permit the term "n----r" because it carries with it so much picturesqueness defines pretty well, I think, our position in the eyes of the white world. Either we are inartistic or we are picturesque and always the inference is implied that we live objectively with one eye on the attitude of the white world as

though it were the audience and we the players whose hope and design is to please. (Fauset, "Some Notes on Color" 76)

In the decades following Carolyn W. Sylvander's biography, *Jessie Redmon Fauset: Black American Writer* (1981), and Deborah McDowell's essay "The Neglected Dimension of Jessie Redmon Fauset" (1985), there has been renewed interest in Fauset, especially within the past couple of decades. Susan Tomlinson's "Teaching Jessie Fauset's *Plum Bun*" (2008) and "'An Unwonted Coquetry': The Commercial Seductions of Jessie Fauset's *The Chinaberry Tree*" (2003) demonstrate such an interest. Other examinations of the author and her work, such as Cherene Sherrard-Johnson's 2009 introduction to the republication of Fauset's *Comedy: American Style*,[5] Masami Sugimori's "Black Subjects' 'Literal' Resistance in Jessie Redmon Fauset's 'Emmy' and 'There Was One Time!'" (2018),[6] and Morgan Jerkins's 2017 *New Yorker* article, "The Forgotten Work of Jessie Redmon Fauset,"[7] as well as her 2020 introduction to the newest edition of Fauset's first novel, *There Is Confusion*,[8] together signal a swell of academic attention to Fauset. In February 2021, MSNBC's hit podcast "Into America" with Pulitzer Prize-winning journalist and host Trymaine Lee presented a miniseries called "Harlem on My Mind";[9] its third episode is dedicated to Fauset and features Jerkins and myself discussing the author's life and legacy. The podcast pushes Fauset beyond the walls of academia and into the public imaginary, as well it should, considering her vast cultural influence on the New Negro Renaissance. The renewed enthusiasm surrounding Fauset is both timely and necessary, with many scholars wondering why Fauset has yet to receive her due and readers being introduced to her work and legacy for the first time. As scholars begin to reevaluate the common themes in her works, they acknowledge that she provided sharper analyses of color consciousness and white respectability values than previously recognized. Still, as scholars continue to resituate Fauset at the front of the literary and cultural movement, few acknowledge how educating and promoting the well-being of Black children were, in essence, her passion project.

THE MEASURE OF A MOVEMENT

How does one measure a movement as impressive and as memorable as the New Negro Renaissance without evaluating its commitment to its posterity? Certainly, the New Negro era produced some of the greatest writers, artists, musicians, and intellectuals in American history. Yet Fauset, her work, and *The Brownies' Book* remain relatively unheralded in the grand scheme of its cultural history. Though Langston Hughes remembers her as a midwife of the

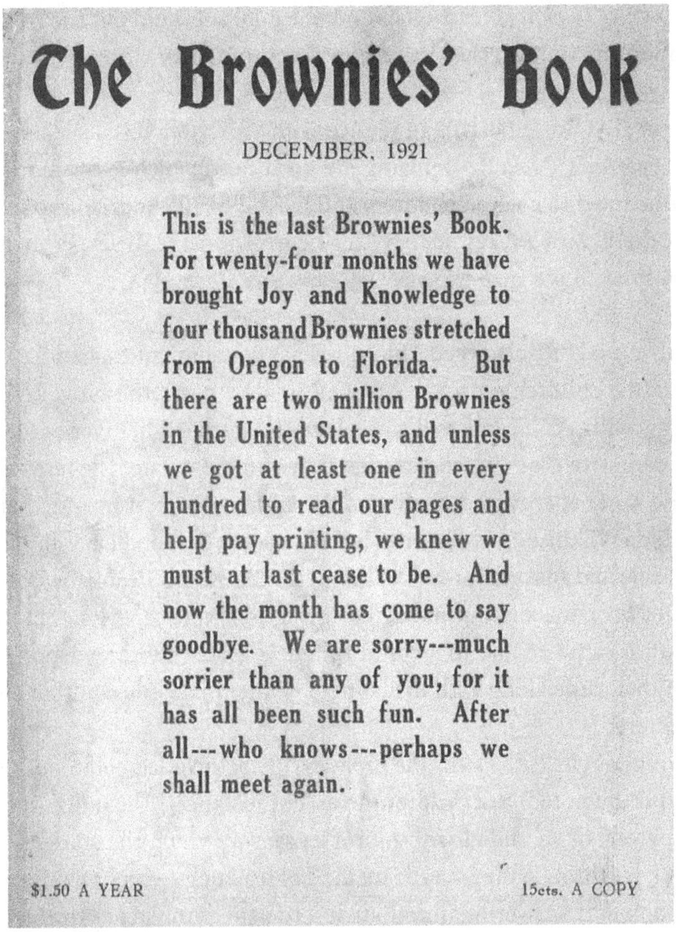

The Brownies' Book

DECEMBER, 1921

This is the last Brownies' Book. For twenty-four months we have brought Joy and Knowledge to four thousand Brownies stretched from Oregon to Florida.   But there are two million Brownies in the United States, and unless we got at least one in every hundred to read our pages and help pay printing, we knew we must at last cease to be.   And now the month has come to say goodbye.   We are sorry---much sorrier than any of you, for it has all been such fun.   After all---who knows---perhaps we shall meet again.

$1.50 A YEAR   15cts. A COPY

Figure 1.1 The message in the final issue of *The Brownies' Book*, announcing the end of the magazine's publication (Du Bois, *The Brownies' Book*, vol. 2).

Renaissance, we still fall short of grasping the laborious beauty of her work with *The Brownies' Book*. Harris reminds us that "Fauset faced a herculean task in her attempts to create an alternative image of blacks in children's literature. Nevertheless, she persevered for two years and helped bring twenty-four issues of *The Brownies' Book* to press. The result of her efforts and the continued support of Du Bois and [Augustus Granville] Dill demonstrate the political nature of *The Brownies' Book*" (37).

Anticipating the financial challenge of publishing two magazines at once—*The Crisis* and *The Brownies' Book*—Du Bois and Fauset called upon friends, intellectuals, and the community to help fund the latter project.[10] While Du Bois's name was on many of the correspondences, Fauset was known to handle much of the administrative work for Du Bois, including work unrelated to either magazine. Despite their efforts, by December 1921

The Brownies' Book had reached its end; the publishers did not release another issue after that time. In the "Valedictory" column, they write:

> Messrs. Du Bois and Dill announce with regret the discontinuance of *The Brownies' Book*. Recognizing the great need which exists for literature adapted to colored children, and indeed to all children who live in a world of varied races, we have for two years made the experiment of publishing at our own expense *The Brownies' Book*. (354)

Later, in 1923, Du Bois urged Dill to release a statement that addressed the fact that the children's magazine was ultimately cost prohibitive (Memo to Augustus Dill). As it came to a close, Fauset continued her work of flooding the readers with Black excellence that they could emulate. The farewell issue kept the same energy and quality as the earlier issues; it included artwork from Hilda Wilkinson, short stories by Yolande Du Bois and Langston Hughes, and "A Selected List of Books Dealing with the Negro Problem." When *The Brownies' Book* was discontinued, the key figures were careful not to indicate that with it came an end to a commitment to Black child readers. The suggestion that came along with the content of the final issue was that children still mattered.

Throughout its entire run, *The Brownies' Book* included columns that were always pertinent to Black children's lives. For instance, "The Judge," a column Fauset wrote, often ended with moral lessons at which the student readers would arrive through the Socratic method of teaching—emphasizing dialogue and asking and answering questions in order to stimulate critical thinking. In this way, "The Judge's wisdom was meant to complement the guidance of the parents. His philosophy of child rearing was that a guided discovery of appropriate ethics and appropriate personal and public actions is more valuable than rules and advice dispensed in an authoritarian manner" (Harris 40). It is easy to detect Fauset's influence here, given how she previously praised the Montessori method and considering her own time as a French and Latin teacher. Although many of The Judge's admonitions indicated a subscription to the respectability politics characteristic of those conservative members of the New Negro Renaissance, Fauset included, they were not intended to condemn the young readers. Instead, The Judge presented the consequences of a given action and allowed the readers to deduce the best course of action. In fact, the lessons were not restricted to the child readers. Harris notes, "Parents received admonition from the Judge as well. He suggested that fathers use less physical punishment and more positive stimulation. Such advice reflects Fauset's adherence to tenets of progressivism that called for nurturant and gentle child rearing techniques" (40).

Other columns, like "The Jury," demonstrated the connection that Fauset desired to make directly with the audience. Readers were encouraged to submit letters to the magazine for inclusion in "The Jury," which served as an advice column. Fauset published these letters from children and even encouraged parents to submit photographs of their babies to be featured in upcoming publications. In by far the most poignant of the early submissions, a girl of sixteen from Fairmount, West Virginia, writes into the February 1920 issue with an enormous request:

> I am an orphan, having neither mother nor father. My mother has been dead eleven years and my father, four years. White people have kept me,— that is, I have worked for them to earn my living. Realizing that I did not always want to be a scrub girl, I have tried to educate myself, as I could not go to school. . . .
>
> Do you think I could through *The Brownies' Book* get a home among a good Christian colored family? I would like to be in a family where they had no large children. I wouldn't mind one small baby, as I love them. I wouldn't mind being with elderly people. Just anywhere among good Christian people, where I could go to good public schools. I can do any kind of work and am a good cook and housekeeper. . . .
>
> I am a dark brown skin girl, with Negro hair, not being very tall nor good to look at. But I wear my clothes nicely.
>
> I would ask you please not to put my full name in *The Brownies' Book*, if you will advertise for a home for me. I don't want anyone to support me. I want to be among MY people, and have a chance for an education. ("The Jury" 52)

The enormity does not lie in her request alone. Rather, it is in the way her request validates the mission of *The Brownies' Book*. Fauset, who was responsible for this and many other sections of *The Brownies' Book*, had succeeded in her mission of rendering Black children and their futures more visible—even possible—through this publication. That she honors this young girl's appeal to be printed for the chance at a good education—the kind for which *The Brownies' Book* advocates—and a home for herself that is among her people is evidence that *The Brownies' Book*—and, dare I say, Fauset herself—was doing critical cultural work in Black communities across the United States.

Honoring this reader's desperate, if hopeful, request to remain anonymous means that Fauset has made the teenager simultaneously visible (by publishing her letter) and invisible (by redacting her name). No doubt, this reflected the Black girl's journey from the home of the white people for whom she worked to the pages of *The Brownies' Book*, where she saw herself and her community.

The fact that this young girl felt compelled to describe herself as "a dark brown skin girl, with Negro hair, not being very tall nor good to look at. But I wear my clothes nicely" is emblematic of the identity-building work that *The Brownies' Book* strived to do. First among their objectives for the magazine, Du Bois and Fauset hoped "to make colored children realize that being 'colored' is a normal, beautiful thing" (Du Bois, "True Brownies" 286). Yet this young girl found it necessary to emphasize her work ethic, suggesting that it somehow compensated for what she was likely taught to believe was an inadequacy and disadvantage on her part. While the magazine, no doubt, nurtured within her a sense of racial belonging that was absent in the home where she lived at the time her request went to press, the unnamed girl's anxiety is palpable through the pages.

This letter in particular makes the end of the publication of *The Brownies' Book* somehow even sadder; it makes one question how many other Brownies would not find homes or how many more would no longer see themselves and the possibilities for their futures catalogued this way because the magazine dedicated exclusively to their needs would soon cease to exist. Yet Fauset—ever the community change agent—continued to advocate for the lives of Black children in the final issue as well. The issue featured a picture titled "These Kiddies Have No Mothers," and it included a caption in which Fauset implored subscribers to help a Black orphanage with funding. In other words, she suggested that the well-being of those pictured should be a community concern and that they ought not be forgotten simply because the magazine was ending. Toward that end, they are the final illustration in the final issue of the magazine, signifying their importance to her and, indeed, the entire Black community. Her final push to find homes and/or funding for Black children in the concluding issue of the magazine confirms her indefatigable commitment to Black children. In many ways, the production of *The Brownies' Book* reimagines for its readership possibilities for bettering their lives through education and community. It inculcates in them an intellectual thirst and a sense of belonging, all routed through the structure of education.

THE BLIND MAZE OF THOUGHT

"Education with a small *e*," writer and activist James Baldwin observes, is "different from Education with a large *e*." In *Dark Days* he tells us, "In the lowercase, education refers to the relations that actually obtain among human beings. In the uppercase, it refers to power" (5–6). Put differently: there exists, in all of everyday human learning, a very real distinction between community education and the apparatus in the United States that is Education. The former refers to the social schooling one receives from family and friends. The latter is the one through which people, Black people specifically, are situated in racialized positions and ultimately forced to remain quiet and submissive to that system. The latter, Education in the uppercase, is about power—dominance to be sure. And, in America specifically, that power is assumed, determined, racialized, and often adjudicated to be white. Baldwin's point in unpacking this "relentless conundrum of your life" (2) is to note that everyone's education begins with the communities to which they belong from birth. For childhood, learning is often about imitation first. Therefore, education in the lowercase is, in a lot of ways, tantamount to identity, especially for Black folks in the United States. And so, *The Brownies' Book* became a harbinger of and cultural tool for Black identity formation. What Fauset attempts with *The Brownies' Book* is to collapse the boundaries between education in the lowercase and the uppercase—between (Black) people and (white) systems of power—in order to embolden a new generation of learners and citizens.

The Brownies' Book existed for more than entertainment alone; it was a pedagogical tool for identity education. As the periodical took shape, Du Bois used an issue of *The Crisis* to publicize the forthcoming publication of a periodical "Designed for all children, but especially for *ours*" (*The Brownies' Book* inside cover). In that issue he delineated seven objectives that he and his team hoped to achieve with the publication of *The Brownies' Book*:

(a) To make colored children realize that being "colored" is a normal and beautiful thing.
(b) To make them familiar with the history and achievements of the Negro race.
(c) To make them know that colored children have grown into beautiful, useful and famous persons.
(d) To teach them delicately a code of honor and action in their relations with white children.
(e) To turn their little hurts and resentments into emulation, ambition and love of their homes and companions.
(f) To point out the best amusements and joys and worth-while things of life.
(g) To inspire them to prepare for definite occupations and duties with a broad spirit of sacrifice. ("The True Brownies" 286)

As young scholars imbibed lessons, religious and educational, from short stories and poems in the children's magazine, they were also introduced to writers of the New Negro Renaissance while Harlem was *en vogue*. The dedication of the inaugural, January 1920 issue of *The Brownies' Book* demonstrates the gap the magazine intended to fill for its young readers: "To Children, who with eager look / Scanned vainly library shelf and nook, / For History or Song or Story / That told of Colored Peoples' glory,— / We dedicate *The Brownies' Book*" (Johnson-Feelings 25). Each issue reflected the atmosphere of the New Negro Renaissance that was happening throughout the country, especially in major cities like Harlem, Washington, DC, and Chicago. In fact, according to Dianne Johnson-Feelings, "the young people who read *The Brownies' Book*—'brownies'—were probably children of NAACP members" (12). The young audience, Fauset anticipated, could mirror the energy and cultural production of this Renaissance. *The Brownies' Book* hoped to groom a new generation of Black scholars and activists. The children's magazine, Johnson-Feelings writes, "assured the children of the sun that their mothers, fathers, teachers and preachers, writers and artists, neighbors and friends, at home and across the oceans, were intelligent and creative" (13).

By the April 1920 issue, *The Brownies' Book* featured work from prominent writers of the New Negro Renaissance, like Fauset's "The Easter Idyl" and Georgia Douglas Johnson's "The Ancestor." The former recounts the story of the life, death, and resurrection of Christ just in time for the Easter holiday. That issue also includes a spotlight on Sojourner Truth, whom Fauset described in the magazine as "A Pioneer Suffragette." Fluent in French, Fauset also translated Jean Aicard's short story "The Return of the Bells" from French to English. This lesson, subtle though it may be, also instructs *The Brownies' Book*'s young readers on the utility of having access to multiple languages.

The periodical was also designed to center children in their own schooling, particularly Black children in their community-based learning. This was an approach to teaching that Fauset had learned and supported early in her teaching career; she published on it in the July 1912 issue of *The Crisis*. Her essay "The Montessori Method—Its Possibilities" encouraged allowing naturally eager children to learn, free from overbearing adults who may unintentionally hinder their innate curiosity. Indeed, Fauset was somewhat preoccupied with how long it takes for a child to "get, so to speak, on his mental feet" (136). In other words, for Fauset, reflection and freedom are the inseparable links necessary for establishing a person's character beyond childhood. She explains the value of such a system by contrasting it with the traditional approach, writing, "the child is trained from infancy to abject dependence on his elders. Secondly, he is girt about with rules and precedents which stifle originality and initiative. He is simply smothered by too much and wrongly applied care and kindness. Now it is exactly this condition of affairs that the Montessori system is seeking to obviate" (137). Put otherwise, Fauset desired the young readers of *The Brownies' Book* to learn in "the pleasant bustle of preoccupation" that is emblematic of the Montessori way (137). Indeed, *The Brownies' Book* included "pictures, stories, letters from little ones, games, and—oh everything!" (inside cover). In her article on the Montessori method she notes, "No one arrives at his majority without beginning that habit of retrospection which is to be with him more or less for the rest of his life" (136). Consequently, Fauset edited *The Brownies' Book* in a way that would foster the type of diverse stimulation that she was convinced every young mind needs in order to, one day, stand on her or his own "mental feet." For her majority-Black young readership, this method was bolstered by an unflinching pronouncement of and respect for Black identity, making *The Brownies' Book* the perfect tool through which to shrink the gaps between Education in the uppercase and education in the lower-case—between Black selfhood and white systems of power and oppression.

Although no one issue of any magazine could completely close the gap between Black and white, the continued deluge of positive Black images and educational assignments could, Fauset staunchly believed, address the Black condition in the United States and, therefore, considerably shrink that gulf—at least in the ways in which Black children could govern their own minds and their ways of thinking about themselves and their people. She and Du Bois supposed that as young readers came face-to-face, as it were, with renowned Black artists—like William E. Scott, Hilda Rue Wilkinson, and Marcellus Hawkins—and New Negro Renaissance authors—like Langston Hughes, Georgia Douglas Johnson, Mary Effie Lee, James Weldon Johnson, Nella Larsen, and Fauset herself—they would be suffused with cultural productions that would foster pride in their evolving Black selves. In a May 1932 interview with *Southern Workman*, she insisted, "it is urgent that ambitious Negro youth be able to read of the achievements of their race" (Starkey 220). While her urgency here is related to the genre of biography—she believed "No part of Negro literature needs more building up than biography" (Starkey 220)—her sentiments about persistently showing Black youth other Black people whom they could admire and, by extension, aspire to become were well documented.

Although *The Crisis* published an annual children's issue, children were not the primary focus of that national journal. Some other national Black magazines also had children's sections or columns for children (Wright 150–51). *The Brownies' Book*, however, was entirely focused on children, and it was rare in its approach. Nineteenth-century American children's literature helped define racial identity for its readers. From film and books to dolls, the nineteenth-century children's market was saturated with images and objects designed to illustrate the import—or lack thereof—of Black children's lives for mainstream consumers. In *Racial Innocence*, Robin Bernstein suggests that Fauset and Du Bois sought to mitigate this through the Black-centered content they published in *The Brownies' Book*:

Dolls of all colors anxiously raise questions about the definitions and limits of humanity. . . . all dolls in play, and all stories about sentient dolls, trouble the boundary between person and thing—the terror at the onto-logical core of slavery. Nineteenth-century black dolls, however, uniquely literalized these functions in that they were owned, insentient things that often explicitly represented enslaved humans. Black dolls marked and eroded the border between person and thing; thus they functioned as devices in the meaning and memory of slavery. (222)

Consequently, when *The Brownies Book* published anything about dolls—such as, for instance, the short story "Dolly's Dream" by Nora Waring or "Merry Christmas to All" by Fauset herself[11]—the magazine was doing corrective work for its young Black audience, who had been inundated with literature and images that assigned value only to white things and, therefore, white people. "Designed especially for Kiddies from Six to Sixteen," *The Brownies' Book* aimed, among other things, "to be a thing of Joy and Beauty, dealing in Happiness . . . to teach Universal Love and Brotherhood for all little folk—black and brown and yellow and white" (inside cover). Recognizing Black children's vulnerability and how the children's print sphere was inundated with stereotypes of Black people,[12] *The Brownies' Book* carved out a space for its young readership to see, to develop, and to grapple with their emerging Black identities, countering those permeating and injurious images charac-teristic of children's literature during the early twentieth century with ones that generated opportunities within the Black children's print sphere for race pride and creativity.

Whereas concerns for Black children were previously addressed in print only as appendages to adult issues and, therefore, only available in the adult print sphere,[13] *The Brownies' Book* as the first periodical published for Black children suggested that Black children's experiences in religion, politics, and identity demanded new paradigms in education. Indeed, prior to the publi-cation of *The Brownies' Book*, *The Crisis* offered only one issue per year solely dedicated to matters facing Black children. Yet, later, there was quite a bit of cross-fertilization between *The Crisis* and *The Brownies' Book*, indicating, as Fauset writes in "Some Notes on Color," that "All of us are passionately inter-ested in the education of our children, our younger brothers and sisters" (76). In "The Children of Double Consciousness," writer Michelle H. Phillips argues,

Du Bois's cross-writing in the children's numbers and in *The Brownies' Book* . . . stage[s], theorize[s], and transgress[es] the duality of youth and age as the center of a new problem for black Americans in the twentieth century: how to responsibly raise black children in the face of inevitable disillusionment and probable despair. And the answer to this question, at first subtle in *Souls*, resounds in this children's literature, which seeks at once to be a source for the black child's entry into double consciousness and to repurpose double consciousness as a model for a resilient black subjectivity beginning in childhood. (592)

The Brownies' Book undeniably captivated and empowered Black youth of the 1920s. Like much of the adult literature of the New Negro Renaissance, the distribution of *The Brownies' Book* affirmed the value of Black life; it effectively shifted the nature of children's literature, especially in how it showcased visual art, spotlighted and lauded young Black scholars, and featured Fauset and other New Negro Renaissance luminaries as creative writers. Under Fauset's direction, it gave young readers the necessary tools to nurture a collective sense of belonging and to theorize their developing Black identities, therefore providing them with critical strategies to navigate a nation in racial turmoil.

Fauset, Du Bois, and indeed all of the Black literati of the New Negro Renaissance perceived how education was inextricable from social and political upward mobility and identity formation for Black folks in the United States. Accordingly, Fauset observes in "Some Notes on Color," "just as deliberately, as earnestly as white people discuss tuition, relative ability of professors, expenses, etc., so we in addition discuss the question of prejudice" (77). As literary editor of both *The Brownies' Book* and *The Crisis*, Fauset's influence was irrefutable, yet she remains understudied and, consequently, has yet to be lauded in the manner befitting literary titans.

The Brownies' Book was imbued with New Negro ideologies reflective of the renaissance that was in full swing during the 1920s. Black students saw themselves in the pages and would often submit to the magazine, praising its content and reflecting on what the publication had taught them. For instance, in the May 1921 issue, two male students from Waco, Texas, M. M. Taylor and M. B. S. Slaughter, are published in "The Jury" section:

> We are two young men striving to be of some service to the race and we are at present attending Paul Quinn College. We are very close pals and in the same grade, and both of us are striving for the leadership of our class.
>
> English is our main study, and our lessons are practically from *The Brownies' Book* which we find very interesting and amusing.
>
> Our teacher, Mrs. Caroline Bond Day, has written several stories in *The Brownies' Book*. We find that this magazine broadens our ideas and increases our vocabularies. We are advising every boy and girl to read it. (156)

Letters such as this one were published to demonstrate the reach of *The Brownies' Book*: not only were Brownies all over the country reading it, imbibing lessons of faith, education, and race pride, but they were also beginning to see the magazine as an instrument for collective political and educational advancement.

The Brownies' Book was filled with pedagogical tools emblematic of Fauset's training as a teacher and a writer, for she would dare not leave the education of Black children in the hands of those who oppressed them. Writer and political activist James Baldwin said it best in his short collection of essays, *Dark Days*:

> To be black was to confront, and to be forced to alter, a condition forged in history. To be white was to be forced to digest a delusion called white supremacy. Indeed, without confronting the history that has either given white people an identity or divested them of it, it is hardly possible for anyone who thinks of himself as white to know what a black person is talking about at all. Or to know what education is. (1)

Fauset was a poet, essayist, novelist, translator, and literary editor concurrent with her boundless work on *The Brownies' Book*. A crucial idea implicit in the publication of *The Brownies' Book* was shifting away from the pernicious, if familiar, white gaze to which Fauset gestured in "Some Notes on Color" and about which Du Bois had famously written, "It is a peculiar sensation, this double-consciousness, this sense of always looking at one's self through the eyes of others, of measuring one's soul by the tape of a world that looks on in amused contempt and pity" (*Souls* 5). Indeed, *The Brownies' Book* embodied Fauset's and Du Bois's intellectual and political investments in the lives of Black children. Therefore, it deliberately facilitated the necessary shift away from the white gaze and toward a decidedly Black one—one which instilled in its readers a fierce pride in their race and expectations of high academic and social achievement. *The Brownies' Book* might well be considered an early articulation of contemporary movements vehemently announcing the value of Black lives. If the annual children's issue of *The Crisis* gestures toward the value of Black youth in the United States, then the publication of *The Brownies' Book* advances that political and theoretical worldview by situating Black children's education and experiences at the forefront of Black cultural production.

The blind maze of thought is this: how one navigates the entanglements of race, education, and class status in order to influence or, where necessary, radically alter Black people's political future. There were many New Negro Renaissance writers who maneuvered through that maze, and Fauset was chief among them. Still, history has not remembered Fauset as the chief architect of this renaissance, despite the fact that her oeuvre bears a radical fervor for Black lives. The work of some of her mentees, though, is deemed downright revolutionary. Fauset's work had the same intensity. The entire arc of Fauset's career is beyond the scope of this essay; further studies could address her poetry, which has yet to receive serious scholarly attention; her short stories, which are often dismissed or relegated to the bottom literary rungs because so many of them were written for a child audience; her adamant illustration of middle-class Black life and her correlating rejection of the notion of Black folks as a monolith (this is the most common and perhaps most condemning way her work is studied, suggesting that her characters did not reflect "real" Black people); and the gatherings she hosted at her house for her accomplished and talented Black friends, most of whom were the faces of the New Negro Renaissance. In addition to acknowledging her for being the first person to publish his poetry, Hughes notes in his autobiography *The Big Sea* the change of pace that her gatherings brought to the revelry that was Harlem then:

> At novelist Jessie Fauset's parties there was always quite a different atmosphere from that at most other Harlem good-time gatherings. At Miss Fauset's a good time was shared by talking literature and reading poetry aloud and perhaps enjoying some conversations in French. White people were very seldom present there unless they were very distinguished people, because Jessie Fauset did not like opening her home to mere sightseers, or faddists, momentarily in love with Negro life. (247)

Fauset was an immensely gifted woman dedicated to reshaping the image of Black people the world over, yet perhaps her most significant—hugely impactful—work, *The Brownies' Book*, has yet to find a place in the mainstream American literary canon. And so, I suggest Fauset as a boon to our understanding of and appreciation for the Black cultural explosion that *was* and the contemporary freedom struggle that *is*. May we return Jessie Redmon Fauset to her rightful place in American literary and cultural history. While other Black writers of that critical moment that shaped much of the African American literary canon were reborn as cultural icons and later added to many literary anthologies—having their poetry and prose taught in classrooms the nation over, in the decades following the end of the New Negro era—Fauset has yet to be thus reborn. For her meticulously written poetry and prose, her publication of the works of Black literary titans, and her purposefully curated friend groups, Fauset not only deserves a new cultural treatment; a life like hers demands it, and she is long overdue.

Notes

1. In his autobiography, *The Big Sea*, Hughes remembered Fauset as a significant figure in the renaissance: "Jessie Fauset at the *Crisis*, Charles Johnson at *Opportunity*, and Alain Locke in Washington were the three people who midwifed the so-called New Negro Literature into being" (218). He went on to remark that while at *The Crisis*, Fauset accepted "The Negro Speaks of Rivers," which was one of his first poems to be published outside of Central High School.

2. Although some anthologies still refer to this cultural moment as the Harlem Renaissance, other major cities in the United States, such as Chicago and Washington, DC, also had a renaissance at the same time. Davarian L. Baldwin's *Chicago's New Negroes: Modernity, the Great Migration, and Black Urban Life* and Treva B. Lindsey's *Colored No More: Reinventing Black Womanhood in Washington, D.C.* both demonstrate how these cities experienced a cultural renaissance that matched—and even predated, according to Lindsey—the one in Harlem. Thus, to acknowledge this fact, many scholars now refer to this moment as the New Negro Renaissance.

3. Fauset noted that she and writers like Walter White, Nella Larsen, and James Weldon Johnson all had similar energies in their subject matter—which is to say that each wrote about mixed-raceness and social upward mobility. See Fauset's "Some Notes on Color."

4. See *That Middle World: Race, Performance, and the Politics of Passing*, in which I introduce and theorize a space called That Middle World, which is distinctly separate from the Black or white worlds and belonging only to and inhabited by mixed-race figures. I argue that That Middle World is the interstitial space that is the location of culture, identity, and often racial performance for mixed-race characters in African American fiction.

5. Sherrad-Johnson, *Introduction to Comedy: American Style*, Rutgers UP, 2009, pp. xv–xl.

6. Sugimori, "Black Subjects' 'Literal' Resistance," *MELUS* 2018, pp. 124–47.

7. Jerkins, "The Forgotten Work of Jessie Redmon Fauset," *New Yorker*, https://www.newyorker.com/books/page-turner/the-forgotten-work-of-jessie-redmon-fauset.

8. Fauset, *There Is Confusion*, Penguin Random House, 2020.

9. Harlem on My Mind: Jessie Redmon Fauset, Ep:3, MSNBC, https://www.msnbc.com/podcast/harlem-my-mind-jessie-redmon-fauset-n1258195.

10. In a letter dated August 14, 1919, Du Bois writes,

My dear Mr. Scott:
As perhaps you know, we are beginning in November a magazine for children to be called "The Brownies' Book." It is designed for all children, especially for colored children. I want very much that you should give us some of your best artistic work. Eventually, we shall pay for all your contributions, but we may not be able to give you any actual cash during the first year. I shall be glad to hear from you on this matter, and to have any suggestions.
    Very sincerely yours,
    WEBDB-CF

11. In it she writes, "But she had three dolls which she had bought herself,—a rag doll, a Japanese doll, and—her favorite, of course—a colored doll, a beautiful brown creature with rosy cheeks and raven hair" (356–57).

12. See *Image of the Black in Children's Fiction* by Dorothy M. Broderick, in which the author describes seven stereotypes of Black people that were present in children's literature.

13. Black periodicals (for instance, *The Colored American*) did have columns for children. Although *The Brownies' Book* is often cited as the first magazine published for African American children, *The Colored American* did its own work to attract young Black readers in the late nineteenth century (Wright 147–63).

Works Cited

Baldwin, James. *Dark Days*. Penguin Random House UK, 2018.

Bernstein, Robin. *Racial Innocence: Performing American Childhood from Slavery to Civil Rights*. New York UP, 2011.

Charles, Julia S. *That Middle World: Race, Performance, and the Politics of Passing*. U of North Carolina P, 2020.

Du Bois, W. E. B., editor. *The Brownies' Book*, vol. 1, no. 1, Jan. 1920. Library of Congress.

Du Bois, W. E. B., editor. *The Brownies' Book*, vol. 2, no. 12, Dec. 1921. W. E. B. Du Bois Papers (MS 312), Special Collections and University Archives, U of Massachusetts Amherst Libraries.

Du Bois, W. E. B. Letter to William E. Scott, 14 Aug. 1919. W. E. B. Du Bois Papers (MS 312), Special Collections and University Archives, U of Massachusetts Amherst Libraries.

Du Bois, W. E. B. Memo to Augustus Dill, 8 Aug. 1923. W. E. B. Du Bois Papers (MS 312), Special Collections and University Archives, U of Massachusetts Amherst Libraries.

Du Bois, W. E. B. *The Souls of Black Folk*. Dover Thrift Editions, 1994.

Du Bois, W. E. B. "The True Brownies." *The Crisis*, vol. 18, Oct. 1919, pp. 285–86.

Du Bois, W. E. B. "Valedictory." *The Brownies' Book*, vol. 2, no. 12, Dec. 1921, p. 354.

Fauset, Jessie Redmon. Letter to W. E. B. Du Bois, 26 Dec. 1903. W. E. B. Du Bois Papers (MS 312), Special Collections and University Archives, U of Massachusetts Amherst Libraries.

Fauset, Jessie Redmon. "Merry Christmas to All." *The Brownies' Book*, vol. 1, no. 12, Dec. 1920, pp. 355–60.

Fauset, Jessie Redmon. "The Montessori Method—Its Possibilities." *The Crisis*, vol. 4, July 1912, pp. 136–38.

Fauset, Jessie Redmon. "Some Notes on Color." *The World Tomorrow*, Mar. 1922, pp. 76–77.

Goff, Florence. "In Black and White." *Bryn Mawr Alumnae Bulletin*, Bryn Mawr College Alumnae Association, Sept. 2015, bulletin.brynmawr.edu/features/hp-primary-feature/in-black-and-white-4/.

Harris, Violet. "Jessie Fauset's Transference of the 'New Negro' Philosophy to Children's Literature." *The Langston Hughes Review*, vol. 6, no. 2, Fall 1987, pp. 36–43.

Hughes, Langston. *The Big Sea: An Autobiography*. Hill and Wang, 1993.

Jarrett, Gene Andrew, and Henry Louis Gates Jr. *The New Negro: Readings on Race, Representation, and African American Culture, 1892–1938*. Princeton UP, 2007, pp. 257–60.

Johnson-Feelings, Dianne. *The Best of "The Brownies' Book."* Oxford UP, 1996.

"The Jury." *The Brownies' Book*, vol. 1, no. 2, Feb. 1920, p. 52.

Lewis, David Levering. *W. E. B. Du Bois: A Biography 1868–1963*. Holt Paperbacks, 2009.

Phillips, Michelle H. "The Children of Double Consciousness: From *The Souls of Black Folk* to *The Brownies' Book*." *PMLA*, vol. 128, no. 3, May 2013, pp. 590–607.

Starkey, Marion L. "Jessie Fauset." *Southern Workman*, vol. 61, May 1932, pp. 217–20.

Sylvander, Carolyn W. *Jessie Redmon Fauset: Black American Writer*. Whitston Publishing, 1981.

Taylor, M. M., and M. B. S. Slaughter. "The Jury." *The Brownies' Book*, vol. 2, no. 5, May 1921, p. 156.

Waring, Nora. "Dolly's Dream." *The Brownies' Book*, vol. 1, no. 11, Nov. 1920, pp. 351–52.

Wright, Nazera Sadiq. "Our Hope Is in the Rising Generation: Locating African American Children's Literature in the Children's Department of the *Colored American*." *Who Writes for Black Children? African American Children's Literature before 1900*, edited by Katharine Capshaw and Anna Mae Duane, U of Minnesota P, 2017, pp. 147–63.

Chapter 2

BLACK HEROES AND "THE JURY"

The Brownies' Book Biographies as Counter-Memories for Black Children

SARA C. VANDERHAAGEN

Biographies occupy a consistent place throughout the brief run of *The Brownies' Book*. Their place was established in the first issue through a story about Katy Ferguson, whom editor Jessie Redmon Fauset identifies as "the founder of the first Sunday School in New York City." The sketch begins by inviting readers to consider their own relationship to the sketch's content: "Did you ever hear of Katy Ferguson? I confess I did not until a very short while ago, and yet without my knowing it, Katy Ferguson must have been exerting a great influence over me for at least sixteen years. And unless I am very much mistaken, she has been influencing you, too." Fauset then recounts Ferguson's early years of enslavement, her loss of family, and her eventual efforts to help care for and educate children. After finishing the story of Ferguson's life, Fauset places her subject in context, reminding readers that Ferguson was "not the only colored woman to do great deeds for her race." Fauset frames her sketch by acknowledging the dearth of information about Black historical figures, which she believes can be remedied through stories like these, and she primes readers to gain more knowledge by declaring, "Think of all the wonderful folks you have still to hear about!" ("Katy Ferguson" 27).

This inaugural biography shares many features with subsequent profiles of figures such as Phillis Wheatley, Crispus Attucks, Denmark Vesey, and Alexander Pushkin. Selected or penned by Fauset and influenced by W. E. B. Du Bois, these sketches reflect the editors' interest in biography as a tool for recovering Black voices from the past and empowering the Black children of their present. In this chapter, I show how these sketches recover and rhetorically reconstruct stories about Black historical figures as counter-memories that critique white memories of Blackness in the early twentieth century and function as tools of resistance for young readers. By reading these sketches alongside published responses to them from readers, I demonstrate that such counter-memories operate by addressing and constituting their audience of African American children as agents and citizens in their own right. I begin by describing how biographies—both within African American children's literature generally and within *The Brownies' Book* specifically—function as counter-memories and by situating my reading within contemporary discussions about child agency. The subsequent analysis explores how the biographies exhibit rhetorical features that enable them to function as counter-memories for young readers. My analysis addresses three features of biographical writing in *The Brownies' Book*: using traditional elements of the biography genre in order to establish Black figures as worthy of remembrance, constructing counter-memories as a critique of white history, and creating continuity between past and present by engaging readers in their contemporary context. I conclude by examining reader letters published in the "The Jury" as further evidence that readers understood and engaged with the biographies as counter-memories and as tools for resistance in their own lives.

THE BROWNIES' BOOK BIOGRAPHIES AS COUNTER-MEMORIES

Since at least the middle of the nineteenth century, the genre of biography has been enlisted creatively by African American communities in a project of popular historical learning for children and young people. Whereas some contemporary biographies for children of all races and backgrounds tend to eschew explicit moral formation in favor of delivering information, biographical sketches and texts written by, about, and for African Americans during the 1920s convey historical accounts with the explicit goal of supplying young readers with politically and racially significant African American models for action (VanderHaagen 35–36).[1] In this way, the conservative genre of biography became a rhetorical resource for achieving (mostly) progressive purposes such as historical recovery and racial uplift. Although audience has been an important consideration in studying texts for all children, it becomes particularly significant for understanding texts for Black children. As Dianne Johnson has persuasively argued, biographies and other texts for African American children historically have functioned as part of a "network of psychological protection, nurturance, and education" cultivated by Black communities (12). These texts emerge in response to unique community needs perceived by their creators, and, for this reason, they are molded powerfully by an accompanying vision of audience. As a magazine intended for the Black

child audience Du Bois described as "the children of the sun," *The Brownies'
Book* was also shaped by these community needs.[2]

The biographies in *The Brownies' Book* reflected the conceptualization of
child audiences espoused by editors Du Bois and Fauset. Du Bois, as Katharine Capshaw Smith claimed, "reinvented conceptions of black childhood"
by treating Black children as "culturally, politically, and aesthetically sophisticated" (*Children's Literature* 1). The young readers of this magazine were
not coddled, protected, or condescended to, but rather were encouraged to
think of themselves as agents of change and, in many cases, "race leaders"
(*Children's Literature* xvi, 5). Du Bois recognized that the magazine would
become a more effective vehicle for political change if it integrated education
and entertainment. Jonda C. McNair and Rudine Sims Bishop have pointed
out that "Du Bois wanted not just to educate and inspire black children but
also to entertain them, to show them the way to joy" (30). Although Du Bois
certainly influenced this editorial philosophy, scholars such as Johnson and
Smith have pointed out that Fauset espoused similar views and implemented
them in the magazine. Fauset's biographer, Caroline Wedin Sylvander, claimed
that Fauset had a long-standing interest in biographies, "especially of historical
Black personages, and especially as corrective models for youth" (106).[3] *The
Brownies' Book* biographies bear the marks of such views. Beyond exemplify-
ing the editorial influence of Fauset and Du Bois, these sketches also reflect
the perspectives of their individual authors.

The vision of the "sophisticated" child audience at play in *The Brownies'
Book* biographies presages contemporary discussion among scholars in children's literature, sociology, and childhood studies that theorize children as
simultaneously influenced and influencing. Outlining this discussion, Allison James explained that studies envisioning children as "social actors" and
"agents" treat them "as 'active in the construction of their own lives'" and as
"having a part to play 'in the lives of those around them' in 'the societies in
which they live'" (41). The analysis in this chapter envisions children in the
same way, both because I find this approach most theoretically compelling and
because it is how Du Bois and Fauset approached their child readers. Although
the biographies deliberately direct interpretation by readers, they also address
children as individuals capable of judging and responding meaningfully to
the action of others. The biographies and letters therefore acknowledge, as
children's literature scholar Marah Gubar argues Victorian children's stories
did, "the belated nature of the child's subjectivity—the fact that young people
are born into a world in which stories about who they are (and what they
should become) are already in circulation before they can speak for themselves." The children addressed by these biographies—and who speak back to
them in revealing ways—thus become, in Gubar's words, "capable of reshaping

stories" in ways that reflect adult influence but also children's capacity for rhetorical influence (6).

These assumptions about children's agency enable the biographical sketches of *The Brownies' Book* to function as counter-memories[4] for young readers. Counter-memories deliberately provide alternatives to and often even critiques of dominant memories. Because the sketches treat young readers as capable of reflection, critical thought, and action, they can also circulate counter-memories that require such capacities in order to dismantle hegemonic memories about Black folks. George Lipsitz explained that counter-memory "focuses on localized experiences of oppression, using them to reframe and refocus dominant narratives" (213). The production and circulation of counter-memories were critical to Black communities of the early twentieth century who were working to challenge, supplement, and replace dominant white narratives of the past that misrepresented Black Americans in harmful ways; they still are today. As Anthony L. Brown argued in his analysis of history textbooks by Black historians such as Carter G. Woodson, educational texts for young readers functioned as particularly powerful sources of counter-memory within African American communities. Published just before the appearance of Woodson's *The Negro in Our History* (1922), *The Brownies' Book* biographies likewise participated in what Brown described as "the process of revising the narrative of African American imagery during the early twentieth century," which "was carefully reconstructed in relation to how various racial discourses and practices constructed African American physicality, intelligence, beauty, and mental capacities" (56). The memories of individuals of African descent in *The Brownies' Book* offered not simple alternatives to white histories but critical engagements with unjust memories. In this sense, the biographies also participated in what Houston A. Baker Jr. described as "critical memory," which "works to illustrate the continuity, at a black majority level, in the community-interested politics of black publicity in America" (4). Both critical memory and counter-memories depend upon addressing—and thereby constituting—an audience of agents able to perceive and dismantle hegemonic historical narratives.

RHETORICAL FEATURES OF *THE BROWNIES' BOOK* BIOGRAPHIES AS COUNTER-MEMORIES

Over the course of its two-year run, *The Brownies' Book* featured a total of twenty nonfiction biographical sketches, most of which were about well-known individuals of African descent such as Harriet Tubman and Frederick Douglass. Yet there were notable exceptions to those general themes. For

instance, there were three accounts of "ordinary" Black folks: Elizabeth Blakesley and Mary Binkley and a reader of *The Brownies' Book* from South Africa
named Olive Plaatje. There are two stories about individuals not of African
descent: a two-installment narrative about white Frenchman Lafayette, written
by white activist Lillie Buffum Chace Wyman, and a sketch of "Saint" Gandhi
by Blanche Watson. Most of the sketches were written by Black women. Of
the sketches appearing in 1920, six were unattributed, most likely written by
Fauset herself. Three sketches were written by Madeline G. Allison, the long-
time secretary of Du Bois. Other Black women authoring sketches included
Elizabeth Ross Haynes, Laura E. Wilkes, Augusta E. Bird, Catherine Deaver
Lealtad, Annette C. Browne, Sarah Talbert Keelan, and Blanche Watson. The
only male author in the group was Arthur Huff Fauset, the brother of Jessie
Redmon Fauset, and the only white author I could verify was Lillie Buffum
Chace Wyman.[5] Most of the sketches run between one and three pages, with
the Frederick Douglass sketch being the longest at five pages. Several of the
sketches also feature illustrations. In the following analysis, I show how these
biographies use traditional elements of the biography genre to represent Black
individuals, critique white history through counter-memories, and engage
readers in ways that connect past and present.

Using Biographical Conventions to Build Counter-Memories

The biographical sketches in *The Brownies' Book* deploy conventional features of biographies to demonstrate that individuals of African descent are
worthy of remembrance, even when measured by white historical standards.
The sketches leverage four conventional elements to establish their subjects'
significance: providing accepted forms of evidence, establishing associations
with prominent—especially white—figures, praising traditional character
traits, and describing the legacy of the subject. By drawing on these conventions, the sketches render potentially unfamiliar figures easily recognizable
as typical biographical subjects and enable them to gain traction within the
traditional scope of history.

Many sketches provide conventional evidence of their subject's significance,
both to capture readers' attention and to ground their argument about the
importance of Black history. The sketches simultaneously celebrate the figures
in their Blackness and supply evidence that they are not only significant "for a
Black person" but are the equals or even superiors of white historical figures.
This strategy can be observed in the sketches of familiar individuals such
as Phillis Wheatley, Crispus Attucks, and Alexander Pushkin. For instance,
when describing the many "reasons why colored Americans should hold Phillis Wheatley in such high esteem," Jessie Redmon Fauset both explains that

Wheatley was "the first Negro in America to win prestige for purely intellectual attainments" and that her story provides ammunition for abolitionists arguing against the presumed inferiority of Black people. Although Fauset identifies Wheatley as a Black "first" in her field, she also judges Wheatley favorably as "the peer of any American poet of those days" ("Phillis Wheatley" 253). As a writer herself, Fauset was well equipped to evaluate Wheatley's literary merits, and she uses that expertise to assess Wheatley's work positively. Fauset likewise compares Attucks to other (white) national heroes who had "distinguished [themselves] in the service of [their] country." Attucks here is not merely an incidental casualty but a deliberate patriot and, according to Fauset, the "first American to die for his fatherland" ("America's First Martyr-Patriot" 216). By making him a "first" and comparing him to other national heroes, she argues that Attucks is at least as significant as white men in other nations and implies that he may actually be *more* significant than white Americans of the period. Catherine Deaver Lealtad's sketch of Pushkin—"The Black Russian"— utilizes a similar strategy in a different national context. She profiles Pushkin because he is a *Black* Russian, yet she recognizes his significance as a Black *Russian*. She hails him as "the creator of Russia's national literature," citing as evidence the fact that, when Pushkin died in a duel, "the Czar regarded his death as a personal loss and the whole nation was moved" (182–83). Lealtad even claims that, before Pushkin, "there was no Russian literature" and the nation's existing literature "imitated and affected things French" (182). While positioning Pushkin as a founder of Russian cultural identity, these claims also subtly reject the notion that Black people were naturally imitative. In this reversal, Pushkin is the original Russian poet, whereas white Russians are mere imitators. His significance, therefore, lies in both his originality and his supposedly innate Russianness.

Arguments for significance are not limited to figures who left historical records, as Annette C. Browne's sketch of Mary Binkley illustrates. The profile of Binkley, a formerly enslaved woman with whom Browne had become acquainted, provided evidence that extraordinary qualities can be observed in "ordinary" people. Browne frames Binkley's significance by explaining,

The sketch of the life of Mary Binkley is no record of great achievements that usually mark biographies, neither is it an attempt to portray the character of one who rose to great heights or even small fame for the simple reason that no such things marked her life; but it is, to me, an impressive story of a soul that was filled with a desire for enlightenment—a desire so strong that many years of bending toil failed to weaken it. (216)

In this passage, Browne signals her recognition of biographical conventions while offering narrative evidence of Binkley's "ordinary" yet "impressive" greatness.

In addition to providing evidence of individual greatness, the sketches advance the case for their subjects' significance by noting their association with prominent (usually white) individuals. This ubiquitous strategy evinces the conservative foundations of such texts (VanderHaagen 78–83). Although relying on associations with white men could imply that white approval is required for remembrance, when read within the context of the authors' other rhetorical choices, these decisions can be understood as strategies for gaining traction with audiences whose very understanding of history was determined by white supremacy. Establishing such connections enables the authors to advance more radical arguments about the influence and importance of Black individuals in global history.

United States presidents, assumed to be familiar to readers, appear as the most common association. Sketches about Sojourner Truth, Blanche Kelso Bruce, Benjamin Banneker, Frederick Douglass, and "Brown Joe" all establish a connection between the subject and a US president. In some cases, such as the sketches of Truth, Douglass, and Bruce, presidents are described in terms of personal familiarity. For instance, Jessie Redmon Fauset explains that Truth "numbered the greatest man in the country, President Lincoln, among her friends" ("A Pioneer Suffragette" 121), and Laura E. Wilkes reports that Douglass "visited with President Lincoln" and his secretary of war to try to secure "commissions for colored men" (269). Bruce enjoys a relationship with the president that enables Bruce to ask "a favor of him"—specifically, a small appointment for his former enslaver (A. H. Fauset 95). Lacking personal relationships with presidents, other individuals such as Benjamin Banneker simply earned their recognition (Haynes 173). Sketches about Douglass, "Brown Joe," and Toussaint L'Ouverture mention other well-known white men with whom they were associated, including abolitionists Wendell Phillips and William Lloyd Garrison and cultural figures such as William Wordsworth (J. R. Fauset, "Toussaint L'Ouverture" 152; Wilkes 268; Wyman, "Brave Brown Joe" 319). A few profiles link their subjects to other prominent Black Americans. For instance, Jessie Redmon Fauset's narrative about Truth introduces Douglass in order to relate the moving (if likely apocryphal) story about her rebuke of a discouraged Douglass: "Frederick, is God dead?" ("A Pioneer Suffragette" 120). This anecdote illustrates Truth's rhetorical power and her influence over the most famous Black man of her time. Douglass also appears alongside Booker T. Washington in the opening paragraph of Bruce's story to situate Bruce within a line of "young slaves" who were "determined to learn somehow" (A. H. Fauset 95). By identifying Washington and Douglass, Arthur

Huff Fauset connects Bruce to better-known Black figures while also establishing that these self-taught men regularly overcame their circumstances. These associations work to bolster explicit claims about the subjects' significance by showing that they were recognized by and, in some instances, influential over prominent figures.

Many biographies for children also praise certain character traits and personal qualities such as intelligence, courage, and generosity, and *The Brownies' Book* sketches are no exception. Although this strategy tends to universalize values, these sketches demonstrate how this strategy can be used in innovative and progressive ways. For instance, these narratives repeatedly insist that supposedly "white" qualities actually coexist with African physiological features such as dark skin. The sketches thus create positive counter-memories of historical Blackness that promote praiseworthy enactments of contemporary Blackness.

Among traditional character traits, determination or self-determination figure most prominently. Some sketches use these words explicitly; others invoke them implicitly. The sketch about Douglass makes most frequent use of the words *determination* or *determined*, explicitly citing one of the two words four times throughout the sketch (Wilkes 266–70). For instance, the narrator explains the story of Douglass's resisting the "slave breaker" by saying, "Douglass' strong resentment at the indignities put upon him by this man gave him the *determination* to resist Covey's second attempt to whip him" (Wilkes 268; emphasis added). This anecdote—perhaps one of the best known from Douglass's first autobiography—illustrates how his determination emerged naturally from being subjected to the undeserved "indignities" of enslavement. Although only the sketch about Paul Cuffee also explicitly describes his "determination" (J. R. Fauset, "A Great Sailor" 39), sketches about Blanche Kelso Bruce and Elizabeth Blakesley illustrate it indirectly (A. H. Fauset 95; Wyman, "The Bravest of the Brave" 338). Some of these examples emphasize not only "determination" but "self-determination"—a critical enacted trait for Black communities dealing with the history of slavery and racial oppression. The value of "self-determination" can also be observed in the story of Katy Ferguson, when Jessie Redmon Fauset reports that Ferguson "did not let her sorrows crush and enfeeble her [but] looked about her to see what her hands could find to do, and having found it, she did it" (27).

Other conventional character traits praised prominently included good sense, kindness, modesty, generosity and humility, courage and bravery, and intelligence and studiousness.[6] Although simply noting these traits in individuals of African heritage serves to counter racist assumptions about white superiority, doing so while simultaneously commenting on the individuals' raced features strengthens the argument. The two most striking examples come from the sketches of Truth and Vesey. In the sketch of Truth, Jessie Redmon Fauset describes the scene in Akron, Ohio, in 1851 when Truth gave her famous speech, saying, "She must have been an impressive figure as she stood there, for she was very tall and dark, with a keen, unflinching eye" ("A Pioneer Suffragette" 121). This description emphasizes Truth's height and "dark" skin, both of which lead Fauset to conclude that she must have looked "impressive" standing before the hostile crowd. Rejecting assumptions about Black folks' "natural" submissiveness, Fauset notes Truth's "keen, unflinching eye," which also contributed to her striking appearance. Madeline G. Allison also associates darkness with good character when she describes Denmark Vesey as "a black man, and handsome," who was also "physically strong" and possessed of "a powerful mentality" (58). Joining these traits in such close proximity demonstrates that Blackness, strength, beauty, and intelligence can coexist in a single individual. These references to Blackness, although not universal across the sketches, appear frequently enough to be notable examples of the ways that these texts use traditional features of biographies to advance counter-memories of the individuals that they commemorate.

The final way in which the sketches use traditional aspects of biographies to articulate counter-memories is by describing the subject's influence, legacy, or commemoration—essentially, their posthumous significance. Closely related to the arguments for significance detailed above, this strategy is often used by creators of twentieth- and twenty-first-century biographies for children in order to invite readers to participate in the creation of shared memory (VanderHaagen 135–41). The discussion of a subject's legacy most often appears at the conclusion of the sketch. However, the one exception to this pattern in *The Brownies' Book*—the inaugural sketch of Katy Ferguson mentioned earlier—demonstrates how this feature works symbiotically with other engagement strategies. After asking readers whether they are familiar with Ferguson (and assuming they are not), Jessie Redmon Fauset reveals her surprise at discovering Ferguson's remarkable influence on her own life. She then turns to readers' experience, saying, "And unless I am very much mistaken, she has been influencing you, too" (27). This opening passage serves several rhetorical purposes. First, by admitting her own ignorance of Ferguson, Fauset emphasizes that lack of awareness does not indicate lack of influence by Black historical figures. Second, by quantifying the influence ("sixteen years"), Fauset indicates the ongoing nature of Ferguson's legacy. Then, by highlighting Ferguson's influence on readers, Fauset prepares readers to consider the scope and persistence of Ferguson's contributions to religious education.

Sketches about figures more prominent than Ferguson take a more conventional approach to describing individuals' legacies. Generally, sketches about familiar individuals such as Crispus Attucks, Frederick Douglass, and

Harriet Tubman feature sweeping pronouncements about influence and vivid descriptions of posthumous recognition. For instance, of sailor Paul Cuffee, readers learn that the world was "truly better because he lived in it" (J. R. Fauset, "A Great Sailor" 39). Likewise, in the conclusion of her sketch of Toussaint L'Ouverture, Fauset declares that "his influence lives on," especially in Haiti, where "the spirit of Toussaint lives eternally among her men, urging them ever and always on to freedom" (152).[7] Other sketches support claims of ongoing influence and legacy by describing how their subjects were mourned and remembered after their deaths. The most extensive of these instances appears in the Douglass sketch, which concludes with several paragraphs describing his well-attended 1895 funeral services and the monument erected to him in Rochester, New York (Wilkes 270). Sketches also document the ways in which figures such as Attucks, Alexandre Dumas, and Alexander Pushkin were memorialized, whether in word or in stone (J. R. Fauset, "America's First Martyr-Patriot" 217; Allison, "Alexandre Dumas" 6, 7; Lealtad 183).[8] By providing different types of evidence to illustrate significance, identifying key associations, praising accepted virtues, and describing legacies, the authors of these sketches make use of the conventional generic features of biographies for children in order to create counter-memorial space for Black figures.

Black Counter-Memory as a Critique of White History

In addition to using generic biographical strategies to build traction for counter-memories, *The Brownies' Book* sketches construct Black counter-memories that together offer a critique of white history. Across the sketches, the authors used three recurring rhetorical strategies to argue that readers could and should challenge white histories: establishing the centrality of Black individuals in history, reframing the history of enslavement, and performing historical reflexivity. These rhetorical moves show readers how to question the history they had been taught in order to replace it with a more accurate, Black-centered account of the past.

First, the sketches treat Black individuals as central agents in history and argue that a complete picture of the past depends on understanding such historical actors. Although many authors of the sketches advanced such ideas, Jessie Redmon Fauset developed the argument most consistently. In several of her sketches, Fauset argues both that Black folks as a group and Black folks as individuals have played important roles in history. Two of Fauset's sketches—about Katy Ferguson and Toussaint L'Ouverture—wax poetic about learning this history. After concluding the narrative about Ferguson, Fauset reminds readers that Ferguson was "not the only colored woman to do great deeds for her race." She builds anticipation for the many sketches to come of "wonderful folks," including, using wry feminist wit, the "many splendid colored men" (27). This passage presents Ferguson as a single representative of a much larger group of important Black historical figures—like the tip of an iceberg providing only a tiny glimpse of what lies below. Although Fauset does not explain what makes these "wonderful folks" worth knowing, her introduction to the story of L'Ouverture details her own views about what makes the best story and, by extension, the best history. Fauset admits that her "favorite" kind of story is "the one where the poor or unknown boy or girl, man or woman, struggles up, up, up until he becomes rich or famous, or useful, or the leader of his people, the saviour of his fatherland." She declares that "all other stories of no matter how splendid adventures and achievements fade into nothing for me beside the heroes who mount—as the Romans used to say—*per aspera ad astra*, 'through rough ways to the stars'!" Fauset does not limit these stories to the standard idea of fame but expresses her even greater "admiration" for those "real people who have passed through real suffering and have achieved real triumph" ("Toussaint L'Ouverture" 149). Fauset clearly outlines her preference for the kinds of rags-to-riches stories favored by Americans during the time. This preference for stories of "real suffering" followed by "real triumph" also dovetails with the many narratives of Black individuals rising "up from slavery," in Booker T. Washington's words. The fraught bootstrap narrative, common in American literature, also provides Fauset and others a means of foregrounding the agency of enslaved persons who freed themselves and/or improved their conditions through hard work and the "determination" praised in so many of the sketches.

Most of the other sketches avoid general reflections on history in favor of relating stories that reveal Black folks' previously obscured roles in key historical events or changes. For instance, when explaining the significance of Phillis Wheatley's poetry, Fauset notes that it provided critical fodder for abolitionists arguing against the racist idea that "Negroes were mentally inferior" (253).[9] Other sketches about early Americans such as Benjamin Banneker and Crispus Attucks reclaim for these figures a central role in revolutionary events. Subtly challenging the historical association between Benjamin Franklin and the early American almanac, Elizabeth Ross Haynes's sketch instructs readers about Benjamin Banneker's contributions to that field. She explains that his study of the stars led him eventually to write an almanac, which was promoted to publishers as being written by "one of the great men of the country." Haynes claims that the publishers deemed the almanac "the work of a genius," which "met the hearty approval of distinguished astronomers" (173). This account links Banneker to well-known scientific advancements of the period and, by using the word "genius," fashions a counter-memory of Black intellectual achievement that undermines white assumptions about Black inferiority.

Fauset's sketch of Crispus Attucks likewise places a Black figure at the center of famous events, in this case the Boston Massacre. She tells readers that, on that "one never-to-be-forgotten day, the 5th of March, 1770, a small band of citizens made an attack on some British soldiers who were marching through State Street, Boston," and "the leader of this band was Crispus Attucks" (216). Although historical records provide no indication of Attucks's leadership position (Kachun 8), Fauset places him unequivocally at the center—and not just by chance but by virtue of his leadership and revolutionary commitments. Both of these examples illustrate the ways in which these authors used narratives to inform readers of Black historical contributions and, in some instances, to leverage the interpretive opportunities provided by incomplete historical records.

The second set of critical counter-memories advanced by these sketches focuses on accounts of slavery. During the early part of the twentieth century, Black Americans remembered the institution—and, in some cases, the firsthand experience—of slavery in diverse ways. To some groups, slavery was a shameful memory that needed to be forgotten, so that African American communities could survive and thrive. To others, the shame of enslavement belonged not to Black Americans but to white Americans, and the time of enslavement ought to be recalled as not only a source of suffering but also a crucible for Black agency (Blight 311–19). *The Brownies' Book* sketches fall almost universally in the latter camp, as they confront the historical reality of enslavement, condemn those who perpetuated it, and celebrate those who resisted it. Rather than viewing enslavement as a source of shame for Black people, many of these authors highlight their subjects' disadvantaged beginnings in order to magnify later achievements. Jessie Redmon Fauset's influence can clearly be seen in this theme, as her sketches emphasize the "horrors of slavery," describe the system as a "curse" ("A Pioneer Suffragette" 120),[10] and posit its inherent connections to "fighting, misgovernment . . . and disaster" ("Toussaint L'Ouverture" 149). This condemnation of slavery can also be observed in sketches by the sole white author in the group, Lillie Buffum Chace Wyman, as when her sketch "Brave Brown Joe and Good White Men" alludes to one company's participation in the illegal slave trade. Relating the story of how enslaved man Joe secretly boarded a boat owned by John H. Pearson and Company in hopes of freeing himself, Wyman notes, "Mr. Pearson is credited, in most of the records, which I have seen, with taking the aggressive and responsible position in certain affairs, which have given the ships and the company a shameful place in history" (318). Pearson's complicity in this "shameful" business marks him as the opposite of the "Good White Men" whom Wyman praises in this and other sketches. Although Wyman's version of events is hardly centered on Black agency, it does provide an important counter-memory that acknowledges white responsibility for the institution of slavery.

Like Fauset, authors such as Augusta E. Bird and Madeline G. Allison emphasized the agency and dignity of the enslaved by carefully selecting certain details and phrases for inclusion in their sketches. Bird's sketch of Harriet Tubman, for instance, describes the marriage of Tubman's enslaved parents, Benjamin Ross and Harriet Green, saying that they were "both slaves, but married and faithful to each other" (84). This short phrase challenges racist images of the enslaved as incapable of fidelity or even basic filial bonds and thereby advocates a counter-memory of enslaved people who were "faithful *to each other*" rather than to a white enslaver. Allison's sketch of Denmark Vesey likewise rejects white notions of slave rebellions as the irrational actions of violent creatures. She insists on using the words of political revolution to describe Vesey's carefully planned slave rebellion, calling it an "organized movement" and an "uprising" (58). Furthermore, she characterizes Vesey as a "cautious" person who took his time to develop a logical "plan" for enslaved people in Charleston to "resist" the "slave system" (58). Such word choices support Allison's concluding judgment that Vesey was a "martyr" for "the cause of freedom" (58). As a whole, the sketch—like Fauset's about L'Ouver-ture—unambiguously argues that planners and executors of slave uprisings are heroes rather than villains. This counter-memory directly confronts white narratives about Black tendencies toward violence, instead condemning the slavery system as the source of violence.

Finally, some of the sketches draw attention to the process of making historical conclusions in order to demonstrate that such conclusions are not fixed but subject to revision based on new information. By performing a measure of reflexivity, the authors model for readers how they, too, might critically examine the historical record that they encounter in school or other white-dominated institutions. Children who understand how historical thinking works may be more open to critical revisions of hegemonic narratives (see Wineburg). Sketches perform reflexivity by interpreting evidence, by qualifying their conclusions, and by drawing attention to gaps in the historical record. For instance, a few authors cite or quote directly from the historical record, as in Jessie Redmon Fauset's sketch of Phillis Wheatley. To provide evidence of her positive evaluation by "many prominent men," Fauset provides an excerpt from the affidavit signed by these men following their interrogation of Wheatley in October 1772 (252). Although this excerpt offers definitive evidence, authors recognize that not all historical evidence offers such clear conclusions. For example, Haynes's sketch about Banneker illustrates his talent as an inventor by describing how Banneker made a clock with "imperfect tools" and "without a model" (172). Haynes then supports this claim with carefully qualified evidence: "An article published in London, England, in 1864, says that Banneker's clock was *probably* the first clock of which every part was made in America" (172; emphasis added). By adding the word "probably," Haynes tempers her claim about Banneker's status as a "first" and shows readers how to make historical claims suited to the available evidence. Other sketches admit complete gaps in the historical record, as in Jessie Redmon Fauset's narrative about Crispus Attucks. Speaking of whether Attucks had escaped enslavement, Fauset says, "Of this we cannot be sure, for history goes blank at this point." She goes on to quote an advertisement for a man escaping slavery presumed to have been Attucks ("America's First Martyr-Patriot" 216). By recognizing the limitations of historical records, Fauset shows readers that she is a careful and trustworthy reporter, and she models how they might make their own informed conclusions about the past. Each of these strategies treats readers not as passive consumers prepared only for predigested information but as active participants in the process of historical judgment and collective remembrance. Young Black readers who view history-making as an active process involving human judgment are better equipped to critically evaluate the white supremacist narratives that systematically ignore Black historical contributions.

Connecting Past and Present

To better prepare readers to appropriate counter-memories as their own, these sketches also use several strategies common in children's literature. Specifically, they address readers directly, facilitate visualization, invite identification with the subject, and make connections to the contemporary context. I view these as rhetorical strategies because they reflect the stated persuasive, public motivations of *The Brownies' Book* editors and authors to form readers' identities and influence their actions.

Many sketches rely on forms of direct address that invite readers to interpret and judge the stories. Sketches about Toussaint L'Ouverture, Katy Ferguson, Elizabeth Blakesley, Samuel Coleridge-Taylor, and Denmark Vesey use various forms of direct address, including rhetorical questions, editorial exclamations, informational asides, and moral lessons. For instance, Madeline G. Allison's sketch of Samuel Coleridge-Taylor is peppered with narrator interjections, evoking a sense that the author is speaking to the readers face-to-face. Allison begins the sketch by describing the impressive accomplishments of Coleridge-Taylor's father, a surgeon originally from Sierra Leone, concluding the first paragraph with an emphatic "Think of that!" Then, after describing the young Samuel, Allison says, "I'd like to have seen him, wouldn't you?" (370). Although not advancing substantive interpretive claims, these

interjections establish trust between author and reader and invite engagement
with the narrative. Directly addressing readers also bids them to judge the
stories.[11] Wyman's profile of Elizabeth Blakesley, an enslaved woman who freed
herself and became an abolitionist, concludes by comparing her to another
historical heroine. She asks whether Blakesley was "not like Joan of Arc in her
courage?" Following this rhetorical question, Wyman instructs her readers
how to respond, saying, "I think every white child and every colored child
in this country should be proud because she [Blakesley] was an American
girl" ("The Bravest of the Brave" 339). In another example, when reporting
Toussaint L'Ouverture's untimely end in jail, Jessie Redmon Fauset minces
no words, saying that "he lay in his cell cold and dead from starvation." She
continues by asking readers, "But does it greatly matter? If he had been asked,
which do you think he would have preferred,—life and ease or the implant-
ing and fostering of the idea of liberty in the Negroes of Hayti? No need to
guess" (152). In this passage, Fauset paints a stark image of the hero's solitary
death, and she uses two rhetorical questions to prompt readers to interpret
his death as a continuation of his work in life. These questions even suggest
that his death was the possible end result of "fostering . . . the idea of liberty
in the Negroes of Hayti" (152). Although the ideas are posed as questions, the
conclusion—though unstated—is implied as obvious with the phrase "no
need to guess." The rhetorical questions work enthymematically, providing
some information so readers can arrive at the "right" conclusion on their own.
Thus, readers are invited to act and think of themselves as nascent judges of
human action.

In addition to typical portraits and illustrations, many sketches also use
vivid description to bring the subject of slavery before the eyes of readers
(see Aristotle 244–48). The framing of this visualization suggests that it is
intended not only to make the sketches livelier but also to prepare readers'
imaginations for the act of judgment. In the story of Katy Ferguson, Fauset
invites readers to imagine slavery and to consider how they might act to
prevent it from recurring. She begins by telling readers that Ferguson was
"born to the cruellest fate that ever awaited a child"—that is, "she was a slave."
Fauset then instructs readers to "*stop and think* about that a little while, *try
to picture* the horrors of such a condition, and *resolve* that in no sense of the
word will you allow such a fate to overtake you and yours" (27; emphasis
added). Rather than avoid the subject of slavery, as most white Americans and
some Black Americans might have preferred, she urges readers to use their
imagination to confront it. Fauset employs a similar approach in her sketch
of Phillis Wheatley, as she invites readers to "*picture* . . . her fear and anguish
when she found herself torn away from everything and everybody whom
she had ever known" (251; emphasis added). In her sketch of Mary Binkley,

Annette C. Browne also invites the audience to reflect and imagine, saying, "In thinking over what you have heard or read about slavery, you, children of a more fortunate age, there will come to your minds no doubt, pictures sad and awful—pictures of children growing up under the oppressor's rod—children whose souls are steeped in ignorance and degradation and in whom every hope is born to be starved out" (214).

Like Fauset, Browne here connects the past of slavery to the readers' present. Browne's sketch, however, prompts more deliberate comparison by emphasizing the deprivation of enslaved children when compared to contemporary children. Although this characterization accurately reflects the immorality of the institution, it obscures the ways in which enslaved people might have educated themselves or resisted their oppression. This opening paragraph also frames Browne's account of Binkley, who was said to have been subject to this same "ignorance" and "degradation" yet nurtured "in her soul a longing for light" (216). Browne employs visualization to advance her lesson: even those in the bleakest situation might resist with hope. Though the lesson is clear, Browne uses visualization to impress upon readers the horrors of slavery and the powers of Black folks who endured them. These authors use descriptions of slavery to help readers visualize and thereby remember—albeit secondhand—the accurate account that the myth of the "happy slave" could never provide. By repeatedly recalling this reality, perhaps the authors sought to ward off the veil of forgetfulness that hung over Americans' memories of slavery.

Some sketch authors also invoke contemporary events to strengthen the link between readers of the present and figures of the past. Fauset's story of Sojourner Truth, for instance, connects Truth's suffrage work to the Nineteenth Amendment, which was then finishing its journey toward ratification (see VanderHaagen 51). The first three paragraphs frame Truth's story in relation to suffrage, beginning, "NOW that the right of women to vote is gradually being conceded throughout the United States, few people stop to realize for how many years women have had to work and fight and wait in order to reach this goal" ("A Pioneer Suffragette" 120). She addresses her audience as informed citizens knowledgeable about this history, saying that "even our boys and girls remember" the challenges faced by women working toward suffrage (120). Using this phrase also emphasizes the proximity of the events, which reinforces the continuity between Truth's life and readers' lives. Likewise, Fauset's sketch of Toussaint L'Ouverture concludes by collapsing the temporal space between his life and early twentieth-century Haiti. After noting that "it was in April, 1803 that he died," Fauset shifts focus rapidly to the nation's present struggles "against a foreign invasion." The sketch concludes by emphasizing L'Ouverture's continuing influence, declaring that Haiti "does not falter" because "the spirit of Toussaint lives eternally among her men,

urging them ever and always on to freedom" (152). This account represents
L'Ouverture as a spirit who has been freed from history in order to ensure
that the victories of the past persist into the future.

CONCLUSION: HOW READERS ENGAGED BLACK
COUNTER-MEMORIES

To conclude this chapter, I turn to the question of how readers responded to
the rhetorical strategies used in *The Brownies' Book* biographies. Although not
comprehensive, the reader letters published in the regular talk-back column,
"The Jury," nonetheless provide evidence of how some readers understood
and engaged with the sketches as counter-memories.[12] Specifically, these letters
demonstrate readers' dissatisfaction with dominant memory practices, their
desire for deeper knowledge of Black history, their enthusiastic engagement
with the biographies, and their growing race consciousness. The authors of
the letters wrote with an expectation that their letters would be read and taken
seriously by the editors of the magazine, which reflects Du Bois's and Fauset's
assumptions about reader sophistication and agency. Indeed, the editors took
some young letter writers, such as Pocahontas Foster, so seriously that they
later published their work in the magazine.

Readers expressed their dissatisfaction with current memory practices in a
variety of ways, including their frustration with the focus on white heroes and
the invisibility of Black ones. Claudia Moore of Pittsburgh wrote in February
1920 that she was "so tired of hearing only of white heroes and celebrating
holidays in their honor." She suggested that communities should instead celebrate Black heroes such as Frederick Douglass and Crispus Attucks and that
The Brownies' Book should advocate such commemorations. Marshalling the
support of her Black peers as evidence, Moore claimed that "all the colored
girls in my class said they wished so too" (83). Pocahontas Foster likewise
reported, "I have never liked history because I always felt that it wasn't much
good" and was "just a lot of dates and things that some men did, men whom I
didn't know and nobody else whom I knew, knew anything about." However,
her encounter with the stories in *The Brownies' Book* about "real colored people, whom I feel that I do know because they were brown people like me," led
her to believe that she did enjoy history (140).

Several readers shared their desire to learn more about Black history,
including specific individuals. Writing in August 1920, Audrey Wright suggested that future magazines include monthly sketches of "Negro heroines,"
which she believed would be "greatly appreciated by those who wish to know
more about their own race women" (256). Readers also recommended specific

biographies: Pocahontas Foster requested a profile of white abolitionist John Brown (140), and Rena Cooper asked for a sketch about Booker T. Washington (24). Although neither request was granted, the letters demonstrate both that writers expected their suggestions to be considered and that writers desired to learn more.

"The Jury" also catalogs the rich array of activities through which readers engaged and became invested in the stories. Willie Brown's letter declared the magazine "just fine!" and indicated his preference for the "stories about the colored heroes." Brown demonstrated his personal investment in the magazine's contents by reporting that he had paid for his "year's subscription by selling lemonade last summer on a very hot street" (208). Ada Simpson wrote about her "scrap-book," which she described as "a large square book filled with sheets of coarse brown paper, with two covers with holes punched through and tied together with a string." She explained that it contained "all the pictures I can find of interesting colored people and the interesting things they do," including "Frederick Douglas [sic], Bishop Allen, Harriet Tubman, Paul Lawrence [sic] Dunbar, and lots of others." She then asked the editors to consider publishing pictures of Katy Ferguson and Paul Cuffee, "so I can cut them out and put them in my book!" (111).

These responses also provide evidence of some readers' expanding race consciousness, bringing the goals of editors Fauset and Du Bois full circle. Several of the writers mentioned their identification with both the trials and triumphs of those profiled in the magazine. Some spoke proudly of the biography subjects as "our own race" (Cooper 24), "brown people like me" (Foster 140), and "race women" (Wright 256). Others described their own aspirations in relation to other Black Americans, such as Paul Cuffee (Murray 111) and Samuel Coleridge-Taylor (Hill 111). Many, as demonstrated above, earnestly affirmed their collective desire for more knowledge about and celebration of the Black past, which they perceived as directly related to their ability to achieve in the present. In this sense, the biographies clearly function as a form of collective memory, which Chris Weedon and Glenn Jordan described as "narratives of past experience constituted by and on behalf of specific groups within which they find meaningful forms of identification that may empower" (143).

These creative, opinionated, and political responses from readers indicate that a significant subset of *The Brownies' Book* readers understood the biographical sketches as a form of Black counter-memory. They understood that the narratives offered an alternative or corrective to hegemonic white memories. They also appeared to recognize that these stories of the Black past mattered for *them* today and that hearing these stories was a matter of social and political utility. The letters in "The Jury," therefore, indicate that

The Brownies' Book biographies operated rhetorically as counter-memory and even, to use the formulation of Houston A. Baker Jr., as the critical memory that works to constitute the Black public sphere. Baker argued that critical memory "focuses the historical continuities of black-majority efforts, strategies and resources for leadership and liberation" and "demonstrates the ever-renewing promise inherent in the contiguity between majority and 'leadership' remembrance" (31). Stories that supply "historically verifiable" accounts of Black leadership, provide a critique of white memories, and construct political resources for members of the Black public sphere—including children—function rhetorically to shape future citizens who are prepared to continue the work of Black public action. The biographies of *The Brownies' Book* appear to have done just that.

Notes

1. On the role of biography in *The Brownies' Book* specifically, see also McNair, "Polar Explorer," and McNair and Bishop.

2. For more on the prominent role of *The Brownies' Book* in relation to African American children's literature, see also Bishop 21–43 and McNair, "Comparative Analysis" 3–7. For a discussion of the earliest history of African American children's literature, see Bishop 1–19.

3. See also Bishop 26 and Johnson 44–45. Katharine Capshaw Smith also claims that Fauset "authored much of the magazine's unattributed or anonymous material" ("*The Brownies' Book*"). All of the unattributed evidence leads me to conclude that Fauset should receive authorial credit for writing these biographies.

4. The term *counter-memory* overlaps somewhat with the concepts of counter-storytelling and counter-narratives. The latter two are derived from critical race methodologies, as developed by Richard Delgado and by Daniel G. Solórzano and Tara J. Yosso, and elaborated in research by scholars such as Sandra Hughes-Hassell, Rema Reynolds and Darquillius Mayweather, and Bronwyn T. Williams. All of these ideas mark the power of stories about nondominant experiences to disrupt dominant narratives. However, I use the term *memory* in order to specifically denote the way in which biographies about Black figures from the past establish memories intended to have broad rhetorical appeal among Black (counter) publics. By using *counter-memory*, this study invokes deliberate efforts to reshape the past in a publicly salient fashion. Furthermore, whereas I treat *counter-memory* as a rhetorical function of the biographies, researchers tend to employ *counter-storytelling* as a strategy for qualitative research. As Reynolds and Mayweather point out, "Counter-storytelling is a methodological tool with a history in communities of color that use oral interpretation to convey stories and struggles often not validated by the dominant culture" (288).

5. Wyman was born in 1847 to a suffragist mother and an abolitionist family and had clear affinities with some of the political commitments of *The Brownies' Book* editors. Her sketches, however, do reveal a problematic and telling focus on "good white people"; indeed, that is the title of one of her sketches (Stevens 2).

6. On good sense, see J. R. Fauset, "Katy Ferguson" 27. On kindness, see J. R. Fauset, "Katy Ferguson" 27; A. H. Fauset 95. On modesty, see J. R. Fauset, "Phillis Wheatley" 252; Haynes 172. On generosity and humility, see Browne 216. On courage and bravery, see Wyman, "The Bravest of the Brave" 338–39 and "Brave Brown Joe" 319. On intelligence and studiousness, see J. R. Fauset,

"A Pioneer Suffragette" 121 and "Phillis Wheatley" 252; and Allison, "Samuel Coleridge-Taylor" 370 and "Alexandre Dumas" 7.

7. For another similar example, see Wilkes 270.

8. A more modest example can be found in Allison's sketch of Samuel Coleridge-Taylor, which reports that "he was laid to rest amidst affection and regret" and his grave "marked by a headstone of Carrara marble, erected by his wife and other lovers of the man and his music" (371).

9. This passage also reframes Wheatley's significance from a purely literary perspective to a political one. This choice deflects the scorn heaped upon Wheatley during the mid- to late twentieth century for supposedly inferior quality.

10. Fauset also uses the word "horrors" to describe Katy Ferguson's experiences as an enslaved child (27).

11. The concept of judgment is woven throughout the periodical, as can be seen in the columns "The Judge" and especially "The Jury," which contains letters from young readers. Using such terms urges children to think of themselves as self-possessed individuals capable of engaging in and judging action.

12. Several letters were published in each issue. For this study, I surveyed all columns of "The Jury" and extracted those letters that explicitly mentioned or alluded to the stories about Black historical figures. This search produced a set of twelve letters published between February 1920 and July 1921, spanning the majority of the periodical's two-year run.

Works Cited

Allison, Madeline G. "Alexandre Dumas, a Great Dramatist: A True Story." *The Brownies' Book*, vol. 2, no. 1, Jan. 1921, pp. 6–7.

Allison, Madeline G. "Denmark Vesey: A Martyr for Freedom." *The Brownies' Book*, vol. 2, no. 2, Feb. 1921, pp. 57–58.

Allison, Madeline G. "Samuel Coleridge-Taylor: A True Story." *The Brownies' Book*, vol. 1, no. 12, Dec. 1920, pp. 370–72.

Aristotle. *On Rhetoric: A Theory of Civic Discourse*. Translated by George A. Kennedy. Oxford UP, 1991.

Baker, Houston A., Jr. "Critical Memory and the Black Public Sphere." *Public Culture*, vol. 7, no. 1, Fall 1994, pp. 3–33.

Bird, Augusta E. "The Story of Harriet Tubman: A True Story." *The Brownies' Book*, vol. 2, no. 3, Mar. 1921, pp. 84–86.

Bishop, Rudine Sims. *Free within Ourselves: The Development of African American Children's Literature*. Heinemann, 2007.

Blight, David. *Race and Reunion: The Civil War in American Memory*. Harvard UP, 2001.

Brown, Anthony L. "Counter-Memory and Race: An Examination of African American Scholars' Challenges to Early Twentieth Century K-12 Historical Discourses." *The Journal of Negro Education*, vol. 79, no. 1, Winter 2010, pp. 54–65.

Brown, Willie. "The Jury." *The Brownies' Book*, vol. 2, no. 7, July 1921, p. 208.

Browne, Annette C. "Sketch of the Life of Mary Binkley." *The Brownies' Book*, vol. 2, no. 7, July 1921, p. 216.

Cooper, Rena. "The Jury." *The Brownies' Book*, vol. 2, no. 1, Jan. 1921, p. 24.

Delgado, Richard. "Storytelling for Oppositionists and Others: A Plea for Narrative." *Critical Race Theory: The Cutting Edge*, edited by Delgado and Jean Stefanic, Temple UP, 2000, pp. 60–70.

Fauset, Arthur Huff. "A Story of a Former Slave Boy." *The Brownies' Book*, vol. 1, no. 3, Mar. 1920, p. 95.

Fauset, Jessie Redmon. "America's First Martyr-Patriot: A True Story." *The Brownies' Book*, vol. 1, no. 7, July 1920, p. 216.

Fauset, Jessie Redmon. "A Great Sailor (Paul Cuffee)." *The Brownies' Book*, vol. 1, no. 2, Feb. 1920, pp. 38–39.

Fauset, Jessie Redmon. "Katy Ferguson." *The Brownies' Book*, vol. 1, no. 1, Jan. 1920, p. 27.

Fauset, Jessie Redmon. "A Pioneer Suffragette: A True Story." *The Brownies' Book*, vol. 1, no. 4, Apr. 1920, pp. 120–21.

Fauset, Jessie Redmon. "The Story of Phillis Wheatley: A True Story." *The Brownies' Book*, vol. 1, no. 8, Aug. 1920, p. 253.

Fauset, Jessie Redmon. "Toussaint L'Ouverture." *The Brownies' Book*, vol. 1, no. 5, May 1920, pp. 149–52.

Foster, Pocahontas. "The Jury." *The Brownies' Book*, vol. 1, no. 5, May 1920, p. 140.

Gubar, Marah. *Artful Dodgers: Reconceiving the Golden Age of Children's Literature*. Oxford UP, 2009.

Haynes, Elizabeth Ross. "Benjamin Banneker." *The Brownies' Book*, vol. 1, no. 6, June 1920, pp. 171–74.

Hill, Augustus. "The Jury." *The Brownies' Book*, vol. 1, no. 4, Apr. 1920, p. 111.

Hughes-Hassell, Sandra. "Multicultural Young Adult Literature as a Form of Counter-Storytelling." *The Library Quarterly*, vol. 83, no. 3, July 2013, pp. 212–88. *JSTOR*, www.jstor .org/stable/10.1086/670696.

James, Allison. "Agency." *The Palgrave Handbook of Childhood Studies*, edited by Jens Qvortrup et al., Palgrave Macmillan, 2009, pp. 34–45.

Johnson, Dianne. *Telling Tales: The Pedagogy and Promise of African American Literature for Youth*. Greenwood P, 1990.

Kachun, Mitch. *First Martyr of Liberty: Crispus Attucks in American Memory*. Oxford UP, 2019.

Lealtad, Catherine Deaver. "The Black Russian: A True Story." *The Brownies' Book*, vol. 2, no. 6, June 1921, pp. 182–83.

Lipsitz, George. *Time Passages: Collective Memory and American Popular Culture*. U of Minnesota P, 1990.

McNair, Jonda C. "A Comparative Analysis of *The Brownies' Book* and Contemporary African American Children's Literature Written by Patricia C. McKissack." *Embracing, Evaluating, and Examining African American Children's and Young Adult Literature*, edited by Wanda M. Brooks and McNair, Scarecrow P, 2008, pp. 3–29.

McNair, Jonda C. "A Polar Explorer, a Pilot, and a Pitcher: Black History in African American Children's Literature." *Social Education*, vol. 81, no. 1, Jan. 2017, pp. 46–49.

McNair, Jonda C., and Rudine Sims Bishop. "'To Be Great, Heroic, or Beautiful': The Enduring Legacy of *The Brownies' Book*." *Horn Book Magazine*, May/June 2018, pp. 28–34, www.hbook .com/?detailStory=great-heroic-beautiful-enduring-legacy-brownies-book.

Moore, Claudia. "The Jury." *The Brownies' Book*, vol. 1, no. 2, Mar. 1920, p. 83.

Murray, Carter. "The Jury." *The Brownies' Book*, vol. 1, no. 4, Apr. 1920, p. 111.

Reynolds, Rema, and Darquillius Mayweather. "Recounting Racism, Resistance, and Repression: Examining the Experiences and #Hashtag Activism of College Students with Critical Race Theory and Counternarratives." *The Journal of Negro Education*, vol. 86, no. 3, Summer 2017, pp. 283–304. *JSTOR*, www.jstor.org/stable/10.7709/jnegroeducation.86.3.0283.

Simpson, Ada. "The Jury." *The Brownies' Book*, vol. 1, no. 4, Apr. 1920, p. 111.

Smith, Katharine Capshaw. "*The Brownies' Book* and the Roots of African American Children's Literature." Accessed 28 June 2019. *The Tar Baby and the Tomahawk: Race and Ethnic Images in American Children's Literature, 1880–1939*, Center for Digital Research in the Humanities at U Nebraska–Lincoln and Center for the Humanities at Washington U in St. Louis, childlit.unl.edu/topics/edi.harlem.html.

Smith, Katharine Capshaw. *Children's Literature of the Harlem Renaissance*. Indiana UP, 2004.

Solórzano, Daniel G., and Tara J. Yosso. "Critical Race Methodology: Counter-Storytelling as an Analytical Framework for Education." *Qualitative Inquiry*, vol. 8, no. 1, Feb. 2002, pp. 23–44.

Stevens, Elizabeth C. *Elizabeth Buffum Chace and Lillie Chace Wyman: A Century of Abolitionist, Suffragist, and Workers' Rights Activism*. McFarland, 2003.

Sylvander, Caroline Wedin. *Jessie Redmon Fauset, Black American Writer*. Whitson Publishing, 1981.

VanderHaagen, Sara C. *Children's Biographies of African American Women: Rhetoric, Public Memory, and Agency*. U of South Carolina P, 2018.

Weedon, Chris, and Glenn Jordan. "Collective Memory: Theory and Politics." *Social Semiotics*, vol. 22, no. 2, Apr. 2012, pp. 143–53. *Academic Search Complete*, doi:10.1080/10350330.2012.664969.

Wilkes, Laura E. "The Story of Frederick Douglass: A True Story." *The Brownies' Book*, vol. 1, no. 9, Sept. 1920, pp. 266–70.

Williams, Bronwyn T. "The Truth in the Tale: Race and 'Counterstorytelling' in the Classroom." *Journal of Adolescent & Adult Literacy*, vol. 48, no. 2, Oct. 2004, pp. 164–69. *JSTOR*, www.jstor.org/stable/40009165.

Wineburg, Samuel S. "On the Reading of Historical Texts: Notes on the Breach between School and Academy." *American Educational Research Journal*, vol. 28, no. 3, Sept. 1991, pp. 495–519. *Academic Search Complete*, doi:10.3102/00028312028003495.

Wright, Audrey. "The Jury." *The Brownies' Book*, vol. 1, no. 8, Aug. 1920, p. 256.

Wyman, Lillie Buffum Chace. "Brave Brown Joe and Good White Men." *The Brownies' Book*, vol. 2, no. 11, Nov. 1921, pp. 318–20.

Wyman, Lillie Buffum Chace. "The Bravest of the Brave: A True Story." *The Brownies' Book*, vol. 1, no. 11, Nov. 1920, pp. 338–39.

Chapter 3

"MY SOUL CALLS FOR LARGER THINGS"

Voice, Vision, and Justice in Children's Letters to the Editor

MICHELLE TAYLOR WATTS

In the February 1920 issue of *The Brownies' Book*, the editors printed the letter of an unnamed sixteen-year-old girl from Fairmount, West Virginia. As an orphan, the young writer had very high hopes for what was surely her first letter to the editors. "White people have kept me," she wrote, "that is, I have worked for them" ("The Jury" 52). The young writer knew there was much more to life and wanted assistance in realizing her dreams: "Realizing that I did not always want to be a scrub girl, I have tried to educate myself" (52). The letter continues with a bold and simple request:

> Do you think I could through *The Brownies' Book* get a home among a good Christian colored family? . . . Just anywhere among good Christian people, where I could go to good public schools. I can do any kind of work and am a good cook and housekeeper. . . .
>
> I would ask you please not to put my full name in *The Brownies' Book*, if you will advertise for a home for me. I don't want anyone to support me. I want to be among MY people, and have a chance for an education. (52)

The young writer longed for the security of a traditional family, and she knew that she could turn to *The Brownies' Book* for guidance. Although there is no evidence to indicate whether this enterprising young woman got the home she wanted, the editors' decision to print the letter illustrates the magazine's overarching goals and W. E. B. Du Bois's ideals for a socially conscious New Negro childhood that would represent the "wide sweep of infinite possibility" that he defined in *Darkwater* (119). In *Children's Literature of the Harlem Renaissance*, Katherine Capshaw Smith reflects on Du Bois's respect for Black children.

Smith writes, "Du Bois reimagined the black child as culturally, politically, and aesthetically sophisticated. This new vision was absolutely necessary to the triumph of the New Negro movement" (1–2). The literature published in *The Brownies' Book* and the letters act as a conversation between adults and readers about the intersection of childhood, race, and social progress.

The letters published in *The Brownies' Book* evoke a holy trinity of Black nation-building: a desire and capacity for education and labor, racial pride, and community. The search for family and safety is reminiscent of the letters published in the *Chicago Defender* during the Great Migration. Like letters written by and for newly arrived migrants, this young writer's letter expressed anxieties about oppression and hopes for a better life, thus becoming a part of the documentation of the Black migrant experience in the urban north during the Progressive Era. The letter is also a clear-eyed rebuke of the immorality of the situation, highlighted by her desire to be among "good Christian people." Importantly, the letter speaks to her awareness of and access to a network of Black people who had a vested interest in the outcomes of her life, given that "black women had a long history of recognizing black children's vulnerability and creating institutions to care for them" (Agyepong 23). Aspiration and racial pride, which are at the heart of this letter, are echoed in nearly all of the letters published in the magazine's column "The Jury." The name of the column speaks to the truthfulness and the importance of children's voices. Indeed, a jury is assembled specifically to render verdicts, and the editors' decision about the name of the column speaks to their pledge to amplify children's voices as arbiters of truth and justice.

This chapter engages questions that have theoretical relevance for *The Brownies' Book* in general and Black childhood studies in particular. First and foremost, what can we learn about Black children by reading these letters? These are not merely letters to the editors. Although they reflect children's engagement with and degree of participation in public life, the letters also represent an archive of Black children's lives, aspirations, and efforts to make sense of a white world that viewed them as a problem and a Black nation that viewed them as a promise. Most of the scholarly examinations of *The Brownies' Book* focus on the stories and columns written for children, but this column focuses solely on the texts written *by* the children. These letters are a crucial milestone as they, for the first time, lift up the voices and firsthand accounts of Black children. These are not the memories of formerly enslaved persons or elder statesmen looking back from a vantage point of experience (Chatelain). These letters represent how children comprehended their lives—overburdened by racism and as advocations for a just nation.

Reading the letters expands our existing notions about the types of readers and writers who participated in the Harlem Renaissance movement. The letters help us interpret how young people navigated and experienced their families, their communities, and, most importantly, their dreams for their futures. By using a framework that I refer to as "insurgent aspirations," we can read the letters as a catalog of their hopes. We can also interpret the letters as the children's own efforts to fight stereotypes and shift the narrative about Black childhood. Insurgent aspirations constitute a framework for understanding the ways in which Black children participate in activist practices. Indeed, all children have hopes and dreams for themselves, but for Black children, aspirations take on a more nuanced meaning because those hopes and dreams are curtailed by systems of white supremacy designed to keep Black children locked in place (Taylor). Insurgency, then, is about the actions and choices Black children use to disrupt systems of oppression. Insurgency also speaks to a functional Black past that empowers and propels young people. Importantly, it is a disruptive tool that alters prevailing notions about the serviceability of Black children's voices and experiences.

The Brownies' Book editors' decisions to publish the letters affirm Black children's intellect and creativity. The urgent appeals for equality and opportunity frame the writers of the letters as part of an emergent citizenry and reiterate the editors' larger efforts to amplify and elevate the diversity of Black children's experiences. The letters establish a blueprint for understanding the role Black children play in the larger projection of Black uplift and public life. Listening to children dismantle cultural ideas about the perceived deficiencies of Black children creates a new narrative of an empowered future. As African American studies scholar Imani Perry notes, "the stories we tell and integrate into our knowledge impact how we see ourselves, how we see others around us, how we treat them, what opportunities we provide, what expectations we have" (187). The letters serve as an ever-present reminder of the stories that Black children have shared about themselves and their communities.

THE SOULS OF BLACK CHILDREN

When the first issue of *The Brownies' Book* was published in January 1920, Black America was still reeling from the violence of the Red Summer of 1919. The memories of racial terror and the power of Black resistance are prominently positioned in the first issue of the magazine. The inclusion of a photo of Black children marching in the Silent Protest of 1917 symbolizes the editors' commitment to a vision of a socially conscious Black childhood. Although the editors felt that all children could enjoy the magazine, the framing and iconography of the protest made it clear that the editors would be in the business of creating content for the children of that race of men and women.

Young Eleanor Holland, from Wilberforce, Ohio, was very sure of her future as a race woman, and although only twelve, she knew that she wanted to be of service to the race: "I am writing to ask you to refer me to some books on the Negro. I want to learn more about my race, so I want to begin early. I am twelve years old and hope to, when I am old enough, bend all of my efforts for the advancement of colored people" (15). What Eleanor may not have realized is that she was already working on behalf of her race. The act of writing a letter to the editor is an important voluntary political act and an entry point into the public sphere. In a study on political engagement and letters to the editor, historian Christopher Cooper and colleagues suggest that these letters provide an important look into the minds of citizens: "Letters to the editor represent a unique opportunity to study voluntary political participation—one where people give rich and detailed explanations for what they believe and why they believe it" (131).

The letters in "The Jury" speak to the ideologically and geographically diverse experiences of Black children as they attempt to navigate the institutions that shape their lives. Rudine Sims Bishop argues that the children's letters "express gratitude for the magazine and its contents, which . . . apparently filled gaps in typical school curricula and was a source of pride and inspiration for parents and children alike" (23). Bishop's assertion establishes an important frame for understanding the cultural work of the letters. As critics have turned to letters and informal texts to understand the lives of Black people in the early twentieth century, we now have new opportunities to learn how they managed the daily realities of Jim Crow life. Historian Cheryl Hicks suggests that these informal texts offer important insight into the lives of regular Black folk who were not part of the Talented Tenth and were more often the beneficiaries of Black uplift projects. She writes, "Historians approach ordinary people's experiences by using a variety of sources, including the annual reports of state institutions, civil rights organizations, and charitable associations; periodicals and newspapers" (4). The children of the "ordinary people" are given a voice in the letters of *The Brownies' Book*.

So who, then, are the New Negro children? These children of the Harlem Renaissance and Progressive Era came of age during a period of sociopolitical upheaval and a precarious hope for a new day. A letter in the January 1920 issue speaks to these complexities. An unnamed fifteen-year-old in Seattle writes, "I am willing to work my way through school. . . . I have tried to do something in Seattle, but the people are very down on the Negro race. In some schools they do not want colored children" ("The Jury" 15). This letter represents both the promise and the peril of growing up during the early twentieth century. The writer's incisive understanding of life in Seattle is important for our understanding of Black migration and the search for home. While the Harlem Renaissance is most commonly associated with movement to the cities of the east coast, many Black families traveled west in search of equality and opportunity, only to be reminded that Jim Crow lived everywhere. Likewise, the Seattle letter writer's respect for hard work and education is an admirable expectation for readers of *The Brownies' Book*. Perhaps what is most important is that despite the cruelties she experienced, she knew that she could find refuge in the pages of *The Brownies' Book* and its community of readers.

Du Bois and Fauset were committed to a type of worldmaking in which Black children could be taught, treasured, and celebrated. Similarly, Alain Locke focused on new ways of documenting and celebrating Black life. In 1925, Locke edited *The New Negro*, an anthology considered by many to be the definitive text of the Harlem Renaissance, which introduced readers to Zora Neale Hurston, Claude McKay, and Langston Hughes. Locke's interpretation of New Negro ideology acknowledged the intersection of Black art and liberation for a new generation of activists and thinkers. Though the term was used in different contexts and eras, the New Negro was an enduring metaphor meant to symbolize diverse responses to sociopolitical inequality at the turn of the century and beyond. This abbreviated genealogy of the term and idea has three important implications for understanding the letters published in *The Brownies' Book* and their relation to the New Negro child's practice of insurgent aspirations. At the core is a yearning for opportunity, joy, access, and intentional emphasis on intellectual history and organizing.

First, the letters in "The Jury" capture the politicized yearning for opportunity and access that was a unifying thread throughout all manifestations of the New Negro. The New Negro became a metaphor for young people's desires to get outside the limiting frames that society attempted to impose on them. Consider, for example, the letter from Pearl Staple, who described herself as "a constant reader of *The Crisis*." Her letter describes her desires for a Black life that is larger than the one she has in Charlottesville, Virginia:

> I read something in *The Crisis* about a mother sitting alone in despair, thinking about her children long ago lost to her. And it reminds me of another mother, our mother country, Africa, and it was that thought which forced me to write the enclosed poem, "Africa." . . .
>
> I will tell you just a little about myself. I live in a stuffy little town, where things go on year after year the same. I was not born here. The place is too small, it's killing me; my soul calls for larger things, so I appeal to you. (111)

Pearl's letter is an intriguing example of a young girl who is desperate to make sense of her oppressive reality. As her letter states, Pearl is an avid reader of

The Crisis and, eventually, *The Brownies' Book*: "I am a constant reader of *The Crisis* and it takes me from six o'clock until nine to read it from cover to cover, and then there remains an endless year of waiting for the next number....it is really a book that never tires one" (111). The "next number" that Pearl refers to is the annual Children's Number of *The Crisis*, which preceded publication of *The Brownies' Book*. Pearl notes her age—fifteen years old—in a postscript, asks that readers have "a little pity," and shares in the body of her letter that many believe her to be odd: "I have been called odd,—in fact, I know that I am odd and I don't like to do things like other people" (111). Her letter does not go into detail about what makes her odd, but we can infer a few things that make her distinctive. Pearl and her family had the money to subscribe, at fifteen cents an issue, and the time to engage with *The Crisis*. Time and money were at a premium for most African American families, especially those living in the Jim Crow South. This is particularly important in light of the 1914 displacement of residents of McKee Row, a Black neighborhood in Charlottesville. Their property was confiscated and deeded to the city. The area became the site of a Confederate monument honoring Thomas "Stonewall" Jackson. Despite the smallness of the city, Pearl's letter represents her investment and engagement with ideas about Black life, which is precisely what the editors had in mind for readers of *The Brownies' Book*.

A second and equally important intersection with New Negro ideologies is the emphasis on intellectual history and social uplift. As literary historian Ann duCille points out, children were almost always the objects of uplift work: "Children were the wealth and the future of the black nation. As the birthplace and nursery of future generations, the home was the focal point of social reform" (63). The letters illustrate that children are not merely the beneficiaries of social reform movements, but also agents of change in their own right. Being of service is at the core of early Black uplift movements. A series of updates from the July issue of *The Brownies' Book*, known as the Education Number, focused on recent graduates. The series showcased their personal achievements and serviceability to the race. One such student, Thelma B. Lewis, mentions her work at the Hiram House: "I entered Central High School of Cleveland, Ohio, four years ago and have never been absent nor tardy for that length of time. For two years I have been a volunteer social service settlement worker at the Hiram Social Settlement House" (qtd. in Allison 206). Another recent graduate, Olive M. Thomas, was very confident of her abilities: "I have a strong ambition toward literature. When I accomplish something worth while [sic] . . . I shall send it to Miss Fauset and I trust it will not be put in the scrap basket" (qtd. in Allison 208). Lydell C. Usher of Commercial High in Brooklyn recounts his achievements, but does so knowing that progress will be bound up in racial struggle:

Although I was not a distinguished scholar, yet I feel as though I was not such a remote star that I could not be seen shining. I was a member of the school's orchestra, in which I played the violin. I participated in the school's band, playing the cornet. If there is anything in this world that I have learned through this training, it is to appreciate education, to be broad-minded and to endeavor to do all that I can to promote the welfare of my posterity. There is only one thing which I regret, and that is that I cannot get into the same sphere as those of the opposite race in regard to work and business activities. I hope that more education, unity and ambition among the Negroes will some day make this possible for all of us. (qtd. in Allison 208)

Usher's personal belief system includes the elements one needs to advance the race—self-determination, self-respect, and commitment to the work of racial progress. Readers do not know what came of Usher's earnest commitment to progress, but another young graduate from Cleveland went on to have an illustrious career as a writer. He writes, "It might interest you to know that I have been elected Class Poet and have also written the Class Song for the graduates. I am, too, editor of *The Annual* and am the first Negro to hold the position since 1901, when it was held by the son of Charles W. Chestnut [sic]." Young Langston Hughes closes his letter with gratitude to the editors, writing, "I thank you for the honor of having my picture in your publication" (qtd. in Allison 206). Fauset's role as editor is particularly important here as she was the force behind Hughes's first publication in *The Brownies' Book*. Usher and Hughes both share their visions for the future, and Hughes in particular recognizes the value of having his picture published alongside his achievements. *The Brownies' Book*, at this point, has become more than just a vehicle for sharing voices of young Black readers. It is also in the business of elevating them as scholars and artists, showing how publication itself can be a tool for uplift. The editors are nurturing a new generation of leaders and showing the depth and breadth of the talent of Black youth.

INSURGENT ASPIRATIONS AND THE PROMISE OF BLACK CHILDHOOD

The Brownies' Book is a product of its social environment and therefore engages with Progressive Era issues; however, it does so in a way that indicts Progressive social welfare policies. Progressive Era views of childhood were focused on ensuring the safety of children and affirming the sanctity of American childhood. To be clear, however, Progressive reformers were focused on white children. As Agyepong points out, the focus on white children was part of a simultaneous effort to criminalize Black children: "The racialized limits of the child-saving movement, as well as the disinvestment in resources for black children at the community level, shaped the evolution of juvenile justice and the image of a dependent and delinquent child" (9).

Du Bois was well aware that responsibility for Black children would have to be grounded in Black uplift. He reckoned with Progressives' deeply held racism in a speech before an all-white audience in Chicago by stating, "There is always that feeling of remoteness, the feeling that it is not their problem" (qtd. in Agyepong 18). Jessie Fauset shared Du Bois's commitment to racial uplift, as evidenced by her work with the National Association of Colored Women. Fauset's editorial work with *The Brownies' Book* follows a tradition of clubwomen's engagement with the lives of Black children. Black women were at the forefront of efforts to organize and provide literal and figurative safe spaces for Black children. For Du Bois and Fauset, working and writing for Black children also meant working *with* them. In many ways, these children were their partners in progress. Katherine Smith considers these power dynamics as they played out in the pages of the *Crisis* in stating: "bearing the weight of social progress on their shoulders, black child readers found themselves exhorted not only to participate in adult political programs but often to lead them" (4). This framework highlights the central premise of *The Brownies' Book* and the centrality of the children's voices. While white Progressives focused on the perceived deficiencies and absences in Black childhood, Du Bois and Fauset centered the abundance, activism, and agency of Black children.

Insurgent aspirations were the New Negro child's language of uplift. This was a way of seeing and existing in the world that resists stereotypes while also affirming the radical power of Black joy, freedom, and possibility. In this context, insurgency signifies the prominence of disruption of power as well as a very deliberate insistence on defining the conditions under which Black children can freely live.

The pleasures of childhood—play, joy, whimsy—can be hard to imagine when you are a Black child living in Jim Crow America; however, a key part of understanding the logic of insurgent aspirations is looking for and finding spaces where children experienced joy and pleasure in a way that was purposeful and powerful. The image of the Black child in the white mind was bound up in the belief that Black children were insensate objects, open to both derision and objectification. The image of the Black pickaninny was a racist holdover from the enslaved past that continued to shape public perceptions of Black children. In *Racial Innocence: Performing American Childhood from Slavery to Civil Rights*, historian Robin Bernstein argues that this cultural effort had devastating impacts on Black children: "In many cases, angelic white children were contrasted with pickaninnies so grotesque as to suggest that only white children *were* children. This is the flip side of the well-known libel of the 'childlike Negro': the equally libelous, equally damaging, but heretofore underanalyzed exclusion of black youth from the category of childhood" (16). The pickaninny was depicted in popular culture as an object completely devoid of sense or feeling and was often shown as being oblivious to danger and pain. The image was recuperated for Progressive child-saving reformers who, as a result, placed Black children outside their sphere of protection. Agyepong notes, "This cultural history of black children's routine construction as subhuman beings who could not feel pain existed alongside the emergence of a redefinition of childhood that made the conception of juvenile justice and a rehabilitative ideal possible" (14). Already mischaracterized in the public sphere, the pleasure and play at work in the letters in "The Jury" took on a new and important meaning.

Children voiced their pleasure with *The Brownies' Book* in ways that acknowledged and redefined the importance of representation. In the first issue, Wenonah Bond of Washington, DC, shared her delight at the prospect of a magazine that would reflect her own life: "Our *Crisis* came a few days ago, and I was very glad to see the advertisement of *The Brownies' Book*. I had just been talking to mother about giving me a subscription to some children's magazine and was delighted to know that we shall soon have one of our very own" (15). Wenonah's letter reflects the social impact of the magazine. Had her mother given her any other magazine, Wenonah would have been bombarded with images of the insensate pickaninny as the only representation of Black childhood. In the April issue, Elizabeth Harris from Atlanta writes, "*The Brownies' Book* has just come and I'm sitting down to tell you about it. I like the second one better than the first,—the drawings of the insects in the story about the fairyland are so funny" (111). Sarah and Helen Woods from Corona, Long Island, made such an impression on the editors that they made a rare editorial intervention in writing, "We feel that we must reproduce, just as they stand, the charming letters of two charming young ladies of four and six years. The elder young lady, Miss Helen A. Woods, sent the drawing as her contribution to *The Brownies' Book*" (Du Bois, "The Jury" 140). The letters in question were indeed charming and sweet and played a crucial role in the editors' actions to elevate the joy of Black childhood. The first letter, addressed to Jessie Fauset, reads, "Dear Miss Fauset: I cannot read very well, but I like pictures." Her older sister, Helen, wrote, "Dear Miss Jessie Fauset: I like *The Brownies' Book* very much. And I read *The Brownies' Book* as much as I can. I hop [sic] some day to be able to write something better than this my self [sic]. Yours respectable [sic], Helen A. Woods" (Du Bois, "The Jury" 140). As

Bishop has argued, the letters from the Woods sisters and other letters published in "The Jury" generally support the editors' vision and illustrate their appreciation for a space just for Black children. But their whimsy and delight mean so much more when we think about the social and political value of Black children's imagination.

Historically, leisure time for Black people and especially Black children has been in short supply. Public spaces were segregated, and congregation in public thoroughfares was also dangerous. As a result, Black people worked to find new pathways of enjoyment and, in doing so, reconfigured the meaning of pleasure, play, and leisure. More recently, researchers have recovered cultural practices relating to the revolutionary acts of leisure. This is most notably reflected in the work of historians Saidiya Hartman and J. T. Roane, whose work offers nuanced readings of Black people's relation to place and pleasure (see, for example, Hartman 239). Likewise, activist adrienne maree brown's work on pleasure activism defines pleasure as a feeling of joy and contentment. She writes, "Feeling good is not frivolous, . . . it is freedom" (qtd. in Gonzalez). Using this modern frame to examine and recover pleasure for Black children like the Woods sisters shifts how we understand their history. They were two little girls who wrote cute letters—letters that their mother mailed to their favorite magazine. The sheer ordinariness of these acts is revolutionary. For Black children like the Woods girls to have laughed and enjoyed their life means that life was not composed of complete drudgery and wholesale racialized trauma. Their lives had meaning outside of white measures of social control, and their joy offered a sliver of respite from a Jim Crow society.

The Brownies' Book was changing hearts and minds, and the letters from later issues indicate that the magazine was achieving its desired effect on readers. As always, the letters reflected readers' keen awareness of racial inequality, but the tone was more impatient, insurgent, and ready for social change. A letter in the May issue from Pocahontas Foster of Orange, New Jersey, begins with confidence about her history and her future: "But since I read the stories of Paul Cuffee, Blanch [sic] K. Bruce and Katy Ferguson, real colored people, whom I feel that do know because they were brown people like me, I believe I do like history" (140). In short, representation matters for Foster. The connection to the histories of intellectual life has a direct correlation to her own engagement with her future, which reaffirms the notion of insurgent aspirations at work in this letter. She goes on to write, "And I wish too, if you can find them, that you would publish the pictures of Katy Ferguson. . . . I just love to think about that nice old lady and all she accomplished, although she began with nothing. When I think how much more happily colored girls start out in life now it seems to me we ought to be able to accomplish almost anything" (140). In this very deliberate articulation of hope and possibility, Foster participated in an important act of storytelling about the future of Black girlhood. She is not alone in thinking about the future of Black girls, as Hannah Maude Barnes from Richmond, Virginia, writes, "I am eleven years old, and I want to be an author. . . . I like your *Brownies' Book* and I wish you would put one of my pieces in it. Then, I feel, I could really see into my future" (83). As Imani Perry notes, the stories we tell about ourselves shape, or reshape, our interpretations of the world around us. As the letters suggest, storytelling can be life-altering and reveal the power of Black children's dreams and visions for changing their world.

A group of letters from the October issue speak to the children's knowledge of inequality and their role in imagining justice for Black people. Thomas R. Reid Jr. of Key West, Florida, recognizes the value of the relationship between *The Brownies' Book* and his own development in writing: "I have just recently become a reader of *The Brownies' Book* and, to say the least, I am much pleased with the publication. It feels for me a long felt need. I am always writing some articles and it is my intention to send some contribution to *The Brownies' Book* that will miss the waste basket" (308). Ida Lockport in Allegheny, Pennsylvania, shares a similar sentiment. She writes, "I am writing to you, not because what I have to say is so important but because I see the other children's letters in *The Brownies' Book* and I should like to have one there too" (308). A letter from John Eastman centers his work ethic:

> Most children are sorry when school opens. But I'm not; I'm glad. Of course, I like summer because it gives me so much spare time, but do you know how I spend it? Working, getting ready for school. Our preacher says I'm the handy man of the neighborhood. I sell papers, run errands, cut the grass and sometimes write letters. . . . When Christmas comes I sell Christmas trees and holly and wreaths. When I'm big enough I'm going to go to college. I'm sure I'll be able to pay my own way through. I think I'll be an engineer. (308)

A letter from Thomas Peterson of Chicago was powerful then and is particularly resonant for current audiences:

> I found "Darkwater" in the library the other day and read a lot of it. I did not understand it all, but I had no trouble with the part where you tell about your life when a boy. I should like to do some of the things you have done, . . . only I want to go to Asia and Africa too. I think colored people are the most wonderful people in the world and when I'm a man, I'm going to write about them too, so that all people will know

the terrible struggles we've had. I don't pay any attention any more to the discouraging things I see in the newspapers. Something just tells me that we are no worse than anybody else. (308)

Although these letter writers had never met, they reflected a commonly reported feeling of pride and possibility. The experiences they wrote about—of being concerned but hopeful about their future, reading and learning from *The Brownies' Book*, being anxious yet excited about the race—fit into a kind of mosaic. This depicts a network of knowledge that sustained an emerging citizenry. The letters underscore the success of teaching Black children their history as a point of personal pride and as a source for rigorous intellectual study. Despite challenges of the moment, the young writers, Peterson in particular, never questioned their ability to survive. The children's faith in their own fortitude is part of a consistently expressed cultural logic that sought to democratize opportunity and create a just world where Black people could live freely.

THE UNBROKEN CIRCLE OF BLACK IMAGINATION

The Brownies' Book was a testament to the joy and promise of Black childhood. The intergenerational dynamics among editors, families, and children marked a shift in the public representation of Black children. But, more importantly, the dynamics shaped how the children understood their lives. In the pages of *The Brownies' Book*, Black children had the space to see themselves, love themselves, and take up space in a world that seemed to be committed to their destruction. In particular, the letters highlighted their intellect and curiosity and served as a blueprint for the practice of citizenship. The cultural work of these young writers reflects Du Bois's mission for the training of Black children detailed in *Darkwater*: "we may teach frankly that this world is not perfection, but development: that the object of education is manhood and womanhood, clear reason, individual talent and genius and the spirit of service and sacrifice" (121). The intellect and the spirit of Black children's voices carry with them a power still felt to this day.

The legacy of Black children's imagination came full circle when eleven-year-old Marley Dias launched the #1000BlackGirlBooks campaign in 2015 (McGrath). Her idea was simple and intriguing: she wanted to collect and donate a thousand books whose primary characters are Black girls. Dias accumulated more than nine thousand books and acquired a book deal to publish her first book, *Marley Dias Gets It Done: And So Can You*. But more importantly, Dias participated in a century-old practice of young Black people examining their world, finding the voids, and using their words and power to fill them. In speaking about her work, Dias said, "Frustration is fuel that can lead to the development of an innovative and useful idea" (qtd. in McGrath). Dias shared a sentiment similar to those described by the young activists in *The Brownies' Book*. Black children as intellectuals and creators have long been a part of American life. Reading the words of "The Jury," modern audiences are forced to acknowledge the long history of Black activist childhoods. Such readings resist the erasure of Black youth power and, most importantly, remind all readers that Black children matter.

Works Cited

Agyepong, Tera Eva. *The Criminalization of Black Children: Race, Gender, and Delinquency in Chicago's Juvenile Justice System, 1899–1945*. U of North Carolina P, 2018.

Allison, M. G. "Brownie Graduates." *The Brownies' Book*, vol. 1, no. 7, July 1920, pp. 204–10.

Barnes, Hannah Maude. "The Jury." *The Brownies' Book*, vol. 1, no. 3, Mar. 1920, p. 83.

Bernstein, Robin. *Racial Innocence: Performing American Childhood from Slavery to Civil Rights*. New York UP, 2011.

Bishop, Rudine Sims. *Free within Ourselves: The Development of African American Children's Literature*. Heinemann, 2007.

Bond, Wenonah. "The Jury." *The Brownies' Book*, vol. 1, no. 1, Jan. 1920, p. 15.

Chatelain, Marcia. *South Side Girls: Growing Up in the Great Migration*. Duke UP, 2015.

Cooper, Christopher, et al. "The Content of Political Participation: Letters to the Editor and the People Who Write Them." *Political Science & Politics*, vol. 42, no. 1, Jan. 2009, pp. 131–37. doi:10.1017/s1049096509009009x.

Du Bois, W. E. B. *Darkwater: Voices from within the Veil*. Dover Publications, 1920.

Du Bois, W. E. B. "The Jury." *The Brownies' Book*, vol. 1, no. 5, May 1920, p. 140.

duCille, Ann. *The Coupling Convention: Sex, Text, and Tradition in Black Women's Fiction*. Oxford UP, 1993.

Eastman, John. "The Jury." *The Brownies' Book*, vol. 1, no. 10, Oct. 1920, p. 308.

Foster, Pocahontas. "The Jury." *The Brownies' Book*, vol. 1, no. 5, May 1920, p. 140.

Gates, Henry Louis, Jr. "The New Negro and the Black Image: From Booker T. Washington to Alain Locke." *TeacherServe*, National Humanities Center, nationalhumanitiescenter.org/tserve/freedom/1917beyond/essays/newnegro.htm.

Gonzalez, Catherine Lizette. "In 'Pleasure Activism,' Adrienne Maree Brown Dares Us to Get in Touch with Our Needs." *Colorlines*, 23 Apr. 2019, www.colorlines.com/articles/pleasure-activism-adrienne-maree-brown-dares-us-get-touch-our-needs.

Harris, Elizabeth. "The Jury." *The Brownies' Book*, vol. 1, no. 4, Apr. 1920, p. 111.

Hartman, Saidiya V. *Wayward Lives, Beautiful Experiments: Intimate Histories of Social Upheaval*. W. W. Norton, 2019.

Hicks, Cheryl D. *Talk with You Like a Woman: African American Women, Justice, and Reform in New York, 1890–1935*. U of North Carolina P, 2010.

Holland, Eleanor. "The Jury." *The Brownies' Book*, vol. 1, no. 1, Jan. 1920, p. 15.

"The Jury." *The Brownies' Book*, vol. 1, no. 1, Jan. 1920, p. 15.

"The Jury." *The Brownies' Book*, vol. 1, no. 2, Feb. 1920, p. 52.

Lockport, Ida. "The Jury." *The Brownies' Book*, vol. 1, no. 10, Oct. 1920, p. 308.

McGrath, Maggie. "From Activist to Author: How 12-Year-Old Marley Dias Is Changing the Face of Children's Literature." *Forbes*, 13 June 2017, www.forbes.com/sites/maggiem cgrath/2017/06/13/from-activist-to-author-how-12-year-old-marley-dias-is-changing-the -face-of-childrens-literature/.

Perry, Imani. *More Beautiful and More Terrible: The Embrace and Transcendence of Racial Inequality in the United States*. New York UP, 2011.

Peterson, Thomas. "The Jury." *The Brownies' Book*, vol. 1, no. 10, Oct. 1920, p. 308.

Reid, Thomas R., Jr. "The Jury." *The Brownies' Book*, vol. 1, no. 10, Oct. 1920, p. 308.

Roane, J. T. "Plotting the Black Commons." *Souls*, vol. 20, no. 3, 2019, pp. 239–66. doi:10.1080/1 0999949.2018.1532757.

Smith, Katharine Capshaw. *Children's Literature of the Harlem Renaissance*. Kindle ed., Indiana UP, 2006.

Staple, Pearl. "The Jury." *The Brownies' Book*, vol. 1, no. 4, Apr. 1920, p. 111.

Taylor, Michelle. *Emergent Identities: The African American Common Woman in United States Literature, 1831–1903*. 2001. Rice U, PhD dissertation. scholarship.rice.edu/handle/1911/18035.

Chapter 4

"LET US MAKE THE WORLD KNOW THAT WE ARE LIVING"

The Brownies' Book, African American Newspapers, and Black Childhood Identity

PAIGE GRAY

In my office, I have a framed image from the first issue of *The Brownies' Book*, the monthly periodical established by W. E. B. Du Bois and members of the National Association for the Advancement of Colored People (NAACP) to further engage the curiosity and creativity of African American children. Extending from the annual Children's Number of *The Crisis*, the primary publication of the NAACP, *The Brownies' Book* reinforces what Katharine Capshaw describes as Du Bois's "faith in the ability of young people to lead the race into the future" (2). As the essays in this collection detail, the magazine included poems and stories telling of Black achievement and history and showcased children's letters and creative writing. Although much of American children's literature during the turn of the last century—and even today—filters ideas of curiosity through the perspective of the middle-class white child, *The Brownies' Book* specifically addressed the lives and experiences of African American children. Its organizing principle centers on the ways in which African American children can more fully embrace their cultural identities, participate in their communities, and become citizens of the world. My beautiful, framed image from that first issue, published in January 1920, epitomizes this effort. In it, a young African American girl stands *en pointe* dressed in a ballet-performance costume (see figure 4.1). Here, we see a radically different vision of Black childhood emerge, as compared to those depicted in previous works of children's literature and culture during the late nineteenth and early twentieth centuries, which were often exaggerated variations of Harriet Beecher Stowe's Topsy. Instead, through the balletic positioning of raised arms

The Brownies' Book
JANUARY, 1920

One Dollar and a Half a Year   Fifteen Cents a Copy

Figure 4.1 *The Brownies' Book* inaugural cover, January 1920. (Library of Congress)

and toes, the girl conveys confident celebration. She communicates the idea of childhood as a space for invention and potential, an idea further emphasized by the blank canvas of the spotless white dress. Yet she also shows her wisdom and skill through the demonstration of her ballet technique—something that inevitably takes hours, if not years, of extended practice and learning.

This image from *The Brownies' Book* sparked my intrigue with not only the publication itself, but also its larger influence on African American childhood, particularity given the paucity of books for Black children by Black authors at the time. Did *The Brownies' Book* help create a larger sense of identity and community for Black children? Did it inspire writers to consider more seriously this large audience of young readers? Rather haphazardly, while

looking through a database of historical African American newspapers, I
came across the children's section of the *Chicago Defender*, perhaps the most
influential African American newspaper of the twentieth century. Its readership extended across the United States, and it played a contributing role in
the Great Migration—a time during which millions of African Americans
left their southern homes for job opportunities in northern industrial cities
like Chicago (Grossman 68). Indeed, it has been said that, "with the exception
of the Bible, no publication was more influential among the Negro masses"
during the first half of the twentieth century (Ottley 8), with newspaper sales
of this weekly publication estimated between 160,000 and 250,000 in the
early 1920s (Grossman 79).

Knowing that the run of *The Brownies' Book* lasted from January 1920 to
December 1921, I searched through digital issues of the *Chicago Defender* from
the early 1920s. Within those pages, I found the Defender Junior and Bud
Billiken, the imagined persona of the section's child editor, on which I have
previously written.[1] After establishing the existence of this children's section,
I determined its first appearance: April 1921. In reading through the Defender
Junior sections over the years following its 1921 debut, I found a supportive
community for Black children from across the country—a prototype for social
media. Young readers could become members of the Bud Billiken Club by
mailing in a form with their name, but they could also mail in letters and
poetry as a way to correspond with their fellow Billikens. In his first out-
ing, Bud Billiken tells readers that he wants to fill "this column with sayings
and doings of we little folks" ("Help Me Out" 5). In this sense, the Defender
Junior takes a cue from *The Brownies' Book* in helping shape an identity and
community for African American children. Moreover, the Defender Junior
section and "The Jury" column of *The Brownies' Book* consisted primarily
of children's letters, essentially functioning as a form of children's literature
written *by* children. Black youth, through these periodicals, could find—or,
at least, attempt to find—their voices.

The Defender Junior proved popular—so popular, in fact, that the Bud
Billiken Parade, first held in 1929 in Chicago's South Side, became a beloved
annual event. It continues to this day, far outlasting the run of the Defender
Junior section, which, near the middle of the century, slowly changed into a
page focused more on school events and news than letters and poetry (Gray
87). Although the youth section of the *Defender* endured for decades, as
compared to *The Brownies' Book*'s two-year run, it is likely that without *The
Brownies' Book*, there would be no Defender Junior or Bud Billiken Parade.

In fact, *The Brownies' Book* seems to have encouraged a number of African American newspapers to launch children's sections in the early 1920s.
Although these sections had limited success, together with the Defender

Junior and *The Brownies' Book*, they show Black childhood and identity as constructed by Black children themselves—they offer a window into how writing and the printed word serve as a means of authentication and agency for young people, particularly young people of color. Here, I want to explore how *The Brownies' Book* promoted curiosity, community, and creativity among its readers, and then consider how African American weekly newspapers of the period reimagined *The Brownies' Book* for their publications—publications with a much larger readership. As such, the ideas of *The Brownies' Book* arguably extended well beyond its initial readership, living on after its publication ceased to further map the contours of Black childhood.

THE BROWNIES' BOOK, IDENTITY, AND CREATIVE AGENCY

In the first issue of *The Brownies' Book*, the pages that follow that striking ballerina photograph include an assortment of fiction, commentary, history, and news that speaks to the magazine's stated mission. *The Brownies' Book*, the opening page tells us, "aims to be a thing of Joy and Beauty, dealing in Happiness, Laughter and Emulation, and designed especially for Kiddies from Six to Sixteen. It will seek to teach Universal Love and Brotherhood for all little folk—black and brown and yellow and white" (Du Bois, inside cover). Although the magazine showcases great literary talent, including that of its coeditor Jessie Redmon Fauset, one of its most compelling parts is that of "The Jury"—children's letters to the editors. Here, we are given a glimpse into Black childhood identity in the making; we simultaneously see young people questioning and refashioning *how* and *who* they want to be in the world. Franklin Lewis writes to ask about "things which colored boys can work at when they grow up" (15). Eleanor Holland wants the editor to "refer [her] to some books on the Negro" so that she "can learn more about [her] race" (15). A fifteen-year-old girl (whose name was withheld) inquires after possible funding sources so that she can attend a boarding school that accepts African American students. The curiosity displayed in "The Jury" underscores a guiding principle of *The Brownies' Book*: the power that comes with self-instigated inquiry and subsequent knowledge acquisition from such inquiry. *The Brownies' Book*, as Capshaw and Marian Wright Edelman have argued, constructs children of color as the means to social reform through their exploration and expression of racial identity. The figure of the Black child functions as one who can challenge the hegemony of white culture.

With *The Brownies' Book*, Du Bois and Fauset "laid the foundation for a new tradition in children's literature, a tradition that challenged the stereotypical depictions of African Americans" (McNair 6). They created a text that simultaneously reflected and encouraged wonder, intellect, and artistry through interweaving mainstream popular culture with African myths and legends, American history and current events, letters and creative works from child readers, and photographs of contemporary African American children and young adults. Children's literature scholars situate the publication of this text, along with Children's Numbers of *The Crisis*, as a significant, if not pivotal, moment in American race and literary culture. Capshaw contends that, during the Harlem Renaissance, "vital discussions about the nature and responsibilities of black childhood originate with Du Bois, and the variety of artistic responses that constitute the nativity of black children's literature fan out from debates initiated in *The Crisis*" (1). She explains, "In contrast to primitivistic images of black childhood like the pickaninny stereotype of nineteenth-century minstrelsy, Du Bois reimagined the black child as culturally, politically, and aesthetically sophisticated" (1).

In her introduction to *The Best of "The Brownies' Book,"* Edelman writes, "The [Harlem] Renaissance began during the same period that *The Brownies' Book* was in existence—a period when black Americans, especially those of the middle class, were critical of the nation but optimistic change could occur" (13). Du Bois and Fauset seized upon this optimism to probe and promote Black identity and issues, both subtly and explicitly. In "At the Zoo," one of her own poems published in *The Brownies' Book*, Fauset uses the breadth of difference seen between animals during a child's adventure at the zoo to underscore the diversity encountered between humans in everyday life and the need for racial tolerance. Reflecting upon his encounters with a variety of strange and intimidating species, the boy speaker resolves "to be to all God's creatures kind. / And kind to them I'll surely be / If only they'll be kind to me!" (86). A later poem in *The Brownies' Book*, "Lighting the Stars" by Robert P. Watts, illustrates how a child's desire to find answers to astronomical and spiritual questions works as a means for her to assert her place in the universe. She asks her mother, "when the starlights wink at me, / If I wink back, could they see?"—only to consider this and later ask, "And do the angels know just where / To get more when they've burned up these? / Oh, Mother, tell me if you please" (250). The poems and short stories published by the magazine also outlined more direct models for African American children to internalize. In the story "Why Bennie Was Fired" by Willie Mae King, an industrious eleven-year-old girl earns extra money by doing house chores for a white woman. The text stresses Bennie's ability to work and save money while excelling in her studies. Here, the story shows curiosity as conflated with ingenuity and enterprise and underlines the importance of financial independence and stability to its readership. In one scene, after Bennie makes a deposit in her new bank account, the narrator tells us that "several people smiled at the independent carriage of that little smiling colored girl as she left the bank" (222). However, the text balances the importance of financial reward with the experiential reward of self-industry, which Bennie finds through her "visits to the library during her recess hours" (222). These visits help Bennie write a composition for an oratory contest that she later wins.

The part of *The Brownies' Book* that I see as particularly influential on later efforts by African American newspapers is "The Jury," which consists of children's letters that validate not only the work of the magazine but also the capabilities of its readers. Moreover, "The Jury" enables its young readers to see that they belong to a wider community of not only Black youth but also Black artists and scholars. A note from fourteen-year-old Selma Ford of New Jersey reads, "I like to write stories, but I had no hopes of ever seeing them in print. Now, perhaps, if I write a very good one, you will let it appear in your magazine" (83). The letters likewise showcase the curiosity of the magazine's readers—a curiosity to learn more about their cultural identity and history, as well as local, national, and world events. Harry Blakeslee from Chicago, who declares that when he "grow[s] up," he is "going to have a newspaper or a magazine," writes that "so many colored folks want to read about the things colored people do and say" (83). He adds that the news section of *The Brownies' Book*, called "As the Crow Flies," is his favorite section. "You can learn such a lot about the whole world in those little paragraphs," he says. "If you always publish that part, I'd be willing to buy it just for that" (83). Harry illustrates genuine curiosity, but it is a curiosity underscored with social consciousness. Because African Americans' lives were largely ignored in the mainstream press, Harry deems it necessary to "have a newspaper or a magazine" so that Black Americans have more opportunities to see their realities depicted and discussed.

Although Du Bois's name most often receives acclaim for the inception and influence of *The Brownies' Book*, it was Fauset who crafted and maintained the publication. Indeed, "Fauset's inclusive attitude dominates the journal," Capshaw notes (25). She cites Thadious M. Davis, who called Fauset the "'functional editor'" of *The Brownies' Book*, as well as Carolyn Wedin Sylvander and Elinor Sinnette, who assert that the magazine is "largely Fauset's accomplishment" (25). Yet the significant cultural work and contributions of Fauset—who, as its literary editor, also helped shape *The Crisis*—remain neglected. "Though she helped to usher in a crucial period of artistic flourishing, and was herself a vital participant in that flourishing," Morgan Jerkins writes in a 2017 *New Yorker* profile, "she was not destined to get much credit for it." Perhaps with the centennial commemoration of *The Brownies' Book*, Fauset will receive more of the scholarly attention she deserves.

The pieces composing the twenty-four-issue run of *The Brownies' Book* "present fictional and authentic models of successful Blacks (and in some cases, of other minorities) who strive for identity and purpose without rejecting their own heritage and cultural values," write Courtney Vaughn-Robertson and Brenda Hill (496). But the magazine's production soon proved financially impossible. These economic woes, coupled with the "controversy over" *The Brownies' Book*'s "somewhat elitist leanings," as described by Vaughn-Robertson and Hill, forced the magazine to fold (495). Though the life of *The Brownies' Book* proved brief, its premise of embracing and bolstering Black childhood identity through the power of the press had taken root. The initial impact of *The Brownies' Book* may have been limited to its near four thousand subscribers (496), but its mission of creating community for Black youth soon found another avenue via African American weekly newspapers—most successfully, the *Chicago Defender*, but attempts were also made in the *Pittsburgh Courier*, Baltimore's *The Afro-American*, and the *Journal and Guide*, published in Norfolk, Virginia. In looking at these newspapers—widely considered the leading African American weeklies—and their children's sections, initiated after *The Brownies' Book*'s first issue, we can see that the legacy, impact, and reach of Du Bois's magazine reveals itself in new and illuminating ways.

THE *CHICAGO DEFENDER*

Indeed, in April 1921, we see how "the *Chicago Defender* adapted and revised *The Brownies' Book* model for a mass audience" (Gray 74). The *Defender* avoided "the implications of and anxiety surrounding uplift ideology" produced by some of the choices made by *The Brownies' Book* editors because it "established a youth section built entirely upon children's contributions," and it did so "within arguably the most influential African American publication of its time, or any time since" (74). Using *The Brownies' Book*'s similar ethos of unity and empowerment among young African Americans, the Defender Junior section was first published under the helm of Bud Billiken, an invented name created for a child-editor position. The first editor, Willard Motley,[2] was a "bright, bespectacled, ten-year-old youngster," writes Roi Ottley, biographer of *Defender* founder and publisher Robert S. Abbott (352). In his debut as Bud Billiken—a name inspired by a popular trinket at the time—Motley implores his peers to submit their poems, questions, and ideas about the world to him so that young people, specifically young African Americans, can have their names in print. His entreaty underscores the validation and legitimacy that come through publication. Bud also encourages children to become members of the Bud Billiken Club by filling out and mailing in the form included in the column (see figures 4.2 and 4.3).

SCHOOL
STUDY
SPORTS

Defender Junior

THE

CHILDREN'S GREATEST NEWSPAPER

HOME
PLAY
WORK

Figure 4.2 Banner for the Defender Junior. (*Chicago Defender*)

JOIN THE
BUD BILLIKEN CLUB

Every boy and girl reader of this column is eligible for membership. Costs nothing to join—you pay no dues. Fill out and return the application blank today and become a member.

Application Blank for Membership

Bud Billiken Club

I wish to become a member of The Chicago Defender's Bud Billiken club

My name is...........................

Address..................., Age....

City................... State........

Parents' name.........................

Figure 4.3 Membership form for the Chicago Defender's Bud Billiken Club. (*Chicago Defender*)

Through the children's letters printed in *The Brownies' Book* and the Defender Junior, children of color could *see themselves* in the stories submitted by their peers, a significant event given that most literature and art for young people at the time focused exclusively on white children. Perhaps even more damaging is that when Black characters were featured, they were demeaning stereotypes. Before publications like *The Brownies' Book*, "children who wanted to read about black characters in children's literature could read about buffoons, mammies, Sambos, or savages, but not about the beauty of 'Children of the Sun,'" explains children's literature scholar Michelle H. Martin (20). But in addition to seeing themselves through these periodicals, young readers were also awakened to their opportunity to *write* themselves into relevance. "Our little doings get lost in the columns of this paper," Bud Billiken asserts in that first Defender Junior section ("Help Me Out" 5). Together, Bud essentially says,

he and the readership can force recognition: "Hereafter get your mamma, papa
or uncle to 'write you up,' and send it to the 'Kids' Department' of this paper,
and 'Bud Billiken,' editor of the Chicago Defender Junior, will take care of it"
(5). With this introductory commentary, the Defender Junior, with that small
phrase "write you up," establishes the notion that language shapes identity
and affirms for Black children that they wield the power to control this (with,
perhaps, the aid of a scribe if they are still working on penmanship).

Although there may be no documented evidence of *The Brownies' Book's*
influence on Abbott and his decision to publish a children's section in the
Defender, it is nearly impossible to believe that, given the "unapologetic black
pride, dignity, and assertiveness" with which Abbott infused the *Defender*,
he would not be well acquainted with all the publications of Du Bois, the
country's leading Black intellectual and activist (Grossman 75). The spirit
of *The Brownies' Book* no doubt permeated the culture of the NAACP and
similar organizations. As such, the concept of creating a feature to unite and
embolden African American children would have easily become embedded in
Abbott's consciousness. But, in addition to being a staunch proponent for racial
justice, Abbott was also a savvy businessman, and the Defender Junior was an
ingenious marketing tool. In outlining Abbott's impetus to launch the Defender
Junior, Ottley writes that "the reason was twofold": Abbott "was probing for a
method by which he could enlist newsboys and maintain their interest in the
paper; and he felt the paper needed reading material of interest to the young
people in general" (351). It should be pointed out that while the Defender Junior
enabled the expression of young Black voices, it also functioned as a vehicle
for revenue. In his second newspaper appearance, Bud's "editorial" encourages
readers to "clean up their lawns and make some pretty gardens," a task that
may require the purchase of "one of those sets of garden tools in the 5 and 10
cent stores." This entreaty from Bud, suggested by the "head editor" to "all the
readers of the Defender Junior," was likely included to entice those "5 and 10
cent stores" to advertise in the *Defender* ("Help Me Out" 5).

In the early days of the Defender Junior, each feature usually began with an
introduction from Bud Billiken, which often stressed the importance of readers
joining the Bud Billiken Club and mailing in their news, requests, and creative
work. Bud also solicited birthday party notices: "If you are planning on giving
a little party soon just let your friends know it by sending word to me. Give
your name, date and home where it will take place. (P. S.—You may send some
cake to me after the party is over)" ("Help Me Out" 5). As such, notices for both
upcoming and past parties were not uncommon. Following this example of
Bud's request for birthday information, he included the following: "Mrs. Amy
Jones, 2349 West Lake street, gave a party Sunday, April 3, in honor of little
Mary Allen Carter, age 9, of Columbia, Mo. There were 20 children present.

They played games and danced. Refreshments were served and each kiddie had lots of fun. One little boy wanted to know when she would give another party" ("Listen to Me" 5). Given that "Mrs. Amy Jones" is indicated first, it is reasonable to conclude that she wrote and submitted the notice, not Mary Allen Carter. This suggests that adults as well as children paid attention to the Defender Junior, and they wanted their children recognized in it. Along these same lines, we can also assume that many parents played secretary for their children and wrote down the stories and questions they wanted sent to Bud—in some letters, the children are listed as three or four years old, likely too young to compose legible correspondence.[3] But all this highlights the community fostered by the Defender Junior, and not just a community for African American children living in the Chicago area. The *Defender* was mailed to all parts of the country; its wide reach enabled a shared sense of identity among its young Black readers across the nation, both literally through membership in the Bud Billiken Club and figuratively or conceptually in that they formed what Benedict Anderson calls an "imagined community."[4]

In his reminders for reader submissions, Bud Billiken subtly nods to the significance of this imagined community among African American children— that through sharing and publishing their letters and creative work, the Bud Billiken Club forces acknowledgment. An introduction from Bud in the April 23, 1921, issue further clarifies this conceit, and it does so with both urgency and solemnity. Bud begins by relating the story of a fly that "sat on the axle of a chariot wheel and said, 'What a dust I do make'" ("Let's Do Something" 5). "The fly imagines that he is causing the wheel to go around" and bring about all that dust, Bud explains to readers. Here, Bud shifts to a kind of homily, imploring, "Let us not be like the fly, thinking we are doing something when really we only move as the world moves us," before remarking,

> The world would move on if we were not in it. This paper would be published just the same without our space.
>
>   Let us make the world know that we are living and helping to make the noise and dust. Make the readers of this "Defender" feel that it is incomplete without our department. ("Let's Do Something" 5)

I find this astonishing and poignant on many fronts. Bud adeptly articulates the potential force that young people possess through their words, echoing convictions that Fauset underlaid in each issue of *The Brownies' Book*. Here, Bud evokes and attempts to dismantle the power dynamic between children and adults by making the Defender Junior indispensable. But this plea also speaks to the racial injustice that defines these young people's daily lives. This is the devastating part: nearly a century later, the "Black Lives Matter" chants of our current cultural moment essentially echo Bud's 1923 plea to "Let us make the world know that we are living" ("Let's Do Something" 5).

THE *PITTSBURGH COURIER, THE AFRO-AMERICAN,* AND THE *JOURNAL AND GUIDE*

Arguably, *The Brownies' Book*'s legacy extended well beyond its original readership through its likely influence on the Defender Junior and that section's considerable audience of young readers throughout the United States. This legacy enabled children of color to see themselves in the letters printed each week in the Defender Junior as well as other African American weeklies. In the January 7, 1922, issue of the Defender Junior, Bud Billiken tells his audience that "we are increasing our Junior page of the Chicago Defender" and then boasts, "We have the best Junior column of any of the weeklies" (8). Several other African American weeklies started children's sections that seemingly took inspiration from *The Brownies' Book* or the Defender Junior (or both).

In 1923, another prominent African American weekly newspaper, the *Pittsburgh Courier*, briefly published a section called the Scatterat League, which closely resembles the model of the Bud Billiken Club. The editorial voice provided by Bud in the Defender Junior comes in the persona of "Adelaide," and both these editorial voices undoubtedly arise from the standards and style that Fauset set with *The Brownies' Book*. In the June 2, 1923, issue of the *Courier*, the Scatterat League, described as "enjoyment for the children" and "featured by Adelaide" in the section's banner (see figure 4.4), gets nearly a page for its contents. The page includes a membership roll with readers' names and addresses, as well as a few reader photographs and short stories ("All about Betty"; "The Wise Little Mother"). It is not clear if Adelaide is a child or adult, or if she is the author of the stories printed in the section. In a note to readers in the same issue, Adelaide writes, "I got so many letters about the Scatterat League that I felt like an important person. I hope the League grows and grows until we can have a large space in the Pittsburgh Courier for our news" (8). She lays out the basic guidelines of the Scatterat League, stating that membership is free and that all readers need to do to join is send in their names and addresses. "Another thing," Adelaide notes, is that "the age limit is 15 years; and one as young as 5 months can be a Baby Scatterat" (8). Interestingly, the section also features a "Scatterat Model"—a drawing of a young girl wearing French-inspired fashion with the caption "Jaunty suit of biege [sic] Poiret Twill embroidered in a darker shade of soutache braid" (see figure 4.5).

Enjoyment for the
Children

The Scatterat League

Featured by
ADELAIDE

Figure 4.4 Banner for the Scatterat League. (*Pittsburgh Courier*)

Scatterat Model

Jaunty suit of biege Poiret Twill
embroidered in a darker shade of
soutache braid.

Figure 4.5 Illustration featured in the Scatterat League. (*Pittsburgh Courier*)

From the digitized newspapers available on Newspapers.com and Pro-
Quest, as well as the historians and scholarship I consulted, it appears that
the Scatterat League was a periodic feature in the *Pittsburgh Courier* in 1923,
but I could not find sections specifically titled Scatterat beyond that year. The
section changes headings—from Scatterat League to A Section for the Kiddies
or A Page for the Kiddies. Variations of a youth page may have existed after
1923, but the Scatterat League section modeled after elements of *The Brownies'
Book* and the Defender Junior seems to be confined to that year. Nevertheless,
the Scatterat League further evidences the cultural work happening in the

wake of *The Brownies' Book*'s debut as African American children sought to define their experience and identity for themselves through the Black press.

The Scatterat League page in the *Pittsburgh Courier* uses a similar approach to that of the Defender Junior: both rely on an editorial voice that serves as a figurehead for the section, and each deems its section a special group that requires membership. This is important, for it points to children's essential need to see that they belong to a community. For African American children in the 1920s, who encountered few if any positive representations of Black childhood and who were excluded from hegemonic ideals of white childhood, becoming a "member" of an organization sanctioned by the newspaper must have been a validating, significant event. Similar to the letters published in the Defender Junior, those on the Scatterat League page expressed children's enthusiasm for the club. In a letter in the July 28, 1923, section, Marcella Griffin tells Adelaide, "I wish to join the Scatterat League. I have secured two new members and I will also send some news" (9). Membership to these newspaper sections facilitated young people's engagement with the public sphere while supporting individual expression.

The *Courier*'s effort to engage a youth readership, aside from the membership model, feels closer in tone to that of *The Brownies' Book*. The curation of short stories for young readers mimics the editorial guidance of Du Bois and Fauset, though Adelaide's choices prove broader. *The Brownies' Book* published an array of material intended to speak to Black children; while some writing addressed "universal" elements of childhood, the magazine dedicated itself to embracing the specific experience of African American childhood. The Scatterat selections (or those on the later Page for the Kiddies and Section for the Kiddies) are more general, often including fairy stories or jokes.

Another leading African American weekly newspaper initiated a children's section shortly after *The Brownies' Book* run—Baltimore's *The Afro-American*. In its November 24, 1922, issue, the newspaper included A Column for the Children section, which contained riddles as well as an instructional note on "How to Prepare Pelts." The section also included letters from young readers. Laura E. Richards tells a story about a little boy on a hot day, and Julia Jones has a joke about "Johnny's New Shoes." Jefferson writes to the editor with a note about eggs. Judging from its inconsistent appearances, the Column for the Children section did not establish a readership like that of the Defender Junior. But it takes part in a wider cultural conversation working to recognize Black young people, a conversation amplified and intensified by *The Brownies' Book* through Fauset's editorial guidance. In the few instances of *The Afro-American*'s children's section, its letters show Black youth's interest in public engagement and artistic invention analogous to that found in Du Bois's magazine and the *Defender*. The Column for the Children published in the

Figure 4.6 Illustration featured in A Column for the Children section. (*The Afro-American*)

January 12, 1923, issue of *The Afro-American* shares a story from Della Swarm "telling where we first got tinsel for our Christmas trees" (12). It also features the "Typewritten Cat"—a cat made out of letters intended as a new year's greeting—from Naomi C. Hedgeman (see figure 4.6). Naomi's letter indicates she lives in Wyoming; like the *Defender*, *The Afro-American* and other weeklies of the Black press had readerships throughout the United States. And so, a little girl in Wyoming who was likely one of few African American children in her town could feel connected to a larger network of young people through *The Afro-American.*

The *Chicago Defender*, the *Pittsburgh Courier*, and *The Afro-American* could be described as journalism and activism—vehicles to promote social justice and condemn racist policies. Robert Abbott, the *Defender*'s publisher, suffused the publication with an "uncompromising racial idealism" (Ottley 2); the three newspapers have been described as one end of a political spectrum of Black weeklies, with the *Journal and Guide* (Norfolk, Virginia) at the other. Historian Henry Lewis Suggs explains that "Black middle-class detractors contrasted the *Journal and Guide*'s Uncle Tom views of northern migration, job discrimination, lynching, and voter registration with the more militant views of the *Chicago Defender*, *Pittsburgh Courier*, and the Baltimore *Afro-American*" (190).

Regardless of their approach to ameliorating racial injustice, these weeklies viewed Du Bois and the NAACP as the leaders in the fight for equality. The *Journal and Guide*'s editor and publisher, P. B. Young, "regarded the NAACP as the only means in America through which the plight of blacks could be made known" (qtd. in Suggs 165). Young adopted the motto "build up, don't tear down" for his newspaper (Suggs 162), and "as World War I ended, the *Journal and Guide* had the largest circulation of any black-owned newspaper in the South" (168). The influence of Du Bois, Fauset, and *The Brownies' Book* stands apparent in the newspaper's youth section, the Brownies Club, which began appearing in the *Journal and Guide* in May 1922 and was published occasionally throughout the following year.

A column in the May 20, 1922, issue of the *Journal and Guide*, under the headline "Boys and Girls," entreats young readers to "JOIN THE BROWNIES CLUB." "The Brownies Club," writes Miriam Dixon, has one guiding principle—"Do something for somebody"—and "all children under sixteen years are eligible." Dixon goes on to say that the "only rule is to do a real kindly act and let us know about it" (6). The origin and inspiration for the Brownies Club section, given the name and proximity in publication to *The Brownies' Book*, seemed to derive, at least in part, from Du Bois and Fauset's children's magazine. However, the *Journal and Guide*'s section focuses on fostering community and identity for Black youth through philanthropic acts in addition to writing. (In this sense, the "Brownie" name may also refer to the spritely creatures of folklore.) "True greatness lies in service," Dixon tells potential Brownies, a creed that connotes the value of citizenship and carries an undercurrent of patriotism with the use of "service" (6). In later issues, Dixon edited the section renamed Brownie Club Breezes under the accompanying motto "do a good deed every day." It follows a familiar model: short stories and jokes curated by Dixon, along with a few letters submitted by Brownies. In the July 1, 1922, issue, a Brownie writes of being "so glad to see my last letter in print, so soon that I am writing again" (Dixon, Brownie Club Breezes 6). "My Brownie act this week was to help an old lady with a heavy basket," the Brownie Club member informs readers. Once again, here we see how the printed word enables young African Americans to feel validated, and with this reader, it encourages further writing. This, in turn, requires the Brownie to do more kind acts. In the next letter, we learn of a Brownie who identifies as a flapper: "I like the showiest clothes and am anxious that folks should notice me on the street." The letter-writer goes on to say, "I am kind-hearted and haven't been really truly bad, yet I feel my present behavior will lead me wrong. Do you take folk like me into your club?" (Dixon, Brownie Club Breezes 6). These few brief sentences reveal persistent themes of childhood—seeking independence and individual expression while also finding acceptance and community.

The basic conceit of the weekly newspaper or monthly magazine helps us understand the ways African American children have and continue to subvert and reimagine hegemonic constructs of childhood. During the 1920s, Black press publishers and young readers reframed notions of childhood using the literal and figurative concept of periodical production. In her scholarship about Victorian children's literature, Marah Gubar, in a close reading of E. Nesbit's *The Story of the Treasure Seekers* (1899), discerns how the newspaper acts as a metaphor for enacting childhood agency. "In order to participate actively in the shaping of their own lives and life stories," Gubar interprets from Nesbit's text, "children should function like the discriminating editors" (129). Indeed, says Gubar, "Rather than simply accepting everything they receive from the culture at large, they should criticize, edit, rewrite, even reject the endless submissions pouring in from all quarters" (129–30). *The Brownies' Book* and children's sections in African American weeklies illuminate the ways in which Black children found agency, creative power, and kinship via appropriating, reconceiving, and reconstructing mainstream white literature and culture in order to more accurately express their realities, anxieties, and ambitions. The ideas put forward by these children of color in the early 1920s perfectly collapse into one another through that ballerina photograph on *The Brownies' Book*'s first cover. But that ballerina also has a voice. I imagine her saying something similar to Bud Billiken's appeal—"Let us make the world know that we are living," or perhaps, simply, "Black Lives Matter."

Notes

1. See Gray 69–88, or an abridged version of that chapter, which appeared under the title "Join the Club: African American Children's Literature, Social Change, and the Chicago Defender Junior," *Children's Literature Association Quarterly*, vol. 42, no. 2, Summer 2017, pp. 149–68.

2. Motley would later become known as the author of *Knock on Any Door* (1947).

3. A Defender Junior letter printed in the June 21, 1921, issue provides a good illustration of a note that may have been dictated to an adult writer, given the children's stated ages:

> My sister and I are sending in our applications for membership to your club. I am so glad that the children can have a voice in the dear old Defender. Daddie and mother are enthusiastic readers of the paper. Long before the children's column was out I would sit and listen to them discuss the Defender and the news it contained. Now that the children's column is in my interest is doubled since I can see my name and piece in the paper. I live on the farm and am 5 years old, and have finished the first reader. Was promoted to the second grade. I also go to Sunday school. We will stop now and write some more next time. Remaining yours truly.—Hazel and Geraldine Hamilton, ages 5 and 3, Mason, Ark. (8)

4. When examining the relationship between newspapers, community, and identity, one needs to acknowledge the theoretical work of Benedict Anderson. Anderson, critical in understanding how the reading of a text by a specific audience at a specific time works to psychically unite

individuals, probes the ideological force of the newspaper to generate an imagined community. (We could, perhaps, say that for Anderson, newspaper readers internalize Mikhail Bakhtin's concept of polyphony.) In discussing the "mass ceremony" in which individuals participate while reading the newspaper, a "paradoxical" one "performed in silent privacy, in the lair of the skull," Anderson states that "each communicant is well aware that the ceremony he performs is being replicated simultaneously by thousands (or millions) of others of whose existence he is confident, yet of whose identity he has not the slightest notion" (428). This repeated, shared activity then produces the "secular, historically cloaked, imagined community," he adds, and the "newspaper reader, observing exact replicas of his own paper being consumed by his subway, barbershop, or residential neighbors, is continually reassured that the imagined world is visibly rooted in everyday life." Anderson helps us better understand the hegemonic role the newspaper held in the lives of Americans beginning in the nineteenth century, extending and multiplying into today's inescapable mass-media influence. But Anderson also demonstrates the ways in which citizens can feel as though they have an active, participatory role within a specific community.

Works Cited

Anderson, Benedict. "From Imagined Communities: Reflections on the Origin and Spread of Nationalism." *Theory of the Novel: A Historical Approach*, edited by Michael McKeon, Johns Hopkins UP, 2000, pp. 414–34.

Billiken, Bud. "Chicago Defender Jr.: For Young Folks by Young Folks." *Chicago Defender*, 11 June 1921, p. 8. *ProQuest Historical Newspapers*.

Billiken, Bud. "Chicago Defender Jr.: For Young Folks by Young Folks." *Chicago Defender*, 7 Jan. 1922, p. 8. *ProQuest Historical Newspapers*.

Billiken, Bud. "Chicago Defender Jr.: For Young Folks by Young Folks: Let's Do Something." *Chicago Defender*, 23 Apr. 1921, p. 5. *ProQuest Historical Newspapers*.

Billiken, Bud. "Chicago Defender Jr.: For Young Folks by Young Folks: Listen to Me." *Chicago Defender*, 9 Apr. 1921, p. 5. *ProQuest Historical Newspapers*.

Billiken, Bud. "Chicago Defender Jr.: For Young Folks: Help Me Out, Please." *Chicago Defender*, 2 Apr. 1921, p. 5. *ProQuest Historical Newspapers*.

Blakeslee, Harry. "The Jury." *The Brownies' Book*, vol. 1, no. 3, Mar. 1920, p. 83.

Capshaw, Katharine. *Children's Literature of the Harlem Renaissance*. Indiana UP, 2004.

A Column for the Children. *The Afro-American*, 24 Nov. 1922, p. 12. *ProQuest Historical Newspapers*.

A Column for the Children. *The Afro-American*, 12 Jan. 1923, p. 12. *ProQuest Historical Newspapers*.

Dixon, Miriam. "Boys and Girls." *Journal and Guide*, 20 May 1922, p. 6. *ProQuest Historical Newspapers*.

Dixon, Miriam. Brownie Club Breezes. *Journal and Guide*, 1 July 1922, p. 6. *ProQuest Historical Newspapers*.

Du Bois, W. E. B., editor. *The Brownies' Book*, vol. 1, 1920. Library of Congress.

Edelman, Marian Wright. "Preface." *The Best of "The Brownies' Book,"* edited by Dianne Johnson-Feelings, Oxford UP, 1996, pp. 12–15.

Fauset, Jessie. "At the Zoo." *The Brownies' Book*, vol. 1, no. 3, Mar. 1920, pp. 85–86.

Ford, Selma. "The Jury." *The Brownies' Book*, vol. 1, no. 3, Mar. 1920, p. 83.

Gray, Paige. *Cub Reporters: American Children's Literature and Journalism in the Golden Age.* SUNY Press, 2019.

Grossman, James R. *Land of Hope: Chicago, Black Southerners, and the Great Migration.* U of Chicago P, 1989.

Gubar, Marah. *Artful Dodgers: Reconceiving the Golden Age of Children's Literature*. Oxford UP, 2009.

Holland, Eleanor. "The Jury." *The Brownies' Book*, vol. 1, no. 1, Jan. 1920, p. 15.

Jerkins, Morgan. "The Forgotten Work of Jessie Redmon Fauset." *The New Yorker*, 18 Feb. 2017, newyorker.com/books/page-turner/the-forgotten-work-of-jessie-redmon-fauset.

King, Willie Mae. "Why Bennie Was Fired." *The Brownies' Book*, vol. 1, no. 7, July 1920, pp. 222–24.

Lewis, Franklin. "The Jury." *The Brownies' Book*, vol. 1, no. 1, Jan. 1920, p. 15.

Martin, Michelle H. *Brown Gold: Milestones of African-American Children's Picture Books, 1845–2002*. Routledge, 2004.

McNair, Jonda C. "A Comparative Analysis of *The Brownies' Book* and Contemporary African American Children's Literature Written by Patricia C. McKissack." *Embracing, Evaluating, and Examining American Children's and Young Adult Literature*, edited by Wanda M. Brooks and McNair, Scarecrow P, 2008, pp. 2–29.

Ottley, Roi. *The Lonely Warrior: The Life and Times of Robert S. Abbott*. Henry Regnery, 1955.

Scatterat League. *Pittsburgh Courier*, 2 June 1923, p. 8. *Newspapers.com*.

Scatterat League. *Pittsburgh Courier*, 28 July 1923, p. 9. *Newspapers.com*.

Suggs, H. Lewis. "Black Strategy and Ideology in the Segregation Era: P. B. Young and the Norfolk Journal and Guide, 1910–1954." *The Virginia Magazine of History and Biography*, vol. 91, no. 2, Apr. 1983, pp. 161–90. *JSTOR*.

Vaughn-Robertson, Courtney, and Brenda Hill. "*The Brownies' Book* and Ebony Jr.!: Literature as a Mirror of the Afro-American Experience." *The Journal of Negro Education*, vol. 58, no. 4, Autumn 1989, pp. 494–510. *JSTOR*.

Watts, Robert P. "Lighting the Stars." *The Brownies' Book*, vol. 1, no. 8, Aug. 1920, p. 250.

Chapter 5

MILDRED D. TAYLOR'S *ROLL OF THUNDER, HEAR MY CRY*

A Worthy Successor to *The Brownies' Book*

JANI L. BARKER

African American literature for youth has a rich, robust tradition of accurately reflecting the voices and experiences of African Americans in ways that provide entertainment, build positive values, promote race pride, and combat racism by countering distorted narratives of Black lives. Although works in this tradition preceded *The Brownies' Book*, the children's magazine proposed by W. E. B. Du Bois—and coedited by him and Jessie Fauset—is significant because it first delineated "the rationale and objectives at the foundations of the very creation of Black children's literature" to support youth in being "educated, acculturated, nurtured and inspired" (D. Johnson 37). The tradition was reinforced half a century after *The Brownies' Book* with the creation of the Coretta Scott King Book Awards to honor books that "portray some aspect of the black experience" through excellent writing and that "motivate readers to develop their own attitudes and behaviors as well as comprehend their personal duty and responsibility as citizens in a pluralistic society" ("Coretta Scott King Book Awards"). This tradition continues a century after the magazine's publication with a wide array of recent award-winning children's literature across a variety of genres (e.g., poetry, nonfiction) and formats (e.g., graphic novels, chapter books, picture books) by African American authors.

Mildred D. Taylor's historical novel *Roll of Thunder, Hear My Cry* (1976), winner of only the second Newbery Medal to be awarded to an African American author, shares many of the core themes of *The Brownies' Book* and meets the objectives Du Bois articulated for Black children's literature. Although I have seen no evidence that Taylor, who was born over two decades after it ceased publication, ever read *The Brownies' Book*, she was familiar with the work of its founder and coeditor, Du Bois. *Roll of Thunder, Hear My Cry* specifically mentions Du Bois's *The Negro* as one of the few books the Logan family owned, a book Mary Logan used to inform her teaching (76). Moreover, direct linear influence is not required for there to be strong connections between *The Brownies' Book* and later African American literature for children. Rudine Sims Bishop attributes similar "thematic emphases" of the literature following *The Brownies' Book* not to "conscious imitations" but rather to the perception among later writers that "many of the social and literary conditions that had spurred the creation of *The Brownies' Book*—for example, the dearth of books about Black children, the distortion and omission of Black history and Black achievement from school curricula, the inaccurate or caricatured visual or literary images of Black people—had changed but little since the 1920s" (33–34). Despite obvious differences between a multiauthored magazine with a range of features and genres and a unified novel, *Roll of Thunder, Hear My Cry* exemplifies the African American tradition of children's literature articulated by *The Brownies' Book*.

This chapter analyzes a number of elements shared by influential works of Du Bois, Fauset, and Taylor. First, I examine Du Bois and Taylor's shared vision of providing truthful accounts of African Americans and the African American experience for diverse, multiracial audiences. In doing so, I show the ways in which *The Brownies' Book* and *Roll of Thunder, Hear My Cry* demonstrate respect for people of all races, even as both explicitly subvert white superiority. Second, I explore how Du Bois's, Fauset's, and Taylor's publications achieve the first two goals Du Bois set out for *The Brownies' Book*: "a) To make colored children realize that being 'colored' is a normal, beautiful thing"; and "b) To make them familiar with the history and achievements of the Negro race" (286). Third, I analyze the distinct anti-racist agenda prevalent in both *The Brownies' Book* and Taylor's novel. Fourth, I explore core values and themes shared by the two publications. Finally, I conclude by showing how Taylor's award-winning novel serves not only as a worthy successor to Du Bois's vision for positive African American children's literature, but also as inspiration for later writers in an ongoing tradition.

A major impetus for both *The Brownies' Book* and *Roll of Thunder, Hear My Cry* was their creators' recognition of the need for children to receive truthful accounts about African American people and experiences. In "The True Brownies," an article in the 1919 issue of *The Crisis* dedicated to children, Du Bois explains that his idea for having a magazine targeted entirely to children sprang from a letter written by a twelve-year-old girl who expressed both her desire to learn more about her race and her hatred for white people. Du Bois was disturbed by the effects that repeated negative accounts of Black experiences such as lynchings, riots, and other atrocities inflicted on Black people—which were, necessarily, reported in the Children's Numbers in *The Crisis*—had on child readers: "To educate them in human hatred is more disastrous to them than to the hated; to seek to raise them in ignorance of their racial identity and peculiar situation is inadvisable—impossible" (285). His solution was to have a monthly magazine for children that could focus on "Joy and Beauty, dealing in Happiness, Laughter and Emulation" (286), blending these positive, entertaining elements with the goals of instilling racial understanding, pride, and duty. This solution would not have been necessary if such depictions of Black life were readily available. Bishop notes that one function of *The Brownies' Book* was "to lift the veil of invisibility and counteract false images and stereotypes in children's books and magazines" (24), and Violet J. Harris argues that the magazine challenged "a selective tradition in children's literature" that "stereotyped Blacks and Black culture," presenting them in negative, inaccurate, and limited ways (6). In the inaugural issue of *The Brownies' Book*, we find a poem by coeditor Jessie Fauset, "Dedication," that explicitly shows the magazine's purpose of telling stories too often omitted:

> To Children, who with eager look
> Scanned vainly library shelf or nook,
> For History or Song or Story
> That told of Colored Peoples' glory,—
> We dedicate THE BROWNIES' BOOK. (32)

More than half a century later, Mildred Taylor, in her acceptance speech for the Newbery Medal awarded to *Roll of Thunder, Hear My Cry*, similarly speaks to the lack of published tales that authentically represented her family's experiences. As a child, she had no access to books that told of "the small and often dangerous triumphs of Black people" that she heard from adults in her family and community, "stories about human pride and survival in a cruelly racist society that were like nothing I read in the history books or the books I devoured at the local library. There were no Black heroes or heroines in those books; no beautiful Black ladies, no handsome Black men; no people filled with pride, strength, or endurance" (25). Instead, she read "a history of a docile, subservient people happy with their fate who did little or nothing to shatter the chains that bound them, both before and after slavery" (25). Thus, Taylor developed "a driving compulsion to paint a truer picture of Black people" (26); she wanted to show Black endurance, strong, loving families, "happy, loved children," and "a Black family united in love and pride" (26). Taylor's compulsion is realized in *Roll of Thunder, Hear My Cry* and her other Logan family novels.

Just as the editors of *The Brownies' Book* and Taylor desired to provide authentic and complete accounts of Black experiences, the positive as well as the challenging ones, they also envisioned diverse audiences of children of multiple races. Du Bois clearly references a comprehensive audience, primarily targeting Black children but including all races, in his initial announcement in *The Crisis* of the proposed "little magazine for children— for all children, but especially for *ours*, 'the Children of the Sun'" (286). These sentiments are repeated on the frontispiece of every issue, along with the stated objective: "to teach Universal Love and Brotherhood for all little folk— black and brown and yellow and white." Jonda C. McNair designates "the belief that all children, African American children especially, deserve to see accurate and positive representation of the culture, experiences, and history of African Americans in literature" as an "underlying ideological assumption" of *The Brownies' Book* ("Comparative Analysis" 19). Based on evidence in letters from readers printed in *The Brownies' Book*, the actual audience, though predominantly Black, included white and international members (Harris 24). The readership for *Roll of Thunder, Hear My Cry* almost certainly includes a much higher rate of non-Black readers, given the widespread recognition it received as winner of the Newbery Medal, the most prestigious award for children's literature in the United States, and its incorporation into school curricula in North America and Britain (Hardstaff 227). Taylor's stated intention indicates that she, like Du Bois, desired a multiracial audience, one consisting of "children, both Black and white" who would like her characters and identify strongly with them ("Newbery Medal Acceptance" 26), and that her work would "be instrumental in teaching children of all colors" about the work done by Blacks in the generation that laid the groundwork for the civil rights movement (28).

As suggested by the inclusive audiences and the desire to teach children of all colors, *The Brownies' Book* and *Roll of Thunder, Hear My Cry* promote respect for all people. Given the racism pervading American society and the antagonism toward white people that this racism might naturally engender, Du Bois and Taylor both explicitly specify whites among those to whom respect should be given. One of Du Bois's endeavors for *The Brownies' Book* was "to teach [colored children] delicately a code of honor and action in their relations with white children" as opposed to educating them "in human hatred" (285–86). Similarly, the wise Mary Logan counters Cassie's impassioned cry, "Ah, shoot! White ain't nothin'!" with "It is something, Cassie. White is something just like black is something. Everybody born on this earth is something and nobody, no matter what color, is better than anybody else" (Taylor, *Roll of Thunder* 127). The message is clear: opposing racism does not mean hatred or disrespect toward white people.

However, both *The Brownies' Book* and *Roll of Thunder, Hear My Cry* sometimes include moments of poking fun at whites or relishing triumph over them to help counterbalance society's unequal power dynamics. These publications' emphasis on Black pride and self-esteem sometimes mandates an emphatic rebuttal to assumptions of white superiority. As Jonda C. McNair argues, "The creation of feelings of superiority among African Americans functions to challenge notions of white supremacy" ("'I May Be Crackin'" 209). Included in the inaugural issue of *The Brownies' Book* is a poem, "The Origin of White Folks," that mocks white folks for putting on airs "about dem wash'out faces" when the reason for their paleness was distinctly not prideworthy. The original race, the poem explains, was colored, but those guilty of eating the fatal apple in the biblical fall of humanity, disgraced, "turnt so pale dey stayed dat way" (Culbertson 7). A fairy story later in that issue also addresses the origin of races in a way that puts the white race at a disadvantage. In this story, people started out white, but the fairy Gyp played a "pleasing" joke, painting some children their favorite red and brown shades as they napped outside, "knowing they would be delighted." The descendants of "the little red children still love to roam" and "the little brown children can be found most everywhere, carrying happiness and sunshine to all they see," but those children who had stayed home missed out on the fun; their descendants remain white and, by implication, colorless and dull (Kilpatrick 31). A bit more subversively, the Logan family rejoices when, after some secret sabotage from the Logan children, rainwater damages the white students' school bus, which had tormented the Black children on their walks to and from school. Elated at their success, the children "shake with silent laughter" as they watch the bus fall victim to their trap (Taylor, *Roll of Thunder* 54). They continue to laugh all evening, upon hearing that the white children will have to walk to and from school for a couple of weeks, contemplating "how sweet was well-maneuvered revenge!" (56). Even Mama and Big Ma, unaware of the cause of the bus's mishap, acknowledge their schadenfreude at the misfortune of the school bus, symbol of the unfair privilege of the white school, and its driver and students. This humor serves not as a rejection of the previously described messages of respect for all, but as a useful psychological survival tool for those who face persistent disrespect—and worse—from the dominant society in which they live. Dexter B. Gordon notes that humor can foster resiliency and a sense of power, serving as a mechanism for self-affirmation and community solidarity for Blacks (257–48).

Affirming Blacks, individually and communally, is at the heart of publications by Du Bois, Fauset, and Taylor. The first "endeavor" that Du Bois mentions for *The Brownies' Book*, and presumably that of greatest priority, is "To make colored children realize that being 'colored' is a normal, beautiful thing" (286).

The themes of race pride, intelligent Blacks, and beautiful Blacks that Harris found prevalent in the magazine's stories seem to fit under this umbrella. This endeavor is vitally important because truthful, positive depictions of Black children were in direct, deliberate opposition to the negative, stereotyped views that permeated mainstream culture. Children's publications in particular at the time of *The Brownies' Book* were dominated by a selective tradition designed, according to Harris, to "socialize" members of the society and teach them "to assume a status and a role that is influenced by race, gender, and class" (10). This selective tradition upheld white superiority, suggesting "to Whites that they were the natural leaders of Blacks" and providing Blacks with "direct and indirect evidence that they held a low status position in society" (10). The editors of *The Brownies' Book* challenged this selective tradition by presenting content that "countered negative and demeaning images they were likely to find in mainstream children's literature" (McNair, "Comparative Analysis" 5). In short, the photos, lists of achievers, letters, columns, fiction, biography, poems, and other features of *The Brownies' Book* repeatedly sent messages that African Americans were normal, not "Other" or lesser, and thus served as a corrective to the imbalanced, untruthful stories that bombarded readers.

At a glance, anyone flipping through the pages of any issue of *The Brownies' Book* might see photos of a multitude of African American youth engaged in positive activities. Photos included young people playing games and sports, posing individually and in small groups of siblings and friends and larger groups—a swimming class at a YMCA, Girl Reserves, dramatic clubs. Readers could view people in uniform and standing patriotically in front of flags, folks coming home from church, at masquerades and other parties, performing in dances and plays, in individual and class high school graduation photos and shots of college commencements, and in many other situations and settings. The people featured in these photographs vary in body and facial shape and in size, complexion, and hairstyle; facial expressions range from serious to wide smiles. All, however, are presented with dignity, and each is, in his or her individual way, attractive. The cumulative effect of these diverse pictures is to normalize the images of Black people shown in them and to show the various positive, enjoyable activities in which they engage to be regular aspects of Black life. The need for such images is exemplified by a letter from a Philadelphia schoolgirl, Alice Martin, published in "The Jury" in the June 1920 issue, in which she relates her experiences of anger and humiliation over the pictures in her school geography lessons: "all the pictures are pretty, nice-looking men and women, except the Africans. They always look so ugly." She acknowledges the variations in attractiveness of people within different races, noting, however, that although she sees "lots of ugly white people" in the world, "they are not the ones they put in the geography" (178).

Through dignified images of Black faces of both ordinary people and those of more exalted status, such as the empress of Ethiopia, Dianne Johnson argues, "no matter what other images [readers] are bombarded with from the larger community, somewhere in their minds, Black royalty, Black dignity, Black on its own terms exists as a reality" (21). Johnson does analyze some problematic examples of colorism, with lighter shades being deemed more attractive than darker skin and "long wavy hair" noted as the standard for beauty in verbal descriptions in some stories and in advertisements for Madame C. J. Walker's hair care products (24). She also notes attempts by artists and the editors to "address and redress the issue of color stratification" and to "consciously work against blatant in-group discrimination" (25). Overall, physical images and descriptions of "a wide spectrum of Black people, including darker skinned persons" (25), emphasize the attractiveness of the race.

This focus on Black as normal and attractive goes far beyond appearance to include admirable character, intelligence, talent, and accomplishments as typical of African Americans in fiction and nonfiction accounts. Readers who in most other children's literature of the time would either not see Black characters at all or would see stereotyped, derogatory images would find in *The Brownies' Book* story after story spotlighting a wide array of Black characters taking center stage and demonstrating their agency and capability. The regular feature "Little People of the Month" provides real-life accounts, accompanied by portraits, of child after child from all around the nation recognized for a wide range of accomplishments. For example, the February 1920 column features a young girl saving money for her education; a two-year-old who could recite thirty-seven "Mother Goose" rhymes; boys who could play piano, horn, and violin; a ten-year-old graduate; and a girl who earned the highest examination grade in her class (58). The April 1921 column applauds a boy who was awarded a $50 prize from the "Polite Editor" of the *Chicago Tribune* for his fine manners; a ten-year-old whose high examination score earned a college scholarship; a baby declared the healthiest in Meadville, Pennsylvania, by the Baby Welfare League; a broad-jumping champion with multiple prizes; and a boy who won a school prize for composing the best words and music for a song (124). These achievements, although typically more in line with those recorded in family newsletters or local newspapers than in history books, are laudable, but their greatest impact would be in showing that talent and accomplishment were common, accessible feats for "Children of the Sun," ordinary as well as extraordinary.

Roll of Thunder, Hear My Cry is equally effective at showing African Americans as normal and beautiful, although its different genre led to different tactics for doing so. The novel frequently describes members of the Logan family and their community; as in *The Brownies' Book*, a spectrum of skin tones and body sizes is depicted, although no preference for one skin tone over another is ever suggested. Cassie's Big Ma is tall and strongly built, with "clear, smooth skin . . . the color of a pecan shell" (Taylor, *Roll of Thunder* 32), and her mama is "tawny-colored, thin and sinewy, with delicate features in a strong-jawed face" (33). Her Uncle Hammer, like her papa, "had dark, red-brown skin, a square-jawed face, and high cheekbones" (119). An older man who comes to live with and help the Logan family, Mr. Morrison, is described as "a human tree in height . . . his massive body bulged with muscles" with skin "of the deepest ebony" (34). Typically, the novel does not directly emphasize the beauty of Black people, although Cassie does think that her mama "looked very pretty" (131) and the language used in descriptions is positive. Instead, the descriptions serve to highlight a variety of appearance traits, showing each to be acceptable, and the love implicit throughout the narrator Cassie's descriptions of her family and friends highlights their attractiveness.

This attractiveness is even more one of personality and character than of form. Each Logan family member has a distinct personality, and although they realistically combine admirable and more problematic traits, each is appealing. Stacy, the twelve-year-old oldest child, is the leader of his siblings, thoughtful and loyal to siblings and friends. Stalwart enough to take a whipping from his teacher (and mother) rather than tell on a cheating friend whose cheat notes he had confiscated, he has the spirit to then beat up the friend in retaliation. Nine-year-old Cassie is strong, outspoken, observant, and capable of spending a month currying favor with a white girl who had offended her, so that she could learn the girl's secrets and exact her revenge with impunity. Christopher-John, cheerful, sensitive, agreeable, is, at seven, the one most reluctant to go along with the siblings' riskier schemes; the youngest, Little Man, is known for his cleanliness, spirit, and willingness to protest the racism of Black students' being issued schoolbooks only after the books had been discarded from the all-white public school in "very poor" condition. The Logan parents, David and Mary, are unfailingly wise, strong, loving, dignified, and resourceful, but Uncle Hammer is both rash in his quick-tempered responses to racism and incredibly generous in his devotion to family.

Taylor's effectiveness at drawing readers into Cassie's perspectives on her family and community is the key to the novel's presentation of Black as normal and beautiful. Eliciting a strong identification between her readers and characters was a goal Taylor had from her teenage years: "I wanted to show happy, loved children about whom other children, both Black and white, could say: 'Hey, I really like them! I feel what they feel.' I wanted to show a Black family united in love and pride, of which the reader would like to be a part" ("Newbery Medal Acceptance" 26). Taylor certainly reaches her goal in *Roll of Thunder, Hear My Cry*, as the Logan family effectively pulls readers into

their lives and creates strong, personal connections. Literary scholar Sarah
Hardstaff suggests that "perhaps Taylor's greatest achievement is in providing
an opportunity for the audience to share, as the 'fifth Logan,' in acts of collaborative witness and collective agency" (240). Through this strong identification,
this African American family is rendered relatable and thus very attractive
to the readers of all races who see themselves in the characters on the page.

Closely allied with Du Bois's goal of making readers see that being Black
is normal and beautiful is his goal of providing familiarity with the history
and achievements of Africans and African Americans. Such information was
conspicuously absent in mainstream history books, leading children to assume
that members of the Negro race had done nothing noteworthy. *The Brownies'
Book* was committed to challenging this dominant perspective through its
storytelling. McNair notes two ways that it does so. First, it would "subvert
dominant ways of seeing and telling," for example, by providing information
about Africa that directly opposed information provided by dominant sources
such as geography textbooks. Second, it would "provide a plethora of information about aspects of American history related to African Americans that is
typically excluded from mainstream discourse" ("Comparative Analysis" 17–18).

Throughout *The Brownies' Book*, Africa's culture and legacy are depicted
positively. African folktales and stories subtitled "An African Story" appear
frequently, and riddles, pictures, and other features spotlighting Africa are also
common. A notable example of the high esteem given to Africa comes from
Jessie Fauset's "The Judge" column in the June 1921 issue. The Judge surprises
his listeners—who stare and even ask if he is joking—by arguing that Africa
is the greatest continent, the one that had provided the most contributions
to human development. He lists seven reasons that support his judgment,
ranging from Africa's being the site of the beginnings of human culture to its
natural resources, art and music, and trade, and even its providing the "world
labor" (via enslavement) that enabled "modern industrial democracy" (168).
Harris notes that "such contentions were in direct contradiction to the image
of Africa found in children's periodicals" (14–15). Likewise, the children con-
versing with the Judge vividly make the point that his argument runs counter
to their school reference books and textbooks: "How on earth can you say that
Africa is the greatest continent? It is stuck way in the back of the Atlas and the
geography . . . devotes only a paragraph to it" (Fauset, "The Judge," June 1921
168). After gaining more complete information, the children conclude that
those writing the histories and geographies must not be colored! In addition
to highlighting a rich African legacy to provide a foundation for Black pride,
The Brownies' Book countered the inaccuracies of historical records from a
white perspective by focusing attention on historically notable achievements
of people of African descent, especially African Americans. These accounts

extended the more "everyday" commendable accomplishments recorded in "Little People of the Month" to include those of greater fame. For example, in the story "The Wishing Game," three children take turns stating which people "from books" they would want to be. The first two name Betsy Ross and Theodore Roosevelt, but the third argues for Paul Laurence Dunbar, Booker T. Washington, Sojourner Truth, and Phillis Wheatley, specifically noting that these famous people shared the three children's racial identity (Browne 7). Biographies of famous achievers such as Harriet Tubman, Benjamin Banneker, Frederick Douglass, Crispus Attucks, and Toussaint L'Ouverture were regular features, as were accounts of less well-known people with notable accomplishments. One such example was Katy Ferguson, a once-enslaved woman who achieved freedom and then started the first Sunday school in New York City. At the end of her biography, the author emphasizes the magazine's goal of providing an array of positive role models of Black achievement: "So now you know the story of a noble colored woman. But she is not the only colored woman to do great deeds for her race. There are many splendid colored men, too. Think of all the wonderful folks you have still to hear about" ("Katy Ferguson" 27).

In *Roll of Thunder, Hear My Cry*, readers also learn much about Black history and achievements neglected or denied by mainstream historical accounts. The novel includes some information about Black civilization and notable deeds. T. J., the Logan children's companion and one of Mary Logan's students, mentions his interest in what she had taught them about Egypt and "them black kings that was rulin' back then" (76), and David Logan, giving the children books by Alexandre Dumas for Christmas, points out that they were written by a Black man, grandson of someone who was enslaved (153). For the most part, however, Taylor focuses more on the everyday history of African Americans, especially the negative parts glossed over or misrepresented in mainstream histories and the strength of those who endured them, than on achievements of famous Black figures.

This different approach to providing familiarity with Black history and achievements makes sense, given differences in the publication eras and target audiences of *The Brownies' Book* and *Roll of Thunder, Hear My Cry*. *The Brownies' Book* was published in a time when blatant racist discrimination was encoded in the law and race-based attacks were common, so that all readers were likely to be all too familiar with the harm racism caused. The hatred engendered in a young Black girl by accounts of horrific white-on-Black violence had inspired Du Bois to create the magazine to provide ample positive accounts to counter the overwhelming societal messages damaging to Black children. Taylor, writing after notable (though insufficient) civil rights movement victories to a much more racially mixed audience, would have a readership including many with limited understanding of the nation's racist legacy. For these readers, the stories of the decades during and after publication of *The Brownies' Book* were history rather than present-day life, and Taylor set out to write a "history not then written in books but one passed from generation to generation" as she had learned it from her father: "a history of great-grandparents and of slavery and of the days following slavery; of those who lived still not free, yet who would not let their spirits be enslaved" that taught her to respect the past, her heritage, and herself (Taylor, author's note).

Throughout the novel, family histories are recounted by the Logan elders and retold by Cassie as she makes connections between previous stories she has heard and new events and information. The interconnections among generations and between past and present are underscored as the family reminisces about Cassie's great-grandfather who repeatedly ran away from slavery, her grandfather's struggles and triumphs in buying the Logan land, and other family milestones. Mr. Morrison shares his own tales about life in the South during Reconstruction and the struggles, almost as difficult as slavery itself, his family faced then. When Mary Logan starts to question the appropriateness of sharing some of the terrifying details, David assures her, "These are things they need to hear, baby. It's their history" (Taylor, *Roll of Thunder* 148). Mary's own commitment to sharing history is evident in her teaching, as she prioritizes her history lessons, scheduling them first each morning while the students are most awake. She teaches about topics such as slavery as her people had experienced it, emphasizing the cruelty of it and the ways in which it supported a "rich economic cycle" in the United States and Europe, while exploiting the labor of Blacks. Her lesson on the day her teaching is observed by Board of Education members is decidedly not based on the board's approved book, and her refusal to teach from the approved book because the information in it was not "true" serves as pretext for firing her (183–84). Despite the significant differences in how they incorporate Black history into their publications, Taylor's historical focus seems closely aligned to Du Bois's, with both using history to bolster Black self-respect and to correct incomplete or erroneous dominant accounts of the past.

Both *The Brownies' Book* and *Roll of Thunder, Hear My Cry* have distinctly activist, anti-racist agendas. As the discussion of the ways in which these publications fulfill Du Bois's first two endeavors shows, a key strategy for both is the subversion of racism through storytelling that demonstrates Black strength, dignity, and joy. Du Bois argued that "all art is propaganda and ever must be" (qtd. in Bishop 25). The magazine he founded was designed to combat racism through the seven uplifting endeavors he articulated, using methods calculated to dissolve the psychological effects of racism and serve as a prophylactic to its internalization. The positive focus of *The Brownies'*

Book implicitly calls out the racist society. Referring to *The Brownies' Book* as "a magazine with a mission" and "a prime example of literature of social action," Bishop asserts, "To build a magazine on the perceived need—among others—for Black children to recognize themselves as normal, to learn about Black history, and to recognize their own potential was to indict both the sociopolitical environment and the instructional and literary texts available to children of the time" (23). Similarly, McNair describes Du Bois as using *The Brownies' Book* as "a political tool to challenge racism and prepare children to resist it while not letting it destroy their lives" ("Comparative Analysis" 19). The greatest form of social activism in *The Brownies' Book* is its often implicit yet powerful rebuttal of racist narratives.

However, *The Brownies' Book*, like *Roll of Thunder, Hear My Cry*, also more directly exposes the violence of racism and educates readers in the manifold harms it causes. Despite *The Brownies' Book*'s focus on positive affirmations of Black heritage, culture, and people and its stated purpose to be "a thing of Joy and Beauty, dealing in Happiness, Laughter and Emulation" (286), Du Bois acknowledged the inadvisability of ignoring the negative aspects of Black children's "peculiar situation" (285). Thus, although the magazine he coedited highlighted the beauty and strength of the African American people, providing positive portrayals on the majority of its pages, it also included truthful accounts of the negative situations they faced because of racism and calls to work against it. The magazine recognized racism more directly, too, in letters from children and parents describing bigotry aimed at African American youth and in accounts of lynchings and race riots in Du Bois's news column, "As the Crow Flies." It directly addressed the need for change as well as optimism that the change will be effected—for example, in Fauset's column in the January 1920 issue when the Judge tells the children, "The Law is old and musty and needs sadly to be changed. In time the children will change it" ("The Judge" 12). Additionally, *The Brownies' Book* recognized public, collective action to work for that change, for example in showing, in the same issue, a picture of children participating in the "Silent Protest" in New York City.

In *Roll of Thunder, Hear My Cry*, the implicit anti-racist strategy of providing attractive stories of African American people that counter racist narratives is balanced by numerous accounts that explicitly reveal the ugliness of racism and its effects on people. On page after page, the novel educates child readers in how racism functions in society to protect white interests in economic, educational, legal, and psychological realms, doing great damage to African Americans in the process. Mary Logan explains economic and legal exploitation, from the slave trade to unfair labor laws and practices of sharecropping. In doing so, she highlights the many material advantages that accrue to the dominant society from the exploitation of Blacks, supported by the law. Education, perhaps the most directly relevant material cost of racism for youth, clearly affects the Logan children, who experience the very unequal provisions made for Black students compared to white students. The school for Black children, funded largely by Black churches though governed by a white school board, features an abbreviated school year because of the economic necessity of sharecropping child labor, meager facilities and supplies, and only seven teachers for 320 students. The lack of buses means some students walk up to seven hours round-trip. In contrast, the county-funded white school meets for a full academic year in adequate facilities with sports fields and buses. Overt legal discrimination is seen in *Roll of Thunder*: when a witness to three men being doused with kerosene and burned takes her account to the sheriff, she is flatly dismissed as a liar. At the near-lynching in the novel's climax, the sheriff takes his cues from the wealthy white plantation owner, whose only concern is that any lynching take place off *his* property; clearly, the lawman cannot be counted on to uphold the law, to protect African American citizens from violence, or to provide justice for victims. In these and countless other examples, the external effects of racism are laid bare for readers.

The psychological costs of racism are even more vividly delineated. The humiliation of racial discrimination is made painfully personal for empathizing readers when, on her first visit to a neighboring town, Cassie is forced to realize the inferior status the dominant white society assigns her. Politely reminding a shopkeeper filling the order of a newly arrived white girl that her own party had been waiting for an hour, she is commanded to get her "little black self back over there and wait some more" and then called a derogatory racial slur before being evicted from the store (Taylor, *Roll of Thunder* 111). Shortly after, she accidentally bumps into a white girl and is forced to apologize and ordered off the sidewalk. When Cassie resists complying, the girl's father shoves her sprawling onto the road and forces her Big Ma to coerce her into apologizing again to "Miz" Lillian Jean. Cassie describes this experience as the cruelest day of her life.

As *Roll of Thunder, Hear My Cry* invites readers into the lives of the protagonists, leading empathizing readers to deeper understanding of racism, it promotes resistance to racism as well. Kelly McDowell notes that as Mary Logan "unveils the power structure for her children, showing them exactly what power is capable of, who wields it, and who is victimized by it," she "shows them how agency is possible" (218). The novel models mental challenges to racist assumptions through Cassie's refusal to comprehend the customary prioritization of whites and by Little Man's quiet insistence that change in the status quo is needed. After the white children's school bus driver has once again deliberately splashed mud on Little Man, Big Ma comforts him with the assurance that when it stops raining, he will not keep getting muddy. He immediately cuts to the real issue: "Ifn that ole bus driver would slow down, I wouldn't get muddy! . . . Or ifn we had a bus like theirs" (Taylor, *Roll of Thunder* 45). The novel also exemplifies strategies for activism, as the Logans are not presented as victims but as active agents of resistance. Mary Logan models overt, sacrificial opposition to racist oppression, risking her family's precarious financial security to organize a three-month boycott of the Wallaces' store, although she acknowledges from the start that the boycott will neither destroy the Wallaces nor provide real justice: "it'll hurt them and we'll have done something," she claims (151). Similarly, David Logan agrees that the Logans' efforts will not be enough to defeat determined white efforts to crush the boycott but insists on trying in the hopes that their children, witnessing the events, will build on their efforts and find greater success (164–65).

The novel's most successful strategies of resistance are subversive, covert ones that mirror tactics literary scholar Mary Turner Harper, in her analysis of the "rich oral tradition" that infuses Taylor's novels, attributes to African American folktales whose heroes, "usually smaller and certainly less powerful, eventually triumph over their stronger and more powerful foes through sheer cunning and wit" (75). David Logan chooses his battles, suppressing his desire for vengeance when the cost would outweigh the benefits. He validates Cassie's need to take action to retain her self-respect after her encounter with Lillian Jean, while cautioning her to plan carefully with an eye to costs and consequences. Cassie's trickster vengeance is highly satisfying. Most decisively, at the novel's climax, David Logan starts a fire that burns a quarter of his own cotton crop, making the arson appear an accidental result of a lightning storm, to divert the attention of whites from a lynching into an ironically mixed-race collective action to fight the fire and preserve everyone's land. Perhaps most subversively of all, the Logans resist racism and challenge the dominant power system around them by their "quiet strength" as they "force a certain respect from the white people around them" (Smith 269). In "A Chronicle of Family Honor: Balancing Rage and Triumph in the Novels of Mildred D. Taylor," Karen Patricia Smith asserts, "The Logan elders possess an 'elegance of approach,' a self-confidence of which no white person has been able to rob them. Even when forced to accede to . . . all of the elements attendant to racist policy and custom, somehow the Logans still maintain their dignity and their stature" (269). This subtle resistance to racism and its effects is very much in line with Du Bois's agenda and with *The Brownies' Book*'s continuous reminders of Black attractiveness and achievement.

In addition to promoting race pride and uplift and combating racism, both *The Brownies' Book* and *Roll of Thunder, Hear My Cry* model core values for young readers, with significant overlap in these exemplary values. *The Brownies' Book*, Violet J. Harris argues, aimed to mold a "refined colored youngster"

(6) with its objectives proposing "a model of social action or behavior that emphasized achievement, excellence, honor, duty, pride, industriousness, optimism, and tolerance" (5). One of the themes Harris notes in *The Brownies' Book* is "the inculcation of specific values such as kindness, truthfulness, egalitarianism, and love" (32). These character traits and values were modeled in the magazine's fictional stories, its "true story" biographies of famous people, and its "Little People of the Month" features. Similarly, in an essay in *The All-White World of Children's Books and African American Children's Literature*, scholar Donnarae MacCann cites a number of "inner qualities such as self-respect, generosity, common sense, inner direction all presented to the reader through plot, not platitude" as important survival strategies to counteract the racist oppression the Logan family faced in *Roll of Thunder, Hear My Cry* (120). Industriousness, duty, honor, loyalty, and love are other traits demonstrated consistently by the Logans that could be added to MacCann's list.

Additionally, both *The Brownies' Book* and Taylor's novel promote education and reading as intrinsically valuable and a means for advancement. McNair notes that "The importance of literacy and reading was stressed in many ways throughout *The Brownies' Book*" ("Comparative Analysis" 13). The Judge listed reading first among the list of activities advocated to develop children's "characters, minds, and bodies," recommending Pritchard and Ovington's *The Upward Path* for stories and poems by and about Blacks (Harris 13). The magazine also provided advertisements for books to help children start their own libraries (McNair, "Comparative Analysis" 14). The potential of education is also indicated in a letter from Mrs. C. M. Johnson published in "The Grown-Ups' Corner" in January 1920. Writing to ask how to instill "race love and race pride" in her son, bullied as the only colored child in his summer hometown, Mrs. Johnson quotes her son to provide a partial answer to her query: "'Mother, the only way to fight these white people is to get an education and fight them with knowledge'" (25). Likewise, the importance of reading is seen in *Roll of Thunder, Hear My Cry* when the students receive the news that they will receive schoolbooks, apparently for the first time, with great excitement. The Logan children are so delighted to receive a book each for Christmas that none of their other presents compared; even Little Man, "who treasured clothes above all else, carefully laid his new pants and sweater aside" to make a cover to protect his new book and spent the day "looking at the bright, shining pictures of faraway places, turning each page as if it were gold" (Taylor, *Roll of Thunder* 153–54). Education in general is shown to be valued, as some students are willing to walk three and a half hours each way to get to and from school. When Little Man complains about the effects of racism, Big Ma provides him with the same solution Mrs. Johnson's son from

The Brownies' Book endorsed: "'You jus' keep on studyin' and get yo'self a good education and you'll be all right'" (45).

The values discussed above are commonly advocated for children of all races, but *The Brownies' Book* and *Roll of Thunder, Hear My Cry* also promote collaborative agency, which is particularly valued in the Black community. In the January 1920 column "The Judge," the Judge advises a girl to ask herself, when deciding whether to buy a hat, what "is best for me, for mother, for the family, for my people, for the world?" This sets even what might seem a minor, personal choice into a communal context while also encouraging critical thinking by asking her, "Does the choice of this hat represent your freedom of thoughtful taste, or your slavery to what the flambuoyant [sic] Kitty does or to what rich white folk wear?" (Fauset, "The Judge" 13). As Dianne Johnson notes, the Judge "makes it unremittingly clear that each and every individual is responsible to himself or herself, the family, the community, the world. This sense of interconnectedness is an abiding concern of *The Brownies' Book* and of subsequent African American children's literature" (29). We see the same sense of communal responsibility throughout *Roll of Thunder, Hear My Cry* in the Logan siblings' determination to stick together, even when doing so might result in a whipping; in Mary Logan's concern for her students and compassion for a Black man burned by racist white men; and in the effort she and David put into organizing and supporting the boycott of the store belonging to the men behind the burning. We see it in Uncle Hammer's willingness to sell his prized car to ensure that the family retains its land and his brother's family their home, in Mr. Morrison's insistence on working without pay when the Logans face financial trouble, and in David Logan's sacrificial burning of his own crops to prevent the lynching of a neighbor boy. In her study of agency in the novel informed by critical corpus linguistics, Hardstaff notes the frequency of collective subjects and argues that "agency in *Roll of Thunder* is often exercised in partnership. . . . the emphasis is on material action, suggesting the importance of the family and community working together, and perhaps a rejection of individualistic approaches to countering social injustice" (238). This solidarity is, perhaps, the linchpin of *The Brownies' Book* and *Roll of Thunder, Hear My Cry*'s efforts to foster self-respect, race pride, and social action.

Roll of Thunder, Hear My Cry shows a robust continuation of the tradition of African American children's literature first articulated regarding *The Brownies' Book*. As Bishop notes, the historical context of African American children's literature has made this literature "purposeful, intended to serve functions that have not been expected of the larger body of American children's literature" (xii). Central features, as demonstrated above, include building up Black children by centering them on the page, showing them the beauty and ability of people like them, acknowledging their proud heritage despite dominant stories to the contrary, and teaching useful values to help them survive and thrive in a racist society.

Just as it extends the endeavors of *The Brownies' Book*, *Roll of Thunder, Hear My Cry* inspires later children's and young adult literature. Notable twenty-first-century writers, including Jacqueline Woodson and Angie Thomas, saw reflections of their own lives in Taylor's novel and were inspired by it. "I know that I am a writer because Ms. Taylor wrote this book and I saw myself inside the pages of it, the way so many thousands of readers have since seen themselves in the pages. Mildred D. Taylor pointed me toward my own stories. Cassie Logan gave me the strength to write them," writes Woodson in her introduction to the fortieth anniversary edition of *Roll of Thunder, Hear My Cry*. Author of the best-selling, award-winning *The Hate U Give*, Angie Thomas calls *Roll of Thunder, Hear My Cry* her "favorite book of all time" and notes, "when I found out that not only was it about a black girl, but the author herself is a black woman . . . I was in love!" (qtd. in Philyaw). By articulating the distinctive ideologies that undergird African American children's literature a century ago, Du Bois and Fauset laid the foundation for these authors as they continue to add to this body of work.

Works Cited

Bishop, Rudine Sims. *Free within Ourselves: The Development of African American Children's Literature*. Greenwood P, 2007.

Browne, Annette. "The Wishing Game." *The Brownies' Book*, vol. 1, no. 1, Jan. 1920, p. 7.

"The Coretta Scott King Book Awards for Authors and Illustrators." American Library Association, 19 Jan. 2009, www.ala.org/rt/emiert/cskbookawards/slction.

Culbertson, Annie Virginia. "The Origin of White Folks." *The Brownies' Book*, vol. 1, no. 1, Jan. 1920, p. 7.

Du Bois, W. E. B. "The True Brownies." *The Crisis*, vol. 18, no. 6, Oct. 1919, pp. 285–86, library.brown.edu/pdfs/1295989365421875.pdf.

Fauset, Jessie. "Dedication." *The Brownies' Book*, vol. 1, no. 1, Jan. 1930, p. 32.

Fauset, Jessie. "The Judge." *The Brownies' Book*, vol. 1, no. 1, Jan. 1920, pp. 12–13.

Fauset, Jessie. "The Judge." *The Brownies' Book*, vol. 2, no. 6, June 1921, p. 168.

Gordon, Dexter B. "Humor in African American Discourse: Speaking of Oppression." *Journal of Black Studies*, vol. 29, no. 2, 1998, pp. 254–76.

Hardstaff, Sarah. "'Papa Said That One Day I Would Understand': Examining Child Agency and Character Development in *Roll of Thunder, Hear My Cry* Using Critical Corpus Linguistics." *Children's Literature in Education*, vol. 46, no. 3, Sept. 2015, pp. 226–41.

Harper, Mary Turner. "Merger and Metamorphosis in the Fiction of Mildred D. Taylor." *Children's Literature Association Quarterly*, vol. 13, no. 2, Summer 1988, pp. 75–80.

Harris, Violet J. *The Brownies' Book: Challenge to the Selective Tradition in Children's Literature*. ERIC, 1984, eric.ed.gov/?id=ED284167.

Johnson, C. M. "The Grown-Ups' Corner." *The Brownies' Book*, vol. 1, no. 1, Jan. 1920, p. 25.

Johnson, Dianne. *Telling Tales: The Pedagogy and Promise of African American Literature for Youth*. Greenwood P, 1990.

"Katy Ferguson." *The Brownies' Book*, vol. 1, no. 1, Jan. 1920, p. 27.

Kilpatrick, A. T. "Gyp: A Fairy Story." *The Brownies' Book*, vol. 1, no. 1, Jan. 1920, p. 31.

"Little People of the Month." *The Brownies' Book*, vol. 1, no. 2, Feb. 1920, pp. 58–59.

"Little People of the Month." *The Brownies' Book*, vol. 2, no. 4, Apr. 1921, pp. 124–26.

MacCann, Donnarae. "The Family Chronicles of Mildred D. Taylor and Mary E. Mebane." *The All-White World of Children's Books and African American Children's Literature*, edited by Osayimwense Osa, Africa World P, 1995, pp. 115–29.

Martin, Alice. "The Jury." *The Brownies' Book*, vol. 1, no. 6, June 1920, p. 178.

McDowell, Kelly. "*Roll of Thunder, Hear My Cry*: A Culturally Specific, Subversive Concept of Child Agency." *Children's Literature in Education*, vol. 33, no. 3, Sept. 2002, pp. 213–25.

McNair, Jonda C. "A Comparative Analysis of *The Brownies' Book* and Contemporary African American Children's Literature Written by Patricia C. McKissack." *Embracing, Evaluating, and Examining African American Children's and Young Adult Literature*, edited by Wanda M. Brooks and McNair, Scarecrow P, 2008, pp. 3–29.

McNair, Jonda C. "'I May Be Crackin', but Um Fackin'": Racial Humor in *The Watsons Go to Birmingham—1963*." *Children's Literature in Education*, vol. 39, no. 3, Sept. 2008, pp. 201–12. *EBSCOhost*, doi:10.1007/s10583-007-9049-1.

Philyaw, Deesha. "Visible: Women Writers of Color: Angie Thomas." *The Rumpus*, 19 Apr. 2017, therumpus.net/2017/04/visible-women-writers-of-color-angie-thomas/.

Smith, Karen Patricia. "A Chronicle of Family Honor: Balancing Rage and Triumph in the Novels of Mildred D. Taylor." *African-American Voices in Young Adult Literature: Tradition, Transition, Transformation*, edited by Smith, Scarecrow P, 1994, pp. 247–76.

Taylor, Mildred D. Author's note. *Roll of Thunder, Hear My Cry*, Dial Books, 1976.

Taylor, Mildred D. "Newbery Medal Acceptance." *Newbery and Caldecott Medal Books, 1976–1985*, edited by Lee Kingman, Horn Book, 1986, pp. 21–30.

Taylor, Mildred D. *Roll of Thunder, Hear My Cry*. Dial Books, 1976.

Woodson, Jacqueline. Introduction. *Roll of Thunder, Hear My Cry*, by Mildred D. Taylor, Kindle ed., Puffin Books, 2016.

The Brownies' Book

DECEMBER, 1921

This is the last Brownies' Book.
For twenty-four months we have
brought Joy and Knowledge to
four thousand Brownies stretched
from Oregon to Florida. But
there are two million Brownies
in the United States, and unless
we got at least one in every
hundred to read our pages and
help pay printing, we knew we
must at last cease to be. And
now the month has come to say
goodbye. We are sorry---much
sorrier than any of you, for it
has all been such fun. After
all---who knows---perhaps we
shall meet again.

$1.50 A YEAR   15cts. A COPY

STATEMENT OF THE OWNERSHIP, MANAGEMENT,
CIRCULATION, ETC., REQUIRED BY THE ACT
OF CONGRESS OF AUGUST 24, 1912.

of **The Brownies' Book**, published monthly at New York,
N. Y., for October 1, 1921.
State of New York }
County of New York } ss.

Before me, a notary in and for the State and county aforesaid, personally appeared Augustus Granville Dill, who, having
been duly sworn according to law, deposes and says that
he is the Business Manager of THE BROWNIES' BOOK and
that the following is, to the best of his knowledge and belief,
a true statement of the ownership, management (and if a
daily paper, the circulation), etc., of the aforesaid publication for the date shown in the above caption, required by
the Act of Congress of August 24, 1912, embodied in section 443, Postal Laws and Regulations, printed on the re-
verse of this form, to wit:

1. That the names and addresses of the publisher, editor,
managing editor, and business managers are:
Publisher—DuBois and Dill, Publishers,
2 West 13th St., New York, N. Y.
Editor—W. E. Burghardt DuBois,
2 West 13th St., New York, N. Y.
Managing Editor—Jessie Redmon Fauset,
2 West 13th St., New York, N. Y.
Business Manager—Augustus Granville Dill,
2 West 13th St., New York, N. Y.

2. That the owners are:
DuBois and Dill, Publishers,
2 West 13th St., New York, N. Y.
W. E. Burghardt DuBois,
2 West 13th St., New York, N. Y.
Augustus Granville Dill,
2 West 13th St., New York, N. Y.

3. That the known bondholders, mortgagees and other
security holders holding or owning 1 per cent or more of
total amount of bonds, mortgages, or other securities are:
NONE.

AUGUSTUS GRANVILLE DILL,

Sworn to and subscribed before me this 1st day of October,
1921.

FRANK M. TURNER,

Notary Public Queens Co., No. 754.
Certificate filed in New York County No. 164, New York
Reg. No. 2122. Term expires Mar. 30, 1922.

THE BROWNIES' BOOK

Published Monthly and Copyrighted by DuBois and Dill, Publishers, at 2 West 13th Street, New York, N. Y. Conducted by W. E. Burghardt DuBois; Jessie Redmon Fauset, Managing Editor; Augustus Granville Dill, Business Manager

VOL. 2. No. 12.   DECEMBER, 1921   WHOLE No 24

CONTENTS

FIFTEEN CENTS A COPY; ONE DOLLAR AND A HALF A YEAR
FOREIGN SUBSCRIPTIONS TWENTY-FIVE CENTS EXTRA

RENEWALS: The date of expiration of each subscription is printed on the wrapper. When the subscription is due, a yellow renewal blank is enclosed.

CHANGE OF ADDRESS: The address of a subscriber can be changed as often as desired. In ordering a change of address, both the old and the new address must be given. Two weeks' notice is required.

MANUSCRIPTS and drawings relating to colored children are desired. They must be accompanied by return postage. If found unavailable they will be returned.

Entered as second class matter January 20, 1920, at the Post Office at New York, N. Y., under the Act of March 3, 1879.

"Tommie and the Flower Fairies" a BROWNIES' BOOK Play Given by School Children at Birmingham, Ala.

The Brownies' Book

Vol. 2—No. 12   DECEMBER, 1921   Whole No. 24

THE LAND BEHIND THE SUN

YOLANDE DU BOIS

OU didn't know that there was such a place did you? No, neither did Madalen, until she went there. Madalen looked like a little Japanese girl, with a dimpled face, golden-brown in color, and soft jet-black hair. Her pretty almond-shaped eyes usually sparkled and danced with mischief. In fact, one afternoon these black eyes held too much mischief for her own good, and after she had succeeded in breaking two saucers, teased the white kitten, eaten the sugar on the sideboard and tangled her grandmother's knitting, her mother decided to put her to bed. I forgot to tell you that Madalen was a very little girl.

"But, Mamma," she protested, "I'm not sleepy, not a bit," and she opened her eyes very widely indeed.

"You've been a very naughty little girl, and if you don't behave, the Brownies will come and carry you away."

"Are the Brownies bad fairies?"

"Well," replied her mother, "they are little brown elves who catch naughty little boys and girls and carry them away until they promise to be good."

"Oh-oh," gasped Madalen, "and where do they take them?"

"Oh, somewhere down behind the sun," laughed the mother. "Now, Madalen, you really must close your eyes and go to sleep."

"Yes, Mamma," said the little girl, "but I wanna know—is it dark behind the sun?"

"Um-m, perhaps. I've never been there," and her mother closed the nursery door hastily. For quite a while Madalen lay perfectly still, with one chubby brown finger in her mouth.

"I wish"—she said aloud after a few moments, "I wish I could peek behind the sun, just to see what it is like."

"Do you really want to see behind the sun?" piped a small sweet voice.

"Oh," squealed Madalen, "who was that?"

"Look behind you," continued the voice. The words were no more than spoken when Madalen whirled around and there, on her very own bed-post, sat the prettiest little figure you ever saw. It looked like a doll, about eight inches high, but Madalen had never seen a doll who could laugh and swing her feet as this one did. Moreover, this minute figure was entirely gold. Her little hands and face were a dull golden-brown, her eyes were like a topaz, her filmy draperies seemed to shimmer with sunlight, and her hair shone like pure gold spun into threads. As for her wings, have you ever seen a bubble in the sunlight? Well, that's what her wings were like. When Madalen could recover from her astonishment she asked:

"Who are you, and where did you come from?"

"From behind the sun," gaily replied the little figure. "I'm one of the ladies-in-waiting, and my name is Topaz."

"Oh," said Madalen, "do you really live behind the sun—what is it like back there?"

"It's a very beautiful land," said the little creature soberly. "Would you like to visit it for a little while?"

"Yes," hesitated the child, "but how shall I get there? Besides, Mamma would spank me for running away."

"Just hold on to my hand tight and shut your eyes—when I say, 'Open', then you'll be there; and as for your mother, she'll never miss you from your crib."

Madalen obediently shut her eyes and clasped the hand of the tiny fairy. For a second she heard a rushing noise, and some voice, only much louder, bade her open her eyes. Looking around, she was astonished to see that Topaz was now the same size as herself.

"Oh," she cried, "you've grown up."

"No," laughed the fairy, "you've grown down."

"Do you mean," demanded the little girl, "that I'm as small as you were?"

"Yes indeed—you had to be to get behind the sun. Now take my hand and come along if you want to see the court of the Queen."

Madalen placed her hand in the fairy's and to her consternation, they rose in the air.

However, as she seemed to float along quite easily and without any effort, she soon gathered up courage to look about her. First of all, she noticed that although the sky above her was a deep blue in color, there was no sun. She couldn't tell where the light came from, but everything seemed enveloped in a silvery glare as though a full moon were shining over them. The next strange thing that she noticed was that the ground was blue; they were floating swiftly over hills and valleys, and the smooth velvety grass, the swaying trees and dainty cottages—all were delightful shades of blue.

"Why is everything blue?" she inquired of her guide, "and where's the sun?"

"Silly!" exclaimed Topaz with a smile, "you're behind it, so naturally you can't see it, and the back of the sun always gives a silver light. Everything is blue because it's our Queen's favorite color. Her name is Sapphire, and all her ladies-in-waiting are called after precious stones."

Madalen replied to this explanation with a nod because she was so busy looking she just couldn't speak. They were approaching what looked like a crystal city. As they drew near, Madalen could see that each little house was a single sapphire, carved into delicate tunnels and pergolas. The little city spread out, and in the very center stood the palace. It was an immense structure, entirely of blue stones set in silver. At the gate of the city they dropped back to earth, and Topaz touched a tiny bell on the lacy silver gate before them. Almost immediately the gate flew open and they beheld a little brown man dressed in a soldier's suit of blue velvet trimmed with silver.

"Greetings—Lady of the Topaz," he said, bowing low before the golden fairy.

"Gatekeeper, this is Lady Madalen from the Land in Front of the Sun."

At this the quaint little man bowed so low that he nearly tumbled on his nose, and the two girls were obliged to hurry on to keep from laughing and hurting his feelings. That never would have done, you know—it's awfully unkind to hurt people's feelings.

As they passed through the winding streets of the little city, Madalen noticed the cheerful faces of the inhabitants, which were all different shades of brown.

"Why!" she exclaimed, "everybody's brown."

"Yes," smiled Topaz, "didn't you know we are the Brownies—we are all brown, even our Queen."

"Why are the ladies-in-waiting named after stones?" inquired the little visitor.

"Because each one looks after the children born in the month her stone represents. What month were you born in?"

"October," replied Madalen.

"Oh," cried the fairy, "that's Opal's month. She is the most beautiful of us, except the Queen—her wings and her dresses are all changeable just like the Opal. Well, here we are. Now, Madalen, follow me and do exactly as I do."

Madalen obediently followed Topaz, gazing meanwhile with awestruck eyes at the structure which they were entering. Her eyes were dazzled by the light from the innumerable blue stones. Crossing the moat over a high arched bridge, Topaz paused and raised her arms. Madalen did likewise and the gate swung open. They ascended a wide, blue carpeted stairway, with a vast reception room also carpeted and hung with blue. At the far ends Madalen could see two blue thrones cut out of single sapphires.

"This," explained the fairy, "is the throne room. It is nearly time for the Queen to receive, so we'll wait."

She had hardly spoken when the vast doors on each side swung open and the ladies-in-waiting appeared. It would be impossible to describe them all, but they were very beautiful. There was the Amethyst in her robe of royal purple, the Ruby in rich red, the Turquoise in delicate blue, and the Opal, resplendent with her rainbow wings and draperies and flaming hair. Looking at the others, Madalen noticed them eagerly watching the throne, so she gazed also. Suddenly it became enveloped in a puff of smoke and as this cleared away she saw the Queen on the throne. When all the ladies had courtesied, Madalen stood before her.

"Lady Madalen," said a voice like a silver bell, "greetings and welcome, my dear."

The Queen's cordiality and beauty soon quieted the child's fears. She looked like a mere girl, about Madalen's color, wrapped in sheer blue chiffon. Around her plump brown neck was a necklace of blue. Even her sandals were blue and the blackness of her hair seemed to reflect blue lights.

Madalen watched the court proceedings with interest and afterward the Queen turned to her and inquired how she liked their land.

"Oh," cried the visitor, "I think it's just wonderful—but I thought you punished naughty children here."

"No," replied the Queen, "but sometimes we bring them here to show them how nice it is to be good."

"Oh, I see," replied Madalen, "and what *does* become of the bad ones?

"Well, if they insist on being naughty, the Wicked Witch of Bogland gets them."

At this juncture the Queen looked very sad.

"Sometimes," she continued, "we can buy them back as the Witch is very fond of gold and silver, and we have plenty of that because whenever anyone in your world does a kind act a piece of gold drops into our treasury."

The Queen went on to tell how the Wicked Witch of Bogland had captured the young King. He was so handsome that she refused money for him but determined to marry him herself. Her eyes filled with tears as she murmured,

"We've tried lots of earth-children but they've all failed and you're too small."

"Well," offered the little girl, "if you tell me what to do I'll try to help you."

Then the Queen sent for Opal and charged her to direct Madalen on her way. As they went out of the Palace, Opal said:

"I know you don't know me but I've often sung you to sleep."

Soon they came to a hedge of thorns and Opal placed a little blue cap on Madalen's head and bade her good-bye, saying:

"Good luck, little one, I would come also but the fairies of this country may not enter Bogland."

Then she clapped her hands and Madalen found herself in a dark wood. Seeing a dim light in the distance, she followed it and soon found a tiny cabin. By this time she was awfully scared but she managed to knock on the door. A hump-backed dwarf opened it and motioned her to enter and turning to the other figure in the room, he squeaked:

"A tasty morsel, eh, mother?"

Looking past the dwarf, the girl saw the Witch, a bent figure in black with a white distorted face and hard gray eyes.

"Hee-hee," she cackled, "a very fine supper, my son; here, fetch me some water to boil her in."

Madalen looked around her in terror. There was no way of escape, she would be cooked alive!

The elf returned and setting down the pail, motioned her to get in it. As she hesitated, the Witch started toward her in a rage and in a panic of fear the child grasped the pail and flung the water over her.

"Oh, oh, oh," screamed the Witch, "Just look what you've done. I'm melting! Didn't you know any better than to wet me?"

Sure enough she was melting before their eyes. The dwarf fled into the darkness as she sank into a shapeless mass. Almost immediately bells began to ring everywhere and people of all shapes and sizes appeared to thank Madalen for their rescue. After a moment of astonishment she recovered herself enough to ask for the unfortunate "King of the Brownies". After a long search they found him hidden away in a dark garret, weak with hunger. Curtsying, Madalen exclaimed joyously:

"The Witch is dead, your Majesty."

Of course his surprise and joy knew no bounds. He was a handsome little king in spite of his rags, with a clear, kind eye. Bidding the others follow, they hurried through the wood to the thorny hedge where the King clapped three times and they were on the other side. When they reached the court, everyone went positively wild with joy and gratitude and determined to give a magnificent ball in honor of Madalen; but when they went to look for her she wasn't there at all!

And far away, in the land of the sun, Madalen was just waking up.

That night at supper her father looked at her strangely, saying:

"I never noticed that little star-shaped mark on your forehead before, daughter."

"No, replied Madalen, "that's where the Queen of the Brownies kissed me."

"What!" cried her astonished parents, "you've been dreaming again."

"Perhaps," said the child.

But she knew quite well it wasn't a dream and we knew it too, but we aren't telling all we know.

UP TO THE CRATER OF AN OLD VOLCANO

LANGSTON HUGHES

EAR Toluca, Mexico, is an old volcano, Xinantecatl. The fires which once burned within its bosom have long ago gone out and now, in the deep crater that in past centuries held boiling lava and red hot ashes, two calm blue lakes sparkle like dainty jewels in a rough setting. No one knows when the last eruption of this volcano took place but some say that it was long before the time of Christ, and when the Aztec Indians came down from the North to found their powerful empire, Xinantecatl, for so they called it, had long been sleeping. Now, like a dead giant at rest, it is still great and majestic. Rising above the puny cities and little low hills that cluster about its base, it is as some nature king rising above a subject people. The ancient Indians thought it a god and climbed its steep sides carrying gold and jewels and precious gifts on their backs as an offering to the mountain deity. Even today the rural Indians say that when shots are fired in the crater or stones thrown into the blue lakes, the mountain becomes angry and calls the clouds to hide its peaks and send rain down upon its disturbers. We in Toluca, however, are not afraid of Xinantecatl. It is like a well known friend to us and one whom we see every day. On clear mornings its peaks are sharp and distinct in the blue sky; at evening the whole mountain makes a great black silhouette against the twilight colors.

When the boys of the Instituto, Toluca's high school, began to plan a two-day walking trip to the crater, and invited me to go with them, I accepted eagerly. They, with the customary Mexican politeness, put my name first on the list of those who were to go and several of the students went with me to aid in choosing the proper kind of "trumpeate", a sort of bag for carrying food. It is woven from marsh grass and is light of weight. They also saw that I bought a wide Mexican hat, as protection from the sun, and told me all the things that I would need to carry. First, plenty of lunch; then, two warm blankets because we were to sleep in the open mountains; my camera for pictures; a bottle for water; a small amount of cognac or some other liquor in case of mountain sickness in the high altitude; and a pistol. "But above all," they said, "take onions!" Those who had been up to the volcano before claimed that they were the very best things to smell if one began to feel ill in the thin air near the summit. I thought to myself that if I should get sick, the scent of onions would only make me worse. Nevertheless I took them and when the time arrived for their use I found my mind completely changed about their smell.

It was a beautiful sunny morning when we left Toluca. From the platform of the small station, where we were to board the seven o'clock train for Calimaya, we could see the white, sparkling snow peaks of the volcano and they seemed very high and far away. There were forty of us going on the trip and, before leaving time, the first coach of the tiny train was completely filled with Instituto boys. The aisle of the car was one jumble of blanket rolls and fat "trumpeates" of food, and the windows were crowded with faces—mostly brown faces of laughing young fellows, all talking at once and watching the late comers hurrying down the platform. These dark faced, friendly school boys were about like other dark skinned boys of my own race whom I had known in the United States. They made me remember a hike that the colored Y. M. C. A. fellows, in Chicago, took out to the sand dunes one summer. There the car windows were crowded with dark faces, too, and everybody talked at once. The only difference was that in Chicago they were speaking English and when a late member of the party reached the platform, every one cried out, "Hurry up!" while here, when Rudolfo, the tardy, came running through the gates, every one in the window shouted, "Apurese!" which means the same in Spanish.

The little train went click, click, click, down the pretty valley. We passed several small villages: Metepec, with its great church large

enough to hold its whole population; San Francisco, a collection of small huts, and a white temple; M e xicaltzingo, where the country bull-fights are held; and then Calimaya, where the road to the v o l c ano begins.

We found Calimaya a small, clean town w i t h c o b blestone streets and a

strong, sturdy l i t t l e beasts, they did not seem to m i n d. They started off down the road with a trot, the two drivers a n d the boy run-ning behind s h o u t ing, "Burro! Burro!" to make them go fast-er. The mem-bers of the hiking party, freed of their luggage, had n o t h ing to pack now ex-cept the can-

stream of water running down the center of each one, where the cows and long horned oxen stopped to drink.

We piled our blankets and bags in one corner of its arched "Portales" to wait while two of the boys went for the guide and the burros— patient little beasts of burden—who were to carry our things. After a long while the bur-ros came. There had been some disagreemen+ in regard to the money to be paid, so we learned, the guide having set a price and then suddenly changing his mind, saying that he could not risk his animals in the cold mountain air for such a small sum. But finally an agreement was reached and we had three burros, a boy and two men to drive them, and a guide—all for a price that would amount to but five Amer-

ican dollars, and this for a two-day trip!

W h e n the w o r d "Vama-nos" was given, the three small animals w e r e a l m o st hidden u n d e r their loads of blankets and lunch-bags, but b e i n g

teens or water bottles and their guns. Very few having pistols, there was an unusual variety of fire-arms in sight, from a modern rifle to ancient carbines. The reason for so many shooting ma-chines was that we might meet bandits on the road, and, though it was only a *might*, every one should be prepared. During the revolu-tions and until a year or so ago the hills were full of robbers, who, not content with taking travelers' money, would ofttimes take their clothes, even to their shoes, leaving the robbed ones to get home as best they could. Now, though such robberies are infrequent, no one goes far into the country unarmed. The boys of the Instituto, going through the quaint streets of Calimaya, looked like a small militia.

The r o a d leading to the foothills w a s quite bare of trees. High in a cloudless sky, the sun b e a t down upon our heads without pity, while the d u s t rose in clouds from un-der our feet.

On either side the road was lined with maguey and cactus plants which served as a sort of fence around the fields, where lazy, slow moving oxen were pulling wooden plows yoked to their horns, and wide-hatted peons pricked them languidly with sharp-pointed sticks. After about an hour's walking we passed Zaragoza, a small village which, like all Mexican villages, had its tall old church towering sad and beautiful above the miserable little huts. By this time all our water bottles were empty and our throats were dry. The guide promised us that we should come to a river soon and when we finally reached its friendly banks, after what seemed like an eternity of tramping in dust and sun, we lay on our stomachs like dogs and drank the cool clear water that came rippling down from the hills.

Soon the road began to ascend and we found ourselves climbing a slope covered with little pine trees. Before us, when we reached the summit, we saw only pine clad hills and then more hills, hiding the volcano from us. Looking back, we saw the wide valley of Toluca below, dotted with red roofed villages and the white towers and domes of old, old churches. At its opposite side we saw the mountains rising like a wall about the valley, shutting it in from the rest of the world and protecting it with their grey and purple strength.

The road now led upward, and it was not easy climbing through the forest of stunted trees with the sun like a hot ball overhead. About one o'clock, when everybody was aching and tired, the guide showed us a little cañon at one side of the road and said that here was the last water to be found before reaching the crater, the next morning; so he advised us to stop for lunch and to fill our water bottles. The burros were unloaded and everyone searched in the pile of "trumpeates" for his lunch-bag. As each woven sack looked just about like another, there was much opening and exchanging and inspecting before each one had his own. Then we scattered about the slope and prepared to eat. One of the boys from each group went down to the spring for water, and it was deliciously sweet and cool. After lunch we decided to rest a while. The guide said we had made good time and in three hours we could reach the timber line, where we were to make camp on the edge of the woods.

At three o'clock we climbed up to the road, loaded the burros and were off again—up, up,

up. We had left the foot-hills behind us now and were on the very slope of the volcano itself. Here the trees, taller and thicker, made what we call a real forest. Perhaps we had eaten too much lunch, or perhaps we were tired, but anyway the trail seemed difficult. Then, too, we had begun to notice the lightness of the air and at every hundred yards or so we had to stop for breath. Some of the boys began to feel ill and at this juncture the onions put in their appearance. I felt none too well, so I began to search in my pockets for my onions, too,—and when, with a dull ache in my head and a breathless feeling in the lungs, I pressed them to my nose, all the former aversion to their scent disappeared. I kept them under my nose all the way to camp. And whether due to the onions or not, I didn't feel any worse while some of the fellows had to walk so slowly that they were left behind the rest of the party.

In the late afternoon we passed through a part of the forest where it seemed as if more than half the trees had been torn up by the roots. Great tree trunks, so large that we could hardly climb over them, lay across the path. Looking down, I could see whole hillsides strewn with these fallen members of the forest. Some of the boys explained to me how, two years before, a hurricane had swept across the mountains and tried to carry the whole forest off with it. The fallen trees were a bad impediment to our progress because, in an atmosphere where one cannot walk without getting out of breath, to climb over a gigantic trunk is an exercise that is not taken with pleasure.

It was almost six o'clock when we arrived at the spot chosen for camp, just below the timber line, where the trees of the mountain end. We were close to the peaks now and one of them, that looked very near, loomed between us and the sinking sun so that all the mountain-side was in shadow. Down below we saw the valley—far, far beneath—bathed in a twilight mist of rose and purple; the little river, that had been a winding, silver thread all day, had now turned golden in the sunset.

We began to make camp. Some unloaded the burros and tied them fast to trees. Others searched for the dry limbs and branches of the pine in order to make the fires. And still others, too tired and out of breath to do anything, sank down upon the ground to rest, for the last hour of the ascent had been the hardest of all.

The shadows on the mountain-side deepened and the sunset colors faded from the sky. For me, the evening passed quickly. There was supper around the blazing camp-fires, of which each group of fellows had its own; then songs and stories and more songs, to which the two burro drivers contributed a love ballad which they said they had learned down in the "hot country." At nine, the first guards were posted and the camp became still. The only noise to be heard was the occasional sob-like "hee-hooing" of the burros and the strong "Alerta" of the watchers, crying to each other from the four corners of the camp.

At two o'clock, when my turn came to stand guard, the moon had gone down behind the mountain and the forest was in inky blackness. The low burning camp-fires gave a little light. A long way off and deep down in the night-covered valley, we saw the white lights of To-luca, shining like a cluster of sunken stars in the darkness.

The next morning, at sunrise, we were off for the crater. A half hour's walk took us past the timber line, out of the forest, and to the open mountain-side. In a little while we found ourselves at the foot of one of the vol-canic peaks, which, if we chose to climb it, would give us a view down into the crater. About half the party chose to go up; the others took the burro path which led around the side of the peak, entering the crater at the lowest opening. The peak, which near the top was covered with large patches of snow, did not appear to be very high. But we soon found that the steepness of its slope and the lightness of the air made the ascent more laborious than we thought it would be, and at every eight or ten steps we had to stop for breath. It seemed as if we would never reach the summit. The rocks and sand and gravel, of which the moun-tain was made, slipped beneath our feet and made us slide half-way back at every forward movement. We had to cross the snow covered spaces on our hands and knees—they were so slippery. When we finally gained the summit, it seemed as if our last breath had gone. We were very high and, between us and the hills below, the white clouds drifted by.

As we turned to look down into the crater, we saw it as a sort of double one, divided into two parts by a long hump-backed hill. On each side of the hill there was a blue lake with a rocky shore. The sides of the crater were steep and many colored, and the three highest of the tall, jagged peaks that formed its ragged edge had snow upon them. We, on top of our laboriously climbed summit, had an excellent view down into that part of the volcano where La Laguna Chica (The Little Lake) sparkled in the morning sun. Those who had taken the burro path were already resting on its shore and the height from which we saw them made them appear very tiny. Feeling the pangs of hunger, as we had not yet eaten breakfast, and knowing that the burros carrying the lunch-bags were waiting for us below, we began to descend. Half running, half sliding in the loose sand and gravel of the inner slope, we reached the bottom much more quickly than we had ascended. On the sandy shore, scat-tered with big boulders taller than a man, we ate our breakfast and drank the cold, refresh-ing water of the clear blue lake.

After breakfast we decided to see La Laguna Grande (The Big Lake), and so, circling around the side of The Little Lake, we began to climb one of the low ends of the hump-backed hill. In a short while, from the top of its rocky ridge, we saw below us the deep blue waters of La Laguna Grande, so beautiful and lovely and calm that it gave one a thrill of surprise at finding it buried in this old vol-cano's burnt, scarred walls. Some people say that this pretty lake has no bottom and that swimmers who venture far into its cold waters may be drawn down into unknown depths. Its smooth, innocent surface, however, gives no indications of such treachery, and the charm of its beauty makes one think it is a good fairy lake and not the wicked old witch with the pretty face, which reputation has given it.

We walked all around the rocky shore, stop-ping now and then to pick up small queer-col-ored stones or the sulphur coated rocks found on the beach. To reach the other end of the lake's long oval required more time than we had expected, for distances are deceiving in the high clear air. We stopped often to rest, sitting down on the large boulders and admir-ing the beautiful colors in the sides of the crater whose walls were sometimes deep crim-son capped with jagged peaks, sometimes bright red or soft orange streaked with pur-ple, and sometimes just gray rock covered with snow patches near the rim. And the blue lake was always like a jewel in a rough setting. At the other end of the oval we found erected on the sandy shore, a large wooden cross which a band of religious people had carried up the steep trail some years before. They held a mass in the crater. Behind the cross rose "El Pice de Fraile," the highest of the Xinantecatl peaks, glittering snow white in morning sun. From its tooth-like summit on a clear day, one who has a pair of strong binoculars can see, off the coast of Guerrero, more than a hundred miles away, the silver waters of the Pacific.

When we climbed back over the hump-backed hill and down to the wider shore of the Little Lake, the burros were already packed with our blankets and much diminished lunch bags. Before we reached the spot where we had eaten, the first ones started off. We filled our water bottles and canteens from the lake and started after them. When we came to the highest point in the narrow road we turned for a last look at the little blue lake below, the hump-backed hill and the opposite red and purple walls of

the volcano. Then we turned and followed the path which curved, at a dizzying height, onto the steeply sloping outer sides of the crater, where a false step too near the edge would have sent one tumbling down a mile or so into a green tree-covered valley. We took care not to make the false step.

When, at sunset, we unloaded the burros in the clean little "Portales" of Calimaya, although stiff and footsore and weary, everybody was happy and agreed that it had been a fine trip. A few minutes later, sitting on the platform of the country station, awaiting the last train for Toluca, we could see, high and far away, the sharp, jagged peaks of the old volcano faintly outlined against the sunset sky. They seemed so very high and so very far from us we could scarcely believe that just ten hours before we had visited them and drunk the cool snow water of their clear blue lakes.

 PLAYTIME

ORIGINAL PUZZLES

C. LESLIE FRAZIER

THE SLEEPY PRINTER

THE printer was sleepy and ran his words together in printing the names of the compositions by these Negro composers. Can you straighten them out?

1. A. J. Conner: "Mych eris hedho pesmy fon destdre ams."
2. James Hemmenway: "Tha trest sos weetli kerest ab ove."
3. George Melburn: "Li st ent othemo ckin gbird."
4. James Bland: "Car ryme bac k tool dVir gini a."
5. Gussie L. Davis: "Theli ghtho useby th esea."
6. Samuel Milady: "Gran d fath erscl ockwa stooh ighf ort hes helf."
7. De Koven Thompson: "Lovecomesbutonc e."
8. Nathaniel R. Dett: "Listentothelambs."
9. J. Rosamond Johnson: "Sin cey ouwe ntaway."
10. Will Marian Cook: "Therainsong."

FRACTIONS

THE totals of the following fractions are the names of our foremost universities:

1. One-half of show and one-half of away.
2. Three-fourths of fish and one-fourth of kiss.
3. One-third of hollow, one-half of warmth, and one-sixth of reduce.
4. Two-fifths of total, one-fifth of regal, and two-fifths of spent.
5. Two-sevenths of Matthew, four-sevenths of lantern, and one-seventh of swagger.
6. Three-elevenths of willingness, three-elevenths of bereavement, three-elevenths of information, and two-elevenths of insincerely.

7. Six-elevenths of morris-dance, two-elevenths of Abracadabra, two-elevenths of sorrowfully, and one-eleventh of spendthrift.

8. Two-fifths of opals, one-fifth of years, and two-fifths of scene.

9. Three-eights of milliner, one-fourth of falconer, one-fourth of revolter, and one-eighth of windmill.

10. One-sixth of Hebrew, one-third of repaid, and one-half of cradle.

EXAMPLE: 1. SH-ow and AW-ay—SHAW.

CENTRAL SYNCOPATIONS AND REMAINDERS

EACH of the words described contains five letters, and the syncopated letters, placed in the order here given, spell the name of a famous American Negro patriot.

1. Syncopate a step for ascending and leave a commotion: 2. Pertaining to morning and leave principal: 3. The leaf of a flower and leave a loud and repeated sound: 4. A dwelling and leave covering for the leg: 5. A kind of nut and leave a song of praise and triumph: 6. A peddler and leave just: 7. Dispatch and leave aversion.

EXAMPLE: 1. stAir.

PRINTER'S PI

A Byb ahs a thoto ta stla,
   Ybba nithks eh kastl,
Byba dansts ponu ish deha
Nhew eh rites ot kawl.

NUMERALS

ECH number represents a letter. 1 is A, 2 is B, 3 is C, etc. Below are names of streets which are popular thoroughfares for Negroes, and the cities and States in which they are:

(1) 2 5 1 12 5 19 20., 13 5 13 16 8 9 19, 20 5 14 14.

(2) 23 25 12 5 25 1 22 5., 16 9 20 20 19 2 21 18 7, 16 1.

(3) 4 18 21 9 4 8 9 12 12 1 22 5., 2 1 12 20 9 13 15 18 5, 13 4.

(4) 19 20 1 20 5 19 20., 3 8 9 3 1 7 15, 9 12 12.

(5) 19 15 21 20 8 19 20., 16 8 9 12 1 4 5 12 16 8 9 1, 1 1.

(6) 21 19 20., 14. 23. 23 1 19 8 9 14 7 20 15 14, 4. 3.

(7) 12 5 14 15 24 1 22 5., 14 5 23 25 15 18 11, 14. 25.

STARS

EACH star represents a missing letter and when you have placed them you will have the names of singers and musicians who can be heard on phonograph records.

1. B*r* W*l*i*m*.
2. M*m*e *m*t*.
3. N*b*e *i*s*e.
4. M*r* S*a*f*r*.
5. R*l*n* H*y*s.
6. L*c*l*e *e*i*i*.
7. F*s* J*b*l*e*i*g*r*.
8. M*m*e *m*t*'s *a*z *o*n*s.
9. H*n*y'* O*c*e*t*a *f *e*p*i*.
10. M*m*h*s *i*k*i*n* B*n*.
11. B*d*l* U*i*e*s*t* Q*a*t*t.

TRANSPOSITIONS

THE same four letters arranged differently spell the four missing words in the jingle.

The captain sat beside the helm,
   Agazing at a ****,
He never called his comrades salts,
   He always called them ****.
He never studied any ****,—
   Painting nor sharps and flats,
But now he studies very hard
   To rid his ship of ****.

"Hey!" cries Billy, *"Hey!—If this is the last Brownies' Book, how 'bout the answers?"*
"Look on page 356" answers the Judge, *"but don't look until you've tried hard!"*

Bingo

WINIFRED VIRGINIA JACKSON

I HAVE a dog named Bingo,
   That dearly loves to play;
He runs about a-barking,
   And has such fun all day!

One day he chased a kittie,
   Who turned and said, "Scat-scat!"
He ran off crying, "Ki-yi!"
   What do you think of that?

Good-Bye!

THE JUDGE

YEZ! O yez! oyez! All Brownies are herewith ordered on pain of not knowing to read page number 354, and to think about it five whole minutes before saying a single word.

"IT seems to me," says Billie, "mighty funny"——

"By which he means 'extremely curious'," explained Wilhelmina, complacently.

"Aw—I don't neither—I mean——"

"Well, what is it that is so extremely funny?" asked the Judge.

"Well, it's this way: here I've saved my money to pay for the BROWNIES' BOOK and now because somebody else didn't I can't have it any more."

"I don't call that a bit funny," said William. "It's pretty serious business and needs looking into. Here are 4000 Brownies who want the BROWNIES' BOOK awfully. Now, why on earth should it be any of our business if 16,000 other kids don't like it or don't see it or can't buy it?"

"It's life," sighed the Judge.

"It seems to be," snapped Wilhelmina, "that there are a lot of grown-ups who are extremely fond of laying the blame of everything disagreeable on life instead of on themselves."

"True," said the Judge. "Too true. From which fact, however, it does not necessarily follow that life isn't a considerably more complicated and mixed-up affair than even the wisest young ladies of 16 like to admit.

"For instance, Tommie Titmouse steps out of his door in Willipuswalipus City, and waits on the street corner. In five minutes a great giant of a wagon with driver and footman whirls by and for five cents carries him ten miles and puts him down at Smith's Toy Store, just where he wanted to go.

"Now, Sallie Dormouse steps out of her door at Skeesix Corners and she might stand on the corner two years and no street car or carriage would come by and carry her anywhere, even for five dollars if she had it, and she hasn't.

"All of which goes to show that life is not a matter of you and me and him, but rather of all of us together. Ten thousand people working together and living together can arrange to have cheap street cars and cheap newspapers while one person or a hundred persons could afford neither.

"If the Brownies of the United States want a BROWNIES' BOOK enough of them must want it and want it badly enough to pay for printing it."

"But," says Billie, "it doesn't cost any more, does it, for each Brownie to have 4000 Brownies' Books printed than it would to have four million?"

"Ah, there you're mistaken," says the Judge. "To print one BROWNIES' BOOK would cost $500. To print 1,000 BROWNIES' BOOK would cost $750. To print 5,000 BROWNIES' BOOK would cost $1000. To print 20,000, would cost $2500. In other words if only 1000 persons want the BROWNIES' BOOK it would cost them 75 cents a copy or nine dollars a year, while if 20,000 will buy it, it could sell for 15 cents a copy, or a dollar and a half a year."

"So the more you print, the cheaper it is?"

"Precisely."

"Then we ought to get busy and make everybody buy the BROWNIES' BOOK," said Billie.

"Oh, it isn't the Kid's fault—it's the Grown-ups—they're so busy with their own silly conferences and wars and autos they haven't time for real things," said William.

"Besides it's too late now," said Wilhelmina.

"It's never too late," said the Judge.

OLIVE PLAATJE

SARAH TALBERT KEELAN

IT is a far throw from New York to South Africa. A sad bereavement suffered by a well known native family in that far off country has reduced the circulation of THE BROWNIES' BOOK by one interested little subscriber, from Kimberley, South Africa—the diamond city of the world.

Olive Schreiner Plaatje, more intimately known as "Ngoetsi," died on the fourteenth of July, in Bloemfontein, South Africa, at the age of sixteen.

Ngoetsi did her life work at the age of thirteen, during the Fall of 1918—which, by the way, is the South African Spring—when the influenza epidemic swept over Kimberley, and killed in one month, 6,000 people, out of a population of about 30,000. October, 1918, has since been known as the "Black October." All the shops, churches, schools, theatres and market places were closed up and deserted. Drug stores alone were packed with customers, day and night. Nearly all the doctors were ill in bed, and pharmacists had to depend upon one general prescription for all sufferers. Throughout October, when the epidemic raged, the city looked like a huge hospital, for, according to official reports, all but five percent of the entire population of the city of Kimberley had the disease.

Only two Kimberley streets, I learn, were alive with traffic—the road from the City Hall to the hospital, and from the hospital to the cemetery.

The Plaatje household was among those stricken with the "flu" with the exception of Ngoetsi and her father, Mr. Solomon Plaatje, the Brotherhood lecturer, who is well known to many of us Americans. He himself at the time was looking after many of the other sufferers, often leaving his sick family alone with Olive, who, single-handed, was kept busy nursing a household of helpless patients, from her mother and cousins down—to be accurate, eight in all.

Nearly every house in the neighborhood had its funerals, but little Olive, like Mrs. Van Rooyen, over the road, saved every one of her patients.

Three months after the epidemic had passed away, when shops, schools, diamond mines and everything had reopened, and the people were glad it was all over, Olive was seized with an attack of rheumatic fever, which the doctors said was the after-effect of her nursing. She had to give up school and her piano lessons, and on the doctor's advice, her parents sent her to the Hot Springs of Aliwal, North Cape. Upon her arrival there, Olive was not allowed to use the waters, because her skin was not white. However, she eventually got better and resumed her studies at the Wesleyan Methodist High School for colored girls in Natal.

It was there that the rheumatic affection went through little Olive's heart and leakage developed. The teachers sent her home, but she got no further than Bloemfontein, where she died, about one hundred miles from home. Her mother hastened to her side; but her father, being in far off America, did not hear of the end until six weeks afterwards.

It is painful to learn that Ngoetsi most probably would have reached her mother's house but for the shocking "Jim Crow" system, which in British South Africa is even more rigorous than in the United States. It is charged that the sickness was aggravated by the harsh treatment accorded her by the white train men of the South African railways. At a railroad junction, where she waited hours for the Kimberley connection, her escort was not allowed to rest the sick girl in the waiting room or on the platform seats, which are at the disposal of white passengers only. The patient had to wait outside of the depot, without shelter or comfort of any kind.

It will thus be seen that while Brownies are a "problem" everywhere, in their own homeland—Africa—their troubles start rather early in life.

While we are enjoying the benefits of instruction in high schools, conservatories and colleges in New York, Massachusetts, etc., we should remember that in South Africa there are no public schools for colored children. The natives can only get elementary training in the rural and village mission schools. Native children who take advantage of these have to pay their "tickeys" and "tanners" (English nickels and dimes), every week in the primary section, while the fourth and fifth grade pupils pay a quarter or more every Monday morning. In addition to these weekly school fees, the African Brownies have to buy their own books, pencils and slates, which in the South African public schools are supplied to white children free of cost. Therefore, we should appreciate the sacrifices made by Mrs. Plaatje and other African mothers to supply their children with training and strive to make the best use of our superior privileges.

Yet with all these difficulties, our late little Brownie friend had advantages which few of us on this side of the Atlantic will ever be privileged to have. Coming probably from the most polyglot family, of a polyglot country, Olive could write and converse in Sechuana, her father's language, as well as Sixosa, her mother tongue. Her parents, being of two different tribes, have separate languages. Besides these, Ngoetso could read and write English and Dutch.

Her uncle is chief translater in native languages for the Union Government. One of her cousins is interpreter to the South African Native Affairs Commission; another was until lately examiner for the Cape Education (Graduating) Department. To hold any of these posts, one has to be proficient in at least six different languages, and have a

Olive Schreiner Plaatje

working knowledge of a few more dialects. One girl cousin is in training as a nurse at the Scottish Missionary Hospital, of Lovedale—the Hampton of South Africa.

The late Brownie was named after Olive Schreiner, a great South African authoress; "Ngoetsi" is after a native chieftainess in Africa.

I first met Olive's father at London, England, during October of last year. This summer I went to spend my vacation with my friend, Mr. and Mrs. Burton, of Ridgefield Park, N. J. Knowing that Mr. Plaatje was in New York, we invited him to spend a day with us, and on calling him over the telephone, to make the engagement, I learned of his sad bereavement, and of how Mrs. Plaatje faced the sorrow of laying to rest away from home, the dear little girl who, three years before, had saved her own mother from the "flu."

I feel certain that readers of THE BROWNIES' BOOK will sympathise with Mr. and Mrs. Plaatje, and especially with Violet "Teto" Plaatje, the surviving subscriber to THE BROWNIES' BOOK, for by the death of Olive, a promising yuong career has been brought to an end; family hopes have been dashed to pieces, and the Kimberley Women's Sisterhood has been deprived of one of their most useful junior members. Peace be to her ashes!

What Would the Dog Say If He Could Talk?

ONCE there lived a little baby who had no father. His father was killed in the war. One day the baby's mother went out and left the dog to stay with the baby. If the dog could talk he would say "I wish the baby's mother would come home so I could go out, but I must be faithful and stay with the baby." I know the dog will get some good meat. Soon after that the baby's mother came in and the dog got his meat and the baby got his milk. Then the dog went out doors.

WILLIAM VALENTINE (age 7).

"SAINT" GANDHI

The Greatest Man in the World
BLANCHE WATSON

BOUT two thousand years ago there lived a man who said, "He that taketh the sword shall perish by the sword,"—that is, He tried to make people see that war was wrong—that all killing was wrong—because *all* human life was sacred. The world, since that time, has listened to that message, but it has not understood it, or even tried to understand it—all of which means that this man came before the world was ready for Him, and (not being ready) it crucified Him!

When I say the world, I do not mean everybody in it. There were some few people who did understand what Jesus, the Christ, taught, and who tried to live by those teachings.

Now, today, on the other side of the world, in far away India, a man is preaching as did Jesus of Nazareth, "Love your enemies"; "Do good to them that hate you"; "Do unto others as you would that they should do unto you". Like Jesus, he goes out under the blue sky and gathers the people around him. Like Jesus, he says "Follow me!" And the people follow him —not by the hundreds—but by the millions— for India is a nation numbering more than 300 million souls!

The people of India want the right to govern themselves as we govern ourselves in this country—as they governed themselves a great many years ago! Usually when a people decide that they want to be independent (as we call it) they "go to war"—that is, they gather together armies and go out and kill one another—forgetting what Jesus said—forgetting that we are all brothers and that God is our Father.

Now this man, who is leading the Indian people—"Saint" Gandhi as he is called—is giving to his people, after all these years, the message of the Man that we Christians call our leader. He, too, says: "He that taketh the sword shall perish by the sword," and—if you will believe it—the British Empire, that has held India against its will for a hundred and sixty years, is more afraid of this man than any "general", that is, any fighting man—that has ever arisen during that time.

You ask me, "Why?"

Let me tell you. Gandhi, this saint, says, "Don't have anything to do with this government and the people it sends here to rule us; but do not hurt them—do not lift a hand against them: just love them!" That is why the British government is so afraid of this great leader. When a man persists in loving you—in spite of all you do to him—you can't keep on hating and mis-using that man forever! More than that—any group of people that is held together by hate and bitterness *must* fall to pieces sooner or later. Hate is destructive—it kills! But a group of people held together by good-will, by love, is mighty—for love is constructive—that is, it builds.

Gandhi says to his people, "If you follow my way, you will be a free people; and when he speaks thus—this little brown man who has to sit in a chair on a table when he speaks—no one can disagree with him. No one can look in his wonderful eyes and even *think* that he is wrong. Do you know why this is? Because of the strength of his spirit. It is the spirit— the spirit of God himself that blazes there, and his word is the word of God.

The English government (and I do not mean the English *people*—that is a different thing) the English government may not know it, but they are afraid of Saint Gandhi simply because he is speaking with the voice of God, even as did Jesus, the Christ—by the Sea of Galilee— hundreds of years ago.

Will the people of India hold out? Will Gandhi succeed? Is the world to learn the lesson that war is murder—that Christ's way is the better way—that love is the "greatest thing in the world"?

Let us all watch India, and Gandhi!

AS THE CROW FLIES

AM flying my last wide flight and am very, very sad. All the world lies dark beneath its snow and sunshine. Only the children are happy. Children are always happy. That is, most always.

❦ England and Ireland are still trying to make peace. The difficulty is first, Ireland does not trust England and claims that Ireland is a free and independent country. It happens that there is a little piece of Ireland called Ulster which does not want to be free and independent and especially does not want to be connected with the rest of Ireland. So the puzzle is how to make Ireland united and almost independent and yet keep her as part of the British Empire, and at the same time make Ulster satisfied as a part of Ireland. The job of doing this is so difficult that the British Prime Minister, Lloyd George, has not been able to get away and attend the Disarmament Conference at Washington.

❦ In another part of the British Empire, Egypt, the natives, among whom are a number of colored people, want also to be free from the domination of England. England has promised that she never meant to annex Egypt and would give her her freedom; but recently when Egyptians came to England to arrange a treaty of independence they found that England was going to make her free except that she wanted to keep an English army anywhere in Egypt that she pleased, and that she wanted to make it impossible for Egypt to make any treaties with foreign countries without England's consent, and other provisions which made the so-called independence a farce. The Egyptians went home without arranging the treaty.

❦ Still further across the world in India several hundred millions of brown people are much incensed at the injustice of English rule. A large part of them are trying to secure their freedom, not by fighting but by refusing to "cooperate". That is, they will not pay taxes, they will not buy goods in the stores, they will not attend the courts or the English schools, etc. Their leader is named Gandhi.

❦ A Disarmament conference is sitting in Washington. The object of it is to see if the civilized nations of the world cannot spend less money in preparing to fight each other, especially as most of the people of the world do not want to fight. The president of the United States therefore has invited various nations to talk the matter over in Washington. When they got there, Secretary of the State, Hughes, proposed that the American, British and Japanese navies be cut down so that the first two should be equal to each other and Japan should be three-fifths as large. In addition to this they have been trying to talk about China; but the difficulty there is that Great Britain, France and Japan have already seized valuable parts of China, and valuable privileges, and do not want to give them up. The United States would like to have some of these privileges too and therefore is championing the rights of China. Meantime it looks as though China would get chiefly promises.

❦ Europe borrowed a great deal of money from the United States during the war and it is difficult to repay it because there is no international money and international debts have to be paid by goods. Europe cannot export goods to the United States in order to pay her debts unless she has raw materials out of which she can make the goods. The United States controls much of the raw material like cotton and food so the whole matter of paying these debts is very difficult.

❦ The peace treaty between the United States and Germany has at last been signed.

❦ There have been numbers of distinguished visitors to the United States recently; Marshal Foch, the leader of the allied army; Arthur

Balfour, the great English statesman, and Aristide Briand, Prime Minister of France.

¶ The Prince of Wales has gone on a visit to India and Japan. The English are afraid that the Indians will not want to see him.

¶ Two Italians have been sentenced to death for murder in Massachusetts. Many people think that they are not guilty and that they were sentenced because they had radical views of government. There is a wide-spread agitation throughout the world to save these two men.

¶ There has been a revolutionary movement in Portugal by which a new government has been installed and many prominent leaders killed. The former king and queen of Hungary, attempted to seize their former government. They arrived in an airplane but were compelled to leave and are now in exile on the island of Madeira.

¶ Great effort is being made to aid the famine stricken inhabitants of Russia. Sufficient food to feed a million people for five months is on its way and yet this is not enough.

———

 OODBYE, dear kiddies. I do not know whom I shall tell all I see hereafter. Nobody I suppose. Besides if I do not fly I shall not see. No, I am not crying. Crows cannot cry. It's a fine thing to be able to cry— sometimes.

———

¶ Senator Philander C. Knox of Pennsylvania, a prominent American statesman is dead.

¶ A proposed strike of the employees of the railroads has been stopped by the action of the United States Railroad Labor Board.

¶ United States will keep an army of 5,600 troops in Germany; the rest will be gradually withdrawn.

¶ President Harding made a speech in Birmingham, Alabama, where he asked for the right to vote for Negroes, just wages and education. He also said that he did not believe in "social equality," whatever that is.

¶ The extra session of Congress has adjourned and after a few days the same men came back to the regular session. President Harding addressed them on subjects for legislation.

¶ There are 54,421,832 persons 21 years of age and over in the United States, who are thus possible voters.

¶ President Harding has signed a bill which devotes seventy-five million dollars to good roads throughout the United States.

¶ There are in the United States 13,920,692 foreign born inhabitants.

¶ A great strike of clothing makers is in progress in New York because the employers want to pay by the piece instead of by the day.

¶ During the last election two states had colored parties who nominated candidates. In Louisville, Kentucky, colored men were nominated for Mayor and city officers while in Virginia the colored people nominated their own candidates for Governor and all state officers. 20,000 people voted for the colored candidates in Virginia.

¶ The Nobel prize for literature, which is given every year and amounts to about $25,000, has been given this year to Anatole France, a great French writer.

¶ Charges for freight on farm products have been reduced throughout the United States.

¶ People of Porto Rico, a large number of whom are colored, are trying to get rid of Governor Riley who seems to have made himself unpopular by injudicious remarks and actions.

¶ The tax bill recently passed by Congress will raise three and one-fourth billion dollars to pay the expenses of the United States government for the current year.

¶ A treaty has been signed between the United States, Great Britain, France and Japan to guarantee each other's possessions among the three thousand islands of the Pacific.

¶ Fifteen American war ships are to be sold at auction.

¶ A fire in Augusta, Georgia, destroyed two million dollars worth of property.

¶ We sent a military man to be governor of the Philippine Islands and very naturally he thinks that the Philippines should continue to be under the domination of the United States. The people do not agree with him.

¶ Marshal Foch, after visiting thirty States of the Union and being much impressed by the kindness of Americans, has returned to France.

¶ A French Negro, René Marin, who is an employee in the French Colonial service in Central Africa, has written a novel, "Batouala", which is about Negroes in Central Africa. It has received the Goncourt prize as the best French book of the year.

Our Little Friends

THE JURY

 AM a little girl nine years old, residing here now, having recently moved from Columbus, Ga. I am a dear lover of books, and every spare moment I am at the Dryades Street Library, reading.

Seeing THE BROWNIES' BOOK there, I was delighted to read it. For the past six months I've been trying to write little poems. One of them I was asked to send you for publication.

Should you think it not worth publishing in your next edition, please send it to me.

Let me hear from you.

I am in the fourth grade.

BEULAH MARTHA HOWARD,
New Orleans, La.

[This is Beulah's "poem".]
SPRING
Spring is here, Spring is here,
The time we children think so dear,
  When the birds begin to sing,
  And the flowers begin to grow,
Then you know that Spring is here.

Spring is here, Spring is here,
When all the children come so near,
  When I can see
  The little bee,
Then you know that Spring is here.

———

I AM twelve years and have been a little author in my home. I have been writing stories at home ever since the year 1917. But I have never sold them. I once wrote to the Author's Press for their six courses but I saw nothing in them which would do me any good because I was a gifted author. I have some of the most gorgeous stories that anyone would enjoy reading. I am very heart-broken. May I ask one small question? Will you pay me for my manuscripts? If so, I would like to appear at once. Everybody that hears I want to become a writer grants me a success and I hope you do too. I am waiting every moment.

Yours truly,
OBIETH HARDIN,
Gaffney, South Carolina.

———

THERE was once a little girl whose name was Lillian. She always played with her doll. It was a big, beautiful, brown doll with long black curls. Lillian loved it very much and took it everywhere she went.

One day while Lillian was in the yard playing her attention was attracted to a little bird singing in the tree above her. She was so busy watching this little bird that she dropped the doll and broke it. This made Lillian very sad, indeed, for she knew that dollie must go at once to the doll's hospital to be made well again.

With tears streaming down her cheeks, she picked dolly up, put her in her carriage and rushed her to the hospital. There she begged the doll doctor to make dolly well. The doctor told Lillian that dolly would have to have an operation and a new head. This frightened Lillian very much, but after asking him not to hurt her baby she went home.

At the hospital dolly made friends with several other dolls, a big French doll, a Japanese doll and a Scotch lassie. Her stay there was very pleasant. Lillian went to visit her often and carried her messages from the little Chinese doll who lived next door.

On Christmas Eve dolly was sent home in a Red Cross Ambulance. She brought back two of her friends, the French and Japanese dolls.

On Christmas day Lillian gave a beautiful party for all the dolls of the neighborhood. Soon, Lillian's doll married a big brown soldier doll and lived many, many happy years.

MIRIAM ANITA THOMAS (Age 8),
Washington, D. C.

———

Goodbye dear Brownies! How I shall miss your letters! JESSIE FAUSET.

THE MELODY MAN

JAMES ALPHEUS BUTLER, JR.

WHEN the autumn leaves whistle down to the ground, and Old Man Winter promises his arrival, the whole atmosphere of the forest seems to take on a golden aspect, and one finds it unnecessary to await the golden glow of the sunset to notice this. The reddish-yellow of the falling leaves, the dark branches of the trees fast becoming bare, the industriousness of the little denizens of the woods preparing for the long, bleak months to come, are all familiar sights. Yet only a visitor might enjoy the picturesque autumn of the little town of Avondale to the fullest extent, only a stranger might perceive and thoroughly enjoy the wonderful autumn atmosphere which envelops the entire town itself—even to the snug houses—for all of this was familiar to the inhabitants of the village.

Two little children—a boy and a girl—sat upon the porch of one of these snug little houses.

"I'm dreadfully tired of these old piano lessons," Emily Thomas said as she swayed back and forth in her little rocking chair. "Every Monday and Wednesday and Friday—Paul, I think that's too much, don't you?"

"Yes," said Paul, a robust little boy of twelve, "and I'm awfully tired of that old violin professor. He makes me tired with his 'do this, an' do that.' And he always wants me to count aloud. I think that is very silly."

"That's just the way it is with Miss Van Ness."

"And there's old Jack Smith—always guying me about playing ball whenever he sees me going to take my lesson. Always braggin' that he doesn't have to bother with any old stuck-up professor. It makes me angry to have to go in there with him—the professor, I mean—and all the other fellows are out having a good time."

Just then their mother's voice was heard from within.

"Children," she called, "you had better begin your practicing now. You know your teachers say you must devote at least one hour an afternoon to practicing."

Paul said "Pshaw!" but they both went in,

for they were both obedient children, and Paul immediately began playing the scale of C Major on his violin, while Emily began her piano finger exercise.

II

ONE typical autumn day, not very long afterwards, there came into the little village of Avondale a tattered old man, almost dressed in rags. Yet from those garments shone a most benevolent old countenance which seemed to be kindness, and gentleness itself. The hat which he wore was minus a crown, and his shoes were much too large for him. His coat seemed mere drapery around him, for the sleeves were torn into shreds. Still this seemed not to alter in the least the impression which he gave to the few people he met as he came into the town. For, upon looking into his eyes, a strange, intense feeling seemed to come over you, it seemed as if you were gazing into the deep blue of a soul as mighty as the sea, as clear and pure as crystal, as humble as the Dove of Peace. And under his arm he carried a wooden box wrought in the semblance of an ancient violin case. Who knew what compelling melodies might emerge from the instrument which one was confident that the box contained!

At first no one paid very much attention to this little old man with the strange looking box which he held so tightly. It was true that whoever chanced to gaze into his eyes was struck with wonder and awe and often with a strange embarrassment—he gazed so sadly, his stare was so haunting. But these villagers, busy with other affairs, promptly forgot the torn old man, and gave their attention to their own pressing affairs.

No one knew from whence he came nor cared to take the trouble to find out. No one knew his purpose in entering the village, and no one knew where and how he lived while there.

On the second day of his stay in the village he chanced to be walking up Poplar Street, and his step was slow and uncertain. He seemed to be glancing at the houses as if trying to find out who lived in there by merely looking at them. Twice he stopped and seemed as if he would sit down, and twice he shook his head and moved sadly on. Then suddenly a rock came sailing with intense speed from an alley and struck the violin case. Almost at the same time there came a "Yee--ho!" from the same alley and a boy with a sling-shot scampered away. The old man stopped and opened his violin box. And then he withdrew his old instrument, with four patched strings.

Now it was just about time for a school to dismiss. The children, happy at the thought of freedom, emerged in a joyous, boisterous crowd and came down the street in a jolly throng. Among them, leading in the laughter and play, were Paul and Emily Thomas.

Suddenly the crowd spied the old man looking fondly at his violin. Paul ran ahead and shouted in glee:

"Hark, hark, the dogs do bark,
    The beggars are coming to town,
Some in rags, some in jags,
    And some in velvet gown."

The crowd was elated. Every one shouted in glee. "Oh, look at the rag man." "Say, mister, want a coat?" "What a fine derby he has on. No crown!" "Ain't that head bald though." "He's got on rags now. His velvet gown must be in his fiddle-box."

But this did not last very long. Suddenly the old man put his violin under his chin and made several long strokes with his bow. Then he launched into a melody—the most wonderful melody the children had ever heard. They became quiet in an instant. They stared at him with large and incredulous eyes. Paul and Emily hardly knew what to think. A ragged man like that playing such wonderful music!

The old man seemed to have the charm of the Pied Piper. From one and two blocks around the children swarmed around him to hear the wonderful music. He seemed to carry their little minds off into the land of far, far away. It was as if some good wizard had come to them and suddenly crowded them into a crescent boat and sped them to the Land Where Dreams Come True.

But good things must end, and at last the old man finished his melody. When he stopped, it seemed as if the children had been released from a spell. As if awakening from a dream which ended too soon, they clamored around him and cried "More—more—oh, please, just one more piece."

But the Melody Man shook his head and, placing his violin back in his box, silently, sadly went his way.

III

EMILY and Paul saw no more of the Melody Man that day. Paul was rather quiet and thoughtful all of the afternoon. When he took his violin from his box he looked at it a long time before beginning to play. When he did finally begin practicing he drew long bows, and wondered if his violin, too, were capable of bringing forth the melodies which the old man had played.

He thought of the way he had led the crowd into making fun of the old man at their first sight of him. And something seemed to tell him that he had done wrong in doing this—he was almost sorry. All that afternoon he thought of the old man with the violin playing for the enchanted children. All afternoon there was before him the vision of the kindly old face, the bent, but firm, body covered with tattered clothes.

He did not rush out today to play with his little chums, as he usually did as soon as the hour which he was compelled to give to his daily practice ended. Instead he went to his mother who was sewing upon the front porch.

"Mother," he said, "I heard a most wonderful man today."

"Is that so?" asked his mother. "Who was he, Paul?"

"An old man, and he played a violin."

"A violin!"

"Yes, mother. All of the children were just coming from school and they met him, too. He was dressed almost from top to bottom in rags, and he had a violin that must be a hundred years old, and he played in the street for us. I liked it so very much!"

"And I thought my little boy didn't like a violin."

"When I heard the old man play I was sorry I had objected to practicing. If I could just play as he did! Oh, mother, do you think it will ever be possible?"

"Why of course, Paul."

"Will I be able to make people dream as he made us dream?"

"Of course."

"Will I be able to make people cry?"

"Yes, if you practice each day."

"And laugh, too?"

"Why, of course, Paul."

The little fellow jumped up and clapped his hands in glee.

"Oh, mother, I'm going to practice every day—every day! I'm never going to miss one. Maybe some day I can do just like the Melody Man!"

The next day was Saturday and since there was no school Paul set out to look for the Melody Man. Jack Smith had told him just that morning that he had seen him playing a "fiddle" further down the street, and Paul was anxious to hear him again.

He walked down Poplar Street and then turned down a sort of alley that led to the part of town where the poor little boys and girls lived. He hardly expected to find the Melody Man in that part of the town, yet it seemed as if something guided his footsteps in that direction. About a half an hour later he was glad he had come into that part of the town. For suddenly there came to him the soft notes of a violin!

With quickened footsteps Paul headed towards the spot from which the notes came. He turned a corner and seemed to burst upon a gathering which almost startled him.

For there, in the midst of a crowd of poor little girls and boys, was the Melody Man playing his violin. It was a beautiful and inspiring sight even though it was in the poor part of the town. The Melody Man was the center of the group and sat upon the dilapidated steps of an old house. His gray, long hair seemed to wave back and forth as he nodded to the rhythm of his music. He seemed to be in exactly the right atmosphere, and seemed to be filled with indescribable joy at the cheer and diversion he was bringing to the people in this crowded street. Even the grown people were listening to the notes which arose from the soul of the Man. From many windows wearied heads were thrust out, in many shop doors there suddenly appeared faces and bodies transformed and enthralled by the music of the Melody Man. Those notes of the Melody Man, seemingly so gentle and modest, rang out as trumpets in the environment of the slums so unaccustomed to such things.

Paul approached and watched and drank in the notes, until suddenly the man stopped and laid his fiddle aside.

"Little children," he said in a strange, feeble voice that gave the impression of being cracked, "do you want to hear a story?"

Everybody cried out as one, and the Melody Man, nodding his head, began his narrative. All the children settled around in comfortable attitudes.

"I am going to tell you a story," began the Melody Man, "that is not unlike my music. It is going to be a tale of one who set out on a noble mission and of what befell him. It is going to be a tale of cheer, and of sorrow." And the Melody Man stared ahead and seemed to be looking backwards into the past.

"Boys and girls," he continued, "there was once a youth, a fine lad, who had neither mother nor father. But his voice was as fresh as the morning, his brow was massive like the mountains and gave hint of a soul as big as life itself. When he smiled it was as if a thousand fairies cast a spell of joy upon you.

"The greatest ambition of the lad was to bring joy to people who knew not what joy was, to cheer those whose shoulders were laden with worry. And the Almighty had blessed him with a Gift with which he might carry out his noble desires. And this gift was a passionate understanding of the soul of music and its relation to human beings.

"So one day, with the light-heartedness of youth, the lad set out to serve humanity with a violin under his arm. It must have been that the very birds recognized in him a friend, for whenever he happened along the road they would always pour forth their most beautiful songs, and they even seemed not to fear him. And to reward them the lad would sit by the side of the road for hours playing for them and imitating their songs with his magic bow and fiddle.

"Time passed and the lad traveled far and wide with his fiddle playing for all and everyone he met, and especially for those who were poor and downcast and despondent. And there was many a heart which he raised from the mire and muck of despair and worry.

"The lad became an old man. He had traveled all over the land of his home and had seen foreign countries—even to the most remote corners of the earth where savages dwell. And during this time he had made friends with Princes, and Kings, and the Rulers of the earth, and even gathered enough of the world's riches to suffice him for the rest of his life. So he decided to build him a big house in which there could be seen the most splendid things man could make, and live in it for the rest of his days.

"But when the old man went to live in his house a strange thing happened. He never felt at home in it. He had no people around him —no open-eyed children to play for, no worn and worried people of the slums to cheer and bring joy to. In his large, dreary house there was nothing but evidence of worldliness, of gold, and all of his life he had been a vender of dreams. It seemed to the old man that he would go crazy if he had to live there.

"So this old man went into his attic where he had thrown his ragged garments when he came to live in the big house and donned them again. And he found his old violin box which had accompanied him on his journeys, and once more he set out as he had done throughout his life. And to this day he has never returned to the big house that he built for himself."

At the end of his tale the Melody Man arose. His kindly countenance lit up in an all-embracing smile. The children clapped in glee. Then he spoke again. "And, now, my little children, I will have to go on my long journey again. For in some other town there are children just like you waiting on a Melody Man to come into their lives."

The children were sad when he said this. They clung to him and begged him with all the ardor of childhood not to go. But the Melody Man was firm, and sadly shook his head.

IV

THAT evening Paul and Emily sat on their porch with their mother and father. Paul was relating to his father the tale which the Melody Man had told that morning. His father was very interested.

"Well, Paul," he said, at its conclusion, "do you think the tale which the Melody Man told you might be true?"

"Why, no sir," answered Paul. "I thought he just told it for fun."

Mr. Thomas leaned back in his chair and smiled. And then he spoke. "As a matter of fact," he said, "the Melody Man is a great violinist. I knew of him when he was young and famous. At that time his name was on the lips of the world." Mr. Thomas paused. "Throughout his life," he said, "he loved to play for the poor folks who cared to listen. This was what brought him fame and fortune, and besides he seemed to enjoy influencing the poor,

unlucky people. Recently, I heard, he left his mansion to continue his work—his great work. And that is your Melody Man, though few people recognize in him the great violinist of the last century."

"Why— —" began Paul.

But just then he stopped. For, trudging up the road, there was the Melody Man himself.

It was dusk. In the deepening gloom there could only be distinguished the bent figure of an old man, with a case clasped tightly under his arm. He held a staff in his hand with which he helped himself along. A hollow reverberation emanated from the violin case, because there were no plush linings within it and the violin was moving about because it did not fit. As he walked, the thump of his stick was followed by the thump of his boots on the pavement.

He passed under a glowing street lamp, and what the light revealed was an inspiration.

There was first of all the splendid figure— that of a man old but still possessing poise— the poise of one who is distinguished. And there was the countenance—a countenance radiating all that savors of the pathos of life, the joy of service, the grandeur of a life given to humanity and the uplift of children who have scant opportunity for witnessing the most beautiful creations of the mind of man. It was a countenance of contentment brim full of the noble happiness which comes from the consciousness that one has done something for his brother who hasn't had the same opportunities he has had. It was a countenance filled with the expectancy of the greater services which lay ahead to be performed, and which seemed to look forward to the performance of them with an eagerness to serve unparalleled.

And as his figure passed away into the dusk of evening and on, on into the distance, the Thomases felt as if something divine had passed before their vision.

Emily broke the silence.

"Mother," she said sweetly, "I'll never refuse to practice again in all my life."

Paul said, "I wouldn't miss another day of violin lessons for all the gold in the world."

And they all were soon silent with thoughts of the Melody Man who brought joy to inhabitants of this world of sordidness.

May they, too, be as faithful to humanity as the Melody Man!

THESE KIDDIES HAVE NO MOTHERS

If you want to help them send pennies to Miss Amy Chadwick, Leonard Street Orphans Home, Atlanta, Ga.

VALEDICTORY

MESSRS. DuBois and Dill announce with regret the discontinuance of THE BROWNIES' BOOK. Recognizing the great need which exists for literature adapted to colored children, and indeed to all children who live in a world of varied races, we have for two years made the experiment of publishing at our own expense, THE BROWNIES' BOOK. The experiment has cost us about $7,000. The total revenue has been about $4,000, leaving us some $3,000 in debt. The total number of subscribers to THE BROWNIES' BOOK has gradually risen to 3,500 and it is increasing very slowly. The magazine cannot, however, pay expenses with less than 15,000 subscribers. As there is no prospect of getting this number of subscribers within less than four or five years we cannot afford to continue the experiment.

The fault has not been with our readers. We have had an unusually enthusiastic set of subscribers. But the magazine was begun just at the time of industrial depression following the war, and the fault of our suspension therefore is rather in the times, which are so out of joint, than in our constituency. It is possible that at some future time we may see our way to republish THE BROWNIES' BOOK.

In the meantime we intend that no subscriber shall lose anything by the suspension. We can reimburse subscribers in several ways. *First,* by a direct return of the balance due in cash; *secondly* by arranging with the CRISIS magazine to transfer our indebtedness and fill out subscriptions with the CRISIS; *thirdly,* by letting subscribers invest the balance due in the purchase of books; and *fourthly* by letting the subscribers contribute to our debts and thus become co-workers with us in this beautiful venture of the balance in any other way in which they can suggest. We shall be glad to hear from our subscribers on this point.

In the meantime may we express to both parents and children our appreciation of their staunch support.

Little People of the Month

THIS month our little people consist of four high school students, one in Maine, 2 in Ohio and one in Oklahoma.

Doris Madeline Johnson who lives way up among the snows of Bangor, Maine, entered a competition for the music of her class ode. Eight of the nine judges declared her music was the best and when she graduated she conducted the orchestra of seventy pieces which played the ode. Of course Doris had a little advantage over some of the other folks because her family are all musicians. Both her father and mother, who came from Norfolk, Virginia, have musical ability; one brother is a violinist and a sister is a 'cellist while another sister won a gold medal as a drummer and xylophonist.

At the Martin's Ferry High School in Ohio, Kenneth Randall led his high school class with a grade of 95 in a class of 62, the next highest average being 91.

At Odena, Ohio, Alverna Blanchard was the only colored pupil in her high school class and made the highest average, 98.

Passing on down to Oklahoma we meet Miss Annie H. Coffey, who is only 15 years old. She completed the 8th grade at Wewoka at the age of 11 years and was valedictorian. She was the youngest pupil in the whole county, among both white and colored pupils, to take the 8th grade examination. As there was no high school at her home she went to the high school at Muskogee and there graduated in a class of 50 pupils at the age of 15. She is in college at Wiley University now.

Annie H. Coffey
Alverna Blanchard

Kenneth Randall
Doris M. Johnson

ANSWERS TO THIS MONTH'S PUZZLES

THE SLEEPY PRINTER

1. My Cherished Hopes, My Fondest Dreams.
2. That Rest so Sweet Like Rest Above.
3. Listen to the Mocking Bird.
4. Carry Me Back to Old Virgina.
5. The Light House by the Sea.
6. Grandfather's Clock Was too High for the Shelf.
7. Listen to the Lambs.
8. Since You Went Away.
10. The Rain Song.

FRACTIONS

1. Shaw. 2. Fisk. 3. Howard. 4. Allen.
5. Atlanta. 6. Wilberforce. 7. Morris Brown.
8. Payne. 9. Lincoln. 10. Biddle.

CENTRAL SYNCOPATIONS AND REMAINDERS

1. stAir. 2. maTin. 3. peTal. 4. hoUse.
5. peCan. 6. faKir. 7. haSte. ATTUCKS.

PRINTER'S PI.

Baby has a tooth at last,
   Baby thinks he talks,
Baby stands upon his head
   When he tries to walk.

NUMERALS

1. Beale St., Memphis, Tenn.
2. Wyley Ave., Pittsburg, Pa.
3. Druid Hill Ave., Baltimore, Md.
4. State St., Chicago, Ill.
5. South St., Philadelphia, Pa.
6. U St., N. W. Washington, D. C.
7. Lenox Ave., New York, N. Y.

STARS

1. Bert Williams. 2. Mamie Smith. 3. Noble Sissle. 4. Mary Stafford. 5. Roland Hayes. 6. Lucille Hegimin. 7. Fisk Jubilee Singers. 8. Mamie Smith's Jazz Hounds. 9. Handy's Orchestra of Memphis. 10. Memphis Pickaniny Band. 11. Biddle University Quartet.

TRANSPOSITIONS

Star. Tars. Arts. Rats.

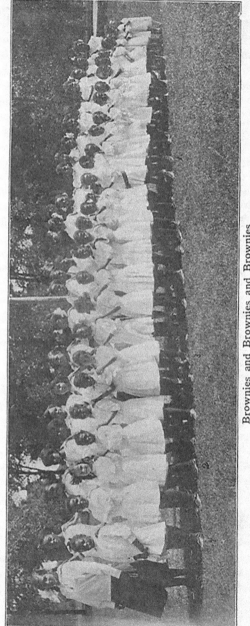

Brownies and Brownies and Brownies

A Selected List of Books

Dealing with the Negro Problem

These prices do not include postage.   Postage extra.

TWO COLORED WOMEN WITH THE AMERICAN EXPEDITIONARY
    FORCES. (Hunton and Johnson) $2.50
THE HEART OF A WOMAN AND OTHER POEMS. (Georgia Douglas
    Johnson) 1.25
NORRIS WRIGHT CUNEY. (Maud Cuney Hare) 1.50
THE SOUL OF JOHN BROWN. (Stephen Graham) 2.00
A NARRATIVE OF THE NEGRO. (Leila Amos Pendleton) 1.50
SOULS OF BLACK FOLK. (W. E. B. DuBois) 2.00
A CENTURY OF NEGRO MIGRATION. (Carter G. Woodson) 1.10
THE CURSE OF RACE PREJUDICE. (James F. Morton) .... .25
HISTORY OF THE NEGRO. (B. G. Brawley) 2.00
THE NEGRO MIGRANT IN PITTSBURGH. (Abraham Epstein) ... .50
GRANNY MAUMEE AND OTHER PLAYS FOR A NEGRO THEATRE.
    (Ridgely Torrence) 2.25
HALF A MAN. (Mary White Ovington) 1.20
AFTERMATH OF SLAVERY. (William Sinclair) .;.......... 1.50
MY LIFE AND WORK. (Bishop Alexander Walters) 1.50
UNSUNG HEROES. (Elizabeth Ross Haynes) 2.50
THE SHADOW. (Mary White Ovington) 2.00
JOHN BROWN. (W. E. B. DuBois) 2.00
NEGRO IN AMERICAN HISTORY. (J. W. Cromwell) 2.00
PRINCE HALL AND HIS FOLLOWERS. (George W. Crawford) .. 1.00
THE VOICE OF THE NEGRO. (Robert T. Kerlin) 2.50
NEGRO CULTURE IN WEST AFRICA. (George W. Ellis) 3.00
THE NEGRO. (W. E. B. Du Bois) .... .90
THE EDUCATION OF THE NEGRO PRIOR TO 1861. (Carter G.
    Woodson) 2.00
THE NEGRO FACES AMERICA. (Herbert J. Seligmann) 1.75
DARKWATER. (W. E. B. DuBois) 2.25
POEMS OF PAUL LAURENCE DUNBAR...................... 2.50
AFRO-AMERICAN FOLKSONGS. (H. E. Krehbiel) 2.00
BOOKER T. WASHINGTON. (Emmett J. Scott and Lyman
    Beecher Stowe) 2.00

Address: **THE CRISIS,** : : **70 Fifth Avenue. New York, N. Y.**

FOUNTAIN OF YOUTH 1513

THE FOUNTAIN OF YOUTH

ONCE DE LEON sailed for many weeks searching for the mythical FOUNTAIN OF YOUTH, located in the newly discovered America. Countless tales had assured him that frequent baths in its exhilirating waters were quite enough to restore his fading youthfulness.

Standing to-day in Neptune Park at St. Augustine, Florida, is the FOUNTAIN OF YOUTH, a show place for visitors, an accepted tradition of old Spain, but without medicinal power and the subtle charm of

MADAM C. J. WALKER'S SUPERFINE PREPARATIONS FOR THE HAIR AND SKIN

Wonderful Hair Grower	Vegetable Shampoo	Cold Cream
Glossine	Vanishing Cream	Antiseptic Hand Soap
Temple Grower	Cleansing Cream	Complexion Soap
Tetter Salve		Superfine Face Powder (white, rose, brown)

Floral Cluster Talcum Powder

Antiseptic Dental Cream   Witch Hazel Jelly

Frequent use of our preparations pre- serves the beauty of fading youth.

Very liberal children's package sent for a dollar and a half

THE MADAM C. J. WALKER MFG. CO., Inc.

640 North West St.   *Dept. 1-X*   Indianapolis, Ind., U.S.A.

CONTRIBUTORS

Jani L. Barker is professor of English and humanities at Southeastern Oklahoma State University, where she specializes in children's and adolescent literature. Research interests include narrative strategies, implied audience, ethics, and African American children's and young adult literature. Her work on historical and contemporary literature has been published in journals including *Children's Literature, Children's Literature Association Quarterly,* and *Children's Literature in Education* and in the edited collections *Internationalism in Children's Series* and *Ethics in Children's Literature.* She can be contacted at jbarker@se.edu.

Rudine Sims Bishop is professor emerita at The Ohio State University. She is the author of *Shadow and Substance: Afro-American Experience in Contemporary Children's Literature* and *Free Within Ourselves: The Development of African American Children's Literature.* Bishop is widely known for her influential article titled "Mirrors, Windows, and Sliding Glass Doors." She can be contacted at bishop.77@osu.edu.

Julia S. Charles-Linen is associate professor of English at the University of Colorado Boulder. She specializes in twentieth-century African American literature, Black Girlhood Studies, and racial passing literature. Charles-Linen is the author of *That Middle World: Race, Performance, and the Politics of Passing* (UNC Press 2020). She can be contacted at Julia.Charles@colorado.edu.

Paige Gray is professor of liberal arts and writing at the Savannah College of Art and Design. She is the author of *Cub Reporters: American Children's Literature and Journalism in the Golden Age* (SUNY Press 2019). Her work has appeared in academic journals such as *Children's Literature* and *Children's Literature Association Quarterly,* as well as popular press outlets including *Time.com, Chicago Tribune,* and *The Conversation,* among others. Her current book project considers how Black youth created community and representation for themselves through periodicals in the twentieth century. She lives in Atlanta and can be contacted at blankPaige@gmail.com.

Dianne Johnson-Feelings is professor of English at the University of South Carolina. She edited *The Best of "The Brownies' Book"* for Oxford University Press and is the author of groundbreaking scholarship recovering the history of African American children's literature. As Dinah Johnson, she is the author of picture books including *H Is for Harlem* (Ottaviano/Little, Brown 2022), *Indigo Dreaming* (HarperCollins 2022), and *Black Magic* (Henry Holt 2010, Square Fish 2021). Find more about her work at www.dinahjohnsonbooks.com. She can be contacted at dianne@sc.edu.

Jonda C. McNair is the Charlotte S. Huck Endowed Professor of Children's Literature at The Ohio State University. She specializes in literature intended for youth with an emphasis on books written by and about African Americans. McNair is a past chair of the Coretta Scott King Book Awards Committee and the 2021 John Newbery Award Selection Committee. Her work has appeared in numerous journals such as *Review of Educational Research*, *The Reading Teacher*, *Language Arts*, *Children's Literature in Education*, and *The Journal of Negro Education*. She can be contacted at mcnair.7@osu.edu.

Sara C. VanderHaagen is associate professor in the Department of Communication and an affiliate faculty member in the Department of African and African Diaspora Studies at the University of Wisconsin-Milwaukee. She conducts research in rhetorical studies, focusing on public memory, African American public discourse, and rhetorics of race. She is the author of *Children's Biographies of African American Women: Rhetoric, Public Memory, and Agency* (2018). Her work has also appeared in journals such as *Children's Literature Association Quarterly*, *Argumentation and Advocacy*, *Quarterly Journal of Speech*, *Philosophy and Rhetoric*, and *Women's Studies in Communication*. She can be contacted at vanderha@uwm.edu.

Michelle Taylor Watts is an independent scholar and a member of the college readiness leadership team in a large urban school district. Her research and practice focus on the intersection of Black childhood, activism, and liberation. Her early publications examined the Transatlantic slave trade and early twentieth-century literary culture. She has taught at Rice University, Miami University of Ohio, and the University of Cincinnati. She can be contacted at mtaylorwatts@gmail.com.

INDEX

References to illustrations appear in **bold**.

Printed in the USA
CPSIA information can be obtained
at www.ICGtesting.com
LVHW080722141123
763836LV00015BA/87